MOSAIC PIECES

Surviving the Dark Side of American Justice

by

Wes Skillings

DORRANCE
PUBLISHING CO
EST. 1920
PITTSBURGH, PENNSYLVANIA 15238

Dorrance Publishing Co
585 Alpha Drive
Pittsburgh, PA 15238
Visit our website at *www.dorrancebookstore.com*

ISBN: 979-8-8860-4030-2
eISBN: 979-8-8860-4933-6

TABLE OF CONTENTS:
Pages of the Mosaic

PREFACE

I've covered a number of murder cases over the years, but I have yet to cover one like the one I came to know intimately starting about three years after the conviction of Kim Hubbard for the October 1973 murder of Jennifer Hill. At that time, as a newspaper reporter, I had not yet reported on a single murder case. I covered my first trials in real time, mostly in the 1980s and 1990s, for another newspaper in another Pennsylvania county.

I have never been able to shrug off this case. You might say this is my shrugging off, but it isn't about repudiating, setting aside or brushing off as much as removing a dead weight from my shoulders that never seemed to lighten. One summer near the end of the previous millennium, I devoted a couple of weeks of vacation time remaking it into a crime novel. I thought it might be better accepted as a work of fiction based on a true crime, because it probably wouldn't be regarded as something that could really happen in our justice system.

As fiction I could come up with my own explanations, with logic based on evidence but not necessarily proof, because the case and its probabilities are, and continue to be, thought-provoking and, at the same time, alarming. What good would a journalistic, nonfiction treatment do by then? Everybody involved had moved on, including Kim himself, and a growing number are no longer with us, among them his father, who devoted the final sixteen years of his life gathering new evidence and tracking down witnesses in pursuit of a new trial or exoneration for his son. My own investigation as a reporter had corroborated much of this evidence, revealing a litany of discrepancies in Kim's prosecution laid out in an investigative series over several weeks in the summer of 1977. I continued to follow the case and its aftereffects for years up to this writing.

Other analyses of the case followed that series, and by the time Kim Hubbard did his time, he had many local supporters who believed at the least he had been unfairly tried and convicted and was not a merciless killer as he had been portrayed in his trial. He was able to start his own business, marry, raise a daughter, recently turned thirty and a success herself, and embark on a fulfilling life. He was still in his early thirties when released from prison and, unlike his father, Joe Hubbard, felt he had spent enough of his life with this albatross weighing him down and walked with his chest out and head held high those first two decades out of prison. He just wanted to lead a semblance of a normal life. He had withstood an entire lost decade—his twenties and into his thirties—and there was much to make up for.

And yet I wanted to get the story out myself and move on with my own life. There was so much there to tell, and I could at least get it out as a based-on-a-true-story novel that I regarded as an obligation to Joe Hubbard who, obsessed with proving his son's innocence and haunted by his inability to do so, died at the age of sixty in the house from which a twelve-year-old girl departed to her death so many years before.

This was the way it was when I forwarded a query letter and a sample chapter to a reputable literary agent who responded in barely a week via phone and seemed quite excited about its prospects. Following up by forwarding the entire manuscript, I immediately regretted doing so. I had turned real people into fictional characters. The protagonist was a reporter who was much like me, and the final chapters revealed the murky figures behind the deception of framing an innocent man for murder. Just to make it more exciting and potential movie material, the climax found me—I mean the protagonist—being pursued by a small-town police chief who was one of a cabal of plotters involved in the frame.

I should note, for the record, that I chose a police chief, something of a master of his domain, as a plot device. Who else could better orchestrate the framing of an innocent man than someone entrenched in the investigation and evidence derived from it? With help from a few key people, here and there, there would be no massive conspiracy required. In the actual murder investigation, there was some assistance from the local constabulary, but it was a retinue of state police in charge with a hands-on district attorney overseeing the case from its inception. The result was a crazy quilt of conflicting evidence that somehow came together to convince a jury to respond with a quick and unanimous verdict on March 1, 1974. It was open-and-shut, it seemed, and all wrapped up on the 124th day after Jennifer Hill's body was found in a cornfield just a few hundred yards east of the borough line of South Williamsport, Pennsylvania, and her own backyard. It may have seemed a done deal at the time, but nobody anticipated the persistence, resolve, and innate intelligence of Joe Hubbard.

Kim Hubbard was barely more than a kid doing time with hardened criminals and bolstering his flagging morale on the reassurances of his father who always seemed on the verge of freeing him from this artificial world into which he had descended.

Despite the therapeutic value of fictionally solving a case very similar to the one that resulted in so many years of frustration and particularly destructive to three generations of the Hubbard family and supporters, I found myself hoping that the agent may have cooled on the prospects of the novel.

I hadn't heard from him for some time, which seemed to denote waning enthusiasm on his end, but I realized I should cut the cord in the event he was deeply involved in analyzing and critiquing my manuscript. I called his office twice, each time leaving a message when no one answered. It seemed odd. I had talked to his secretary on previous calls. She didn't seem the type to ignore a ringing phone during business hours. Not long after that, she called me to let me know that he was critically ill and hospitalized. It didn't seem respectful to talk business, so I muttered something about a hopeful recovery. Her response was that full recovery was not likely since he was well into his sixties. He had been felled by a debilitating stroke with a long recuperation ahead even if he did survive. I never did recover the copy of the manuscript I sent and learned a few months later that his agency was defunct and so, I assumed, was he. It seemed to be a sign that I should tell the real story one day.

In his opening remarks to the jury of February 21, 1974, DA Allen Ertel described the case as "a mosaic" comprised of a lot of disparate tiles that jurors could piece together to construct a "clear picture" that the defendant had motive and opportunity to commit the crime.

Joe Hubbard told me several times that if ever a book were written about the case, it should be entitled "The Mosaic Pieces." It was he who discovered additional exculpatory pieces to create a much different picture. This was the suggested title of the novel that never came to be, so I got to keep it for the true story and a return to the journalistic approach. I don't get to fill in the blanks and create villains as I did as a novelist, other than suggesting possibilities. I can promise a lot of questions, and some of them, now as then, have no conclusive answers and probably never will.

I'll confess I provide subjective, even intimate, details about the Hubbards and others I have interviewed, followed, and researched over the years. If it seems I somehow got inside their heads, I did. I came to know them very well.

Wes Skillings

PROLOGUE

This is a generational chronicle with murder or, more explicitly, a murder investigation and trial, as the keystone of its arching narrative. It is a complex story, as is always the case in a karmic collision of lives past, present and into the future that is now today. The strands of the story, both tragic and life affirming, antedate the murder case by decades and emanate from there for decades thereafter. It is as much about what came after as before. This meticulously investigated and researched story would never have been told had not a young girl been intercepted and murdered while walking home on a bright October afternoon in 1973. By nightfall her body had been carefully placed in a cornfield, as the prosecution presented the crime, where it lay in repose between rows of tasseling corn for nine full days with little shielding from the sun during the day and exposed to seasonally mild nocturnal temperatures.

That was the storyline offered by the prosecution in the Commonwealth v. Kim Lee Hubbard in a February 1974 trial that seemed open-and-shut as presented in the serial coverage of the local press, testimony drizzling drop by drop on public cognizance. Yet it was destined to become one of the more contested capital murder cases in Pennsylvania over the next decade. Had it happened in a big city with a more aggressive press, it might be better known, but, in a way, it could have only happened in a barely metropolitan place like Williamsport. It is a small city surrounded by a rural vastness dotted with villages and the dots connected by two-lane roads more tarred than paved that sprouted from the lumbering industry of the late 1800s and then a dairy farming culture.

I was a twenty-nine-year-old reporter, nine years out of Vietnam and five years graduated from college with a BA in English and one journalism course to my credit, when I received my first assignment as an investigative reporter. I armed myself with the required skepticism when sent forth by my City Editor to take a closer look at Hubbard's murder trial and conviction three years and four months before.

The result was a series of a dozen articles spanning five issues of the newspaper, launched on the last day of July in 1977 and highlighting discrepancies in the evidence while raising questions about the Commonwealth's case. The articles came to an abrupt halt when some sobering revelations were raised in my coverage about, among other things, the improbable sterling condition of the victim's body and a tire print placing the defendant at or near the body scene that hadn't been on his car until after the body was "officially" discovered. It was way too far out on a limb for *Grit*, a Sunday weekly known mostly for its inspirational and comforting human-interest features with a blend of the usual community news fare.

This is not a story solely about that murder case and its many flaws, but it weighs heavily throughout, and it is, in the words of the immortal Reggie Jackson, the straw that stirs the drink. The drink is a potpourri of compelling characters and an intimate look at American justice served up in middle-class America at an interesting time in history.

At the center of it all were the Hubbards. Life hadn't been easy on any of them even before the death of Jennifer Hill—and it got worse for all of them thereafter.

"They're painfully honest people, pretty much unsophisticated and without guile," was the apt description offered by Sandra Wengert, who followed the case closely and was convinced Kim was not the killer.

When I think of the Hubbards, I see a family of character and courage despite some very human flaws. They deserved better than what they got—reeling from one tragedy after another, it seemed, but always expecting life to get better. Sometimes it did, but only long enough to foster fleeting memories they could cling to when the promise of a normal life soured again.

You could fault the Hubbards for naïveté because they believed in concepts like you're innocent until proven guilty and, most of all, that the truth will set you free. They believed in democracy, justice and in neighbors who would be there for them when needed. Some were. In fact, when things got tough financially, even the prospect of the next meal, money or donated food would appear, often anonymously, as if something or someone was watching over them.

Most of the 70,000 residents of the Williamsport Metropolitan Statistical Area, comprised of four adjacent municipalities within a two-mile radius with the county seat, the City of Williamsport, population about 40,000 in the early 1970s, as its hub, would only know what they read in the papers. That would include the arrest of Kim Lee Hubbard fewer than three weeks after the public learned of the murder and implied sexual assault of Jennifer Hill with the report of the finding of her body. There would be updates from the DA's office and state police during the investigation with incriminating details on Kim Hubbard's guilt capped by trial testimony scattered over eight days in February of 1974. The verdict was pronounced after a brief jury deliberation on March 1.

There were Joe and Dorisann, the parents, both gone now. Joe died a slow and painful death in, of all places, the living room of his house, converted into a bedroom as his final resting place. He was only sixty, his life extinguished in a death watch of eighteen excruciating hours.

When I think of Joe Hubbard, I remember a man who never seemed to get a break. And nobody deserved a break more than he did. He grew up dirt poor, drank too much for a time and married a kind, long-suffering woman he rescued from an abusive father. After losing six-year-old son, Donald, in a horrible accident outside a neighborhood elementary school, Joe embarked headlong into an abbreviated Christian ministry to atone for his perceived sins. He lost two sons—one to death, another to the criminal justice system—and a daughter he never got to hold mortally trapped in the birth canal. The second son, the convicted murderer, was returned to their lives, but Joe could not shake the injustice and his inability to overcome it.

He was a little guy with a square chin and a crooked nose, looking as one might expect a man to look who had been a lightweight boxer in the Navy. He could have been Popeye, the cartoon, in human form. He had a raspy voice, as if he may have taken too many punches to the throat, most likely due to the thousands of packs of cigarettes smoked over a span of more than four decades. The voice was surprisingly calming and deliberate in normal conversation but, when impassioned, as it often was during the bleak years of Kim's incarceration, it rose in volume as clear as a sunrise bugle call.

He had given so much of himself to vindicate his son, digging up mountains of vindicating evidence and, it seemed, always so close to a new trial that he knew would erase Kim's conviction from the record. All the appeals, before state and federal judges, had been exhausted over a decade. When Kim got out of prison, focused on getting on with his life and seemingly not interested in revisiting the case and exoneration, the obsession that had driven Joe Hubbard for more than a decade slowly waned.

As the cops closed in on their one and only acknowledged suspect in the murder of Jennifer Hill, Joe succumbed to a mental breakdown, brought on by anxiety, stress and depression, and was lying helplessly under heavy sedation in the unit for patients with mental disorders at the Williamsport Hospital.

Meanwhile, state police criminal investigators and the district attorney himself were interrogating his naively cooperative wife and son, gathering evidence in his house, some of which would prove to be flawed if not contrived. Joe himself, in his drugged vulnerability, was being questioned while convalescing with probing interrogators at his bedside intent on getting him to implicate his son. Something he never did.

Dorisann, always the hopeful one, would live another twenty-one-and-a-half years after losing Joe. She was able to spend lost time with son, Kim, released in 1984 after nine years in prison and almost a year in a halfway house in Johnstown, all preceded by almost four months in the Lycoming County Prison prior to and during his trial and conviction. She also got to enjoy the company of her three granddaughters—two from daughter, Ruth, and the youngest from Kim and his wife, Susan, who he married in 1990.

Dorisann was ultimately able to put the tragedies behind her. Not Joe. He was still consumed with the case and the injustices he felt were perpetrated on him and his family right up until his death. He did get to see Kim get out of prison and start a new life back in his hometown.

Kim just wanted, during those first two decades of freedom, to get on with his life and make up for a nightmare that had wiped out the promise of his twenties. In a way, Kim's freedom signaled the end of his father being able to prove his son was not a murderer, because, after all, nobody cared anymore. It even seemed that Kim didn't care. He did care, as he later confessed, but he was stepping on the neck of his anger, keeping it from rising and consuming his life as it had his father's.

"I wasn't even going to come back to this town," he conceded, sitting casually on the rail of his parents' porch in South Williamsport in the summer of 1984, a few months after serving out his sentence. "My father's business is here and everything, and he needed help. I owed him that much. He took care of me for ten years. They got me all my legal counsel, ran themselves in debt over me. They just went above and beyond."

His sister, Ruth, sees herself as something of an angel of death, because she had been enveloped in it since she was a child. She was, however, more an angel of mercy, because she was the one who nursed both of her parents over their final hours, days, and months. Disease claimed two husbands and it was Ruthie, as everyone calls her, who cared for them.

Jennifer Hill's last day alive had been spent with Ruthie. Both were twelve years of age and had been close friends since they were toddlers. On October 19, 1973, they were thirteen unlucky blocks apart—a dozen of them along one quiet residential street. A walk home that afternoon culminated in Jennifer becoming a missing person and, finally, a murder victim. Kim was arrested and convicted for committing the crime in what remains an increasingly unlikely and improbable scenario. Ruth would lose virtually all of her friends, ostracized at school in the ensuing years as the sister of a murderer.

All the pain, tragedy and triumph seemed to set the table for the one thing that brought them the fame—make that infamy—they never sought. Like most American families, they would have passed without much notice beyond an immediate circle of family and friends, but what happened in

October 1973, changed all that. It changed all the history that had come before and refuses to let go of the surviving Hubbards to this day.

As for the murder trial, you have the rare opportunity to check out all the evidence, including photos (some of which are graphic and not advisable for the young or easily dismayed), all the testimony in the trial itself, new evidence and affidavits that shed a different light on the value of convicting evidence. They show an assortment of disputed physical evidence. There were expert witnesses who came along after the trial to provide convincing proof that the body that supposedly lay in a field in warm October weather where rodents, insects and other creatures abound, couldn't have been there more than forty-eight hours and was probably refrigerated and returned to be found a second time. By whom and why are questions still debated.

The website is *Kim Hubbard: The Real Story* and can provide an interactive experience for readers of the book interested in a more detailed inspection of the evidence and testimony. I wrote the overview of the case and various contradictions in the case on the website's Home Page, and it was Kim's interest in exoneration after years of trying to forgive and forget what happened to him that convinced me to tell this story before senility claims what writing skills remain.

CHAPTER 1: THE HUBBARDS

"They were Expendable; All of Them"

He doesn't remember much of what would become the most important—and most devastating—days of his life. The trial. He does remember the odd feeling of blood departing his body, through his feet and into the floor when he heard the word, "Guilty!" The newspaper said he didn't react, which may have been true on the outside. Then, after the judge spouted some legal mumbo-jumbo, meaningless at this juncture with numbness clashing with disbelief, he was escorted out of the courtroom, barely conscious of what was going on around him.

It was weird. Right up to the verdict he was thinking they were going to stop this whole drama. The judge would say it had all been a big mistake and then he would apologize on behalf of the court.

He was a convicted murderer, and he still didn't understand how and why he had come to be here in handcuffs, escorted back to his old cell in the county jail where he had spent the previous four months. He held on to the feeling that someone, anyone, would step forward and say, "Wait! You can't do this!"

Then it would all go away or he would wake up from a bad dream. He would be back home—barely a mile away as the crow flies; just across the river—and finishing his senior year in high school. They would find the real killer and he would go home. No harm done. He hadn't paid much attention to the evidence they presented in court. He probably should have, but he was dumb enough to believe, at the time, that innocent people don't go to jail for crimes someone else commits. His whole family fell for that piece of fiction.

Looking back, his life was finally heading in the right direction in October 1973. There was promise something good was coming his way.

All the misery his family had endured prior to and since he went in the Army at the age of seventeen, then returning home on a hardship discharge, was a memory—a recent memory but safely behind them.

Or so it seemed.

He was getting his shit together, as they say in the Army when some screwup finally starts figuring out the mystery of being a soldier. Don't make it complicated. Keep it simple, stupid! He should have known better. The only thing simple about what had happened to him since October 19, 1973, was how simple he and his family had been to get duped the way they had by a prosecutor so firmly fixed on a conviction, a career boost, that he was willing to destroy him and his family. That's how he felt then and still feels today. Today is literally a lifetime later for Kim Lee Hubbard, husband, father, successful contractor and convicted murderer, in the very town where he had been arrested and convicted more than forty-eight years before. He was barely older than a child then. Ten years younger than his daughter, Kyrstin, is today.

They were expendable. All of them. Expendable. In an odd sense, he may have fared better than his parents and his sister, Ruth. They had all been locked in their own prisons, unable to get on with their lives. His father, Joe, now gone, was unable to escape the prison of his mind. He couldn't continue to serve the self-imposed sentence of guilt. But, at the same time, he would do so much to clear his son's name—even if it did not officially beget a new trial or exoneration.

Kim would serve his time, return to his hometown, and start anew with his life—something the rest of the Hubbards had been unable to do. His mother, Dorisann, had her trust violated time and again. She never lost her faith in God, but it had been violated by just about everyone else outside of her family. Ruthie somehow survived being the little sister of the proclaimed killer of her best friend, but tragedy and depression seemed to haunt her over the years.

What was it she said to me back in 2018 when she was fifty-six years old, a mother and a grandmother who had been widowed twice by husbands claimed by terminal disease?

"I envy Kim. I watch him today and I think I'd give anything to have his life. He has a bucket list and his toys and takes vacations all the time.... All I do is work and can't even get ahead. Sometimes it doesn't seem fair."

It's not that she's begrudging her older brother's happiness. It's just that everything seems to go back to one day that started as a sublime Friday, playing with her friends on a school holiday, a sparkling autumn day. She can't escape it. Somehow Kim can, even though he wants nothing more than to be absolved and his hands washed clean of being legally branded a convicted killer of a twelve-year-old girl. Some conscientious newspaper editor will undoubtedly include it in Kim's obituary. That was, after all, a claim to fame he disdains. He wants exoneration more in his father's memory than for himself, and then there are his wife and daughter. Better that the obituary includes "vindicated" or "absolved" if the murder case is mentioned at all. Most everybody else intimately connected with the case is gone anyway.

Otherwise, he's doing okay.

So, who was to blame for all this suffering and tragedy? Was it Kim for mistakes he'd made in his young life? Was it his father for falling apart when everything was collapsing around his family and police closing in on them? Maybe it was his mother for being the naïve and trusting person she had always been—his clinching alibi for the precious span of minutes they had given him to murder a child and dump her body in a cornfield just outside of town?

Good guys don't let people get away with murder, whether premeditated or spontaneous, and then frame someone else who is easy prey. That's what they did to him. The rationalization of co-conspirators might have been that he was young, could do the time and still return to lead a productive life. Kim Hubbard did just that and that undoubtedly salved some consciences. Anyway, if he did do it, as one skeptic said to me, "No harm. No foul."

Fast forward forty-seven years. Both his mother and father are gone now. Kim has been happily married to Susan, an elementary school teacher, for more than three decades. They are parents of a grown daughter who has embarked on a career as a pharmacist. He repairs and replaces roofs and chimneys, his specialty being slate roofs that flourish on homes throughout the Northcentral Pennsylvania's Lycoming County and adjacent municipalities.

It was something of an inheritance from his father. Just about everything else of his parents' material worth had been expended over the years in a quest for a new trial with newly discovered evidence. It had drawn the interest of renowned forensic experts, who disputed key evidence against Kim. Still, he remains a convicted murderer, though far from a pariah in his hometown.

He celebrated his sixty-fifth birthday on April 29, 2018, reaching traditional retirement age. The ten years he lost make him resistant to retirement. Anyway, he could easily pass for forty-five, and he loves physical activities like skiing, working out in the gym and taking long rides on his motorcycle. He works hard and he plays hard. You might say he is still trying to make up for a chunk of life he missed all those years ago. This is something Ruth, for various reasons, can't have.

He has many customers, a great reputation and plenty of friends, despite what most everyone knows about his past. He is not a "hang out with the boys" kind of guy and chooses his companions carefully. His experience as a murder suspect and subsequent trial and conviction taught him to always be where he had someone to alibi him. His life, especially the first decade out of prison, has been one long alibi. Who knows when a convicted killer might come in handy in resolving another murder case?

Kim Hubbard is the convicted murderer of a twelve-year-old girl, and it is incredible, looking back at the investigation and prosecution, that he was never granted a new trial or exonerated after he served his time. He came close on several occasions, mostly due to his father's obsessive crusade to prove his innocence.

There may never have been a murder case with more discrepancies and what appear to be multiple instances of mishandling, manipulation, or manufacturing of evidence. In fact, there may have been too many flaws in the prosecution's case, apparently unnoticed or ignored by his defense attorney and the jury that declared him guilty. So many mistakes, misinformation, and misconduct, but the one thing they have been good for was perhaps a little vindication.

How could too much evidence of prosecutorial and police misconduct or incompetence have stymied a string of appeals all the way up through the Pennsylvania Supreme Court? How could investigative reporting in three regional publications, each bringing out glaring flaws in the Commonwealth's case, fail to affirm his innocence or, at the least, convince a higher court that he could get another shot at justice? The justice system had reversed on him. Innocent until proven guilty had become the much tougher legal objective of proving innocence after a proclamation of guilt by a jury of his peers.

Back in 2013, Hubbard put up a website (kimhubbardstory.com) that lays it all out, including evidentiary photos, trial transcripts, affidavits from witnesses disputing police and witness testimony, as well as convincing evidence and expert commentary elicited over the decade Hubbard was serving his time in state correctional facilities.

His father, Joe, and his faithful ally, Charlie King, among the most recent to die, started literally the day after the jury delivered its verdict, returning to the body scene and uncovering discrepancies almost immediately.

Why didn't someone step forward during all these years to clear his name? The answer may lie in the following question sent to Hubbard at his website by an archaeologist who said he had once received training as a "death scene investigator":

> If the police, coroner/medical examiner, pathologist, and prosecutor all conspired against you, what was the catalyst? In my "victimology" training I learned that there must be some germ that allows a theory (even a fabricated story / conspiracy) to be built off of it... Essentially, my question is, "Why you, Kim?"

Although it didn't necessarily require all of the aforementioned to be knowingly involved in a conspiracy, it is a very telling question and has always been a stumbling block in subsequent judicial appeals and calls for exoneration. The concern is no longer how the evidence doesn't add up or how severely defective it may be. It morphs into why "they" would do it, who would have to conspire to do it and, of course, the question, "Why you, Kim?"

The more plausible answer to that question might have better been asked of the district attorney as he proceeded to target the Hubbards even before the public learned there was a murder. What about the state police who abandoned the murder investigation protocol of starting with those closest to the victim before moving outward? Why would the victim, a child, walk almost a dozen blocks toward home and then, within sight of her destination, turn and walk in another direction, not to be seen by anyone for a half an hour before getting into a vehicle that allegedly resembled Kim Hubbard's car? The Commonwealth identified the car with at least one glaring omission by an eyewitness who was, unknown to the jury and the defendant, hypnotized to refresh her recollection after being shown the impounded car twice.

The only other explanation for all of this was massive incompetence mixed with an abundance of dumb luck throughout the entire investigation by the police, as well as during the trial itself by both the prosecution and defense. They would therefore have been fortunate that their poorly constructed evidence had not fallen apart, burying their case like hay in one of those collapsed barns so sadly a part of Lycoming County's pastoral countryside. There was certainly a whole bunch of bad luck for Kim Hubbard and some amazing coincidences for the Commonwealth of Pennsylvania. By following the trial transcript and looking at how the evidence was presented, we can see that it wasn't necessarily the fault of the jury. The so-called hard evidence was confusing, conflicting, and ultimately circumstantial while witness testimony was contradictory. The investigators and county coroner seemed resolute in their testimony. For starters, you have to believe the evidence and investigators. Most juries do, and that tends to counterbalance the one thing a defendant has going for him—reasonable doubt.

But the jury must have suspected something was not quite right. The prosecution's scenario was of a violent crime, the perpetrator intent on sexually assaulting the young girl and, when thwarted, strangling her to death and dumping the body. And yet, the jurors chose to convict on a lesser charge of homicide, which called for a sentence of ten to twenty years. That sentence would later protect the verdict from being overturned due to ineffectiveness of counsel. It appears reasonable doubt at least led to a lesser sentence and allowed Kim Hubbard to return to a normal and productive life while still a young man.

There was no sign of molestation, as the pathologist conceded, and there were no injuries indicating a struggle, as well as underwhelming external signs of manual strangulation, the stated cause of death. The only thing that was clear in retrospect was that her airway was shut off, collapsed, in what may have been a brief unpremeditated act. The few imprints and discoloration on her neck didn't reveal much—no defined ligature marks or telling bruises on the front of her neck from powerful thumbs pressing in. It could have been a sudden blow delivered in anger or a push and fall against a table or counter ledge, fracturing cartilage and collapsing the airway. The jurors, despite the confusing sleight-of-hand presentation of the body scene evidence, could at least see that.

Kim Hubbard is not sitting on death row or serving out a life sentence. He was out in ten years. This is not a cold case, because it has been adjudicated and officially resolved, though the crime itself seems far from solved. There was no urgency to correct a miscarriage of justice. His life was not destroyed. He was accepted back into his community, mostly because of investigative news coverage after his conviction that provided ample demonstration that, at the least, he did not receive a fair trial.

With the exception of this one thing hanging over his head and the first decade of his adulthood lost, he can't, and doesn't, complain about the detour his life has taken since Jennifer Hill was officially declared a murder victim. He is luckier than the growing number of falsely imprisoned men—mostly poor and black—who never got to start a family and a career because they were old or infirmed by the time they were freed, if freed at all. This story may revolve around a murder, arrest, trial, and conviction forty-seven years ago, but those surrealistic nineteen weeks of his life are only part of the story.

This is the story of an American family who belatedly came to believe they were the perfect patsies for an ambitious district attorney who would soon be elected to Congress and subsequently seem destined to even higher political office. There are a few blanks to be filled in because those who know the truth have gone to their graves or are not talking.

It is about Joe and Dorisann Hubbard, the path that took them to see their son, Kim, convicted of murder, and its consequences on their lives. Ruth's childhood was virtually demolished as the sister of an accused and convicted murderer, and her adult life hasn't been much better. Now a middle-aged woman nearing retirement age, she is more accepting of the course her life has taken, but still wonders what could have been.

The crime is older than the national median age today, which means most Americans are younger than the murder case itself. The convicted killer has been out of prison for more than three-and-a-half decades, belatedly picking up where his father left off by turning his attention to the case in 2013.

Finally, there is the cold case detective, a self-proclaimed seeker of the truth, who, in a flawed, sloppily investigated, and prejudicial book, claimed to have finally proven Kim Hubbard's guilt more than four decades after his trial. But, as you'll see, the former policeman showed himself to be an opportunist and an ex-cop unwilling to concede that, as he contradictorily stated in his book, "police don't always do the right thing." He then went on the proclaim that, in this case, they always did. His book, entitled *Unsolved No More*, could be more accurately entitled *Framed Once Again*.

For those of us who have covered this case, there was always an expectation that someone involved would step forward and break the case wide open. From a journalistic perspective, there seemed to be enough new and contradictory evidence to do just that.

Many of the primary characters involved in the investigation and trial of Kim Hubbard have passed away, including the prosecutor, defense attorney, several state police criminal investigators, key eyewitnesses for both the Commonwealth and the defense, and the man who discovered the body of the twelve-year-old murder victim, Jennifer Hill, and came to regard it as "the sorriest day of my life."

I never caught Joe Hubbard in a lie in the thirteen years I knew him. Not that I agreed with all of his theories and observations about certain evidence and testimony. He had been a trusting man who had served his country, church, and community unselfishly, only to see friends and neighbors abandon him and his family when he was most vulnerable. I would occasionally question some of his interpretations about the motives of witnesses and investigators involved in the case, but I understood his skepticism. He never forgave himself for some of his missteps and shortcomings as a husband and parent.

As for Dorisann Hubbard, she may be the most authentic and trustworthy person I have ever met. Like her husband, she had not enjoyed the easiest of lives, but she never complained. She accepted all setbacks as the Will of God and trustingly moved on, patiently waiting for God to help her understand. She lost one child prenatally, barely escaping with her own life. She went on to have Ruth Marie fewer than two years later. She lost the other, just a little boy of six, in a freak after-school accident.

The final indignity for this incredibly sincere woman was being portrayed as a liar because she was her son's only alibi for several crucial minutes in an otherwise ordinary afternoon. It is a cruel irony that she was abandoned by members of her church as the mother of a murderer, evoking words of admiration from one juror as "doing what any good mother would do to save her son."

CHAPTER 2: JOE

"Planting Churches" and Planted Evidence

"I think his last breath, his last thought, was about the case."
– Ruth Marie (Hubbard) Day on her father, Joe Hubbard

Joseph Riley Hubbard, Jr., was born on Feb. 12, 1929, in one of the most sparely populated sections of Pennsylvania's rural Clinton County to Joseph Sr. and Anna Hubbard. Situated west of the small city of Lock Haven and comprised of just two square miles, Allison is one of Pennsylvania's smallest townships in both size and population. Even today, at last report, it was home to barely 200 residents.

He grew up in poverty, a casualty of a broken family who survived and prevailed over some intimidating odds. His birth father, Joseph, Sr., was a hunchback, one of his sisters later revealed. Joe never used "Jr." as an appendage to his name or talked about his biological father, but his older sisters called him "Junior" as a child. In truth, he never talked about his childhood at all. Son, Kim, knows virtually nothing about his father's life growing up. The fact that his father was married, briefly, to a woman named Mary before meeting his mother, was something Kim learned quite recently.

Joe Hubbard's biological father was still the head of the household in 1930 when he was just a year old. Junior spent some time, as a child, in a county institution for those who couldn't take care of themselves or their children in those tough economic times. These were known as poorhouses in those days before political correctness when rural America was slowly recovering from the Depression. They were regarded as an early form of welfare and, historically, a byproduct of the carnage of the Civil War that radically altered families for generations through death and disability. It had engendered a growing army of the elderly who could no longer be cared for by their families because of special needs they couldn't accommodate.

Those old institutions evolved into poorhouses and county nursing homes by the time Joe Hubbard arrived in an unwelcoming world in which he was viewed as another mouth to feed. Joe's time as a ward of the state around the ages of nine and ten was likely a temporary solution for his overburdened mother before being returned to his family and a recent addition to the family, a stepfather.

Joseph Hubbard, Sr., a gambler from Tennessee, had been abusive to his wife, Anna, his namesake's mother. In the vernacular of the times, he was remembered by his daughters as a "wife beater." Anna left with the three kids and retreated to Pennsylvania. Hubbard, Sr., stayed in Tennessee, no longer a part of their lives.

Then Anna met Joseph Davis, and they went on to have Delores, the youngest of the siblings, later in life. They never married because Davis had a wife in either an institution for the mentally ill or nursing home in Texas and was apparently paying for her ongoing care.

In the 1940 Census, when Joe was eleven, his parents were listed as Joseph and Anna Davis, though his stepfather was never able to legally marry his mother without committing bigamy. That, too, may have been the case with Anna, because there was no record of her divorce from the elder Hubbard or that he provided any further monetary support to her or their children. Davis and his stepson never got along and were known to fight, physically and verbally. Perhaps the young man was resented as a drain on the family budget after returning to the fold from institutional care.

I found little biographical information on Davis, but one interesting tidbit stands out. Davis was regarded as a sharpshooter, his one claim to fame being as an escort and protector of President Woodrow Wilson on a European trip after World War I.

Sisters Louise and Betty were, respectively, two and four years older than their brother. They were spared the poorhouse. It was Joe's much younger half sister, Delores, who would be the only one of his siblings to continue a relationship with Joe and wife, Dorisann, in later years.

Whatever happened in those early years, he didn't talk about much, even to his own family. It was Delores who apprised them of what she knew about his childhood. He was barely beyond childhood himself when he made his first attempt at marriage, which didn't last very long. How long? He never talked about that either, but it was apparently a matter of months.

Dorisann and Joe married on January 23, 1951. She was nineteen and he eleven days shy of his twenty-second birthday. She gave birth to their first child, Kim Lee, on April 28, 1953, while his father was still in the Navy in Newport, Rhode Island. Joe had lied about his age to join the US Navy in 1946. It appears his last assignment before being honorably discharged from the Navy in 1954 was aboard the *USS Hickox*, a destroyer. They returned to civilian life and a home on Hastings Street in South Williamsport. They were three doors away from another family, Jack and Norma Hill, and the wives would become friends, never suspecting the tragedy that awaited them with two of their children, one yet to be born. Kim, just a toddler, would have a younger brother, Donald Joseph, named jointly after his maternal grandfather and father, born in 1956.

Joe Hubbard was small and wiry, weighing in at around 135 pounds with his pockets full of change. A splayed nose betrayed his years as a boxer in the US Navy. He hadn't benefited from much of a role model when it came to husbands in his own life so, perhaps, he hadn't been much of a husband himself in that first union. Then he met and fell in love with a dark-haired beauty, Dorisann Forsburg, three years and nine months younger than he when he was working as a steeplejack for her father, Donald Forsburg. As steeplejacks, they spent much of their time on the road, often high above the landscape surmounting steeples, smokestacks, and other lofty industrial structures in western Pennsylvania hours away from Williamsport.

Joe and Dorisann lost two children—a daughter at birth and their son, Donald, whose death would consume Joe with guilt and send their lives in an entirely different direction. It was late afternoon on February 13, 1962, when Donald died in a tragic accident in front of the old Mountain

Avenue Elementary School, a block south to Mountain Avenue and a dozen blocks east on that street from his house. A front-page story in the Williamsport *Sun-Gazette* on Valentine's Day, February 14, reported that it was the first fatality involving a school bus in Lycoming County and the only one so far in Pennsylvania five-and-a-half months into the 1961–62 school year.

Ruthie, born June 13, 1961, was only eight months old when Donald, six, died. He was crushed under the dual rear wheels of a loaded school bus near the school at the end of a day of classes. He was on a street corner across from the school entrance, having just been assisted there by a crossing guard. According to witnesses, he appeared to slip on a sidewall of plowed snow, sliding under the bus filled with children as it was backing up. It was reported that he was "instantly killed" from what was essentially a crushed skull.

Joe would take full responsibility for the death of Donald. He hadn't been there to pick up the boy because he had surrendered to a familiar temptation, staying too long at the neighborhood tavern. Donald, as little kids will do, decided he could navigate the handful of blocks home. Ruth remembers her mother telling her years later how Joe had howled in grief, demanding over and over again why it had to be Donald. The only other person in the house old enough to understand at the time was Kim who was two months shy of his eighth birthday.

There is little logic in abject grief. Maybe Joe Hubbard, overwhelmed by guilt, was actually wailing that it should have been him. But a young boy, struggling to comprehend death, may have come to a different conclusion hearing these lamentations. Did Kim sustain any emotional scars from this tragedy? If so, it is buried in his subconscious. He says he has no recollection of this and few memories of Donald at all for that matter.

"I should remember more about him. He was my brother. We lived together for six years," Kim, then in his sixties, confided, shaking his head and grimacing as if disgusted with himself. He rarely mentions Donald and only when someone else brings him up. "I get these little, I don't know, snapshots, but it's not like I can sit here and tell you he was this kind of kid or that kind of kid."

He does concede that he couldn't do much to please his father over the next eleven years and nine months before Kim himself would become the subject of front-page news.

After Donald's death, Joe turned to a radically different way of life, dedicating his whole family to "service to the Lord," in what was undoubtedly an act of penance. The Hubbards would move from South Williamsport shortly thereafter when, Joe, overwhelmed with grief at the loss of Donald, would turn to religion. It sustained his life, assuaging his grief and guilt, but it turned everyone else's lives upside down.

He enlisted his entire family into the work of the Lord at Christian Ministries for the Florida-based New Tribes Mission, established in 1942. The young family apparently lived in Florida, to "train" for one year, as was part of the organization's program. Then they returned to Pennsylvania where New Tribes had a 100-acre mission camp not far from Williamsport. It was just outside Jersey Shore, whose only shores were along the West Branch of the Susquehanna River and Pine Creek, which flowed into the river from the north through picturesque state forestland. It was a place where future missionaries and their families lived together, became immersed in the Bible, and conditioned their souls to bring God's word to primitive people.

Joe was thriving, finding self-worth in religion he'd never before experienced, but Dorisann, who had always been the religious one, struggled with living that way and fretted that it was not how she wanted the kids to grow up.

What was New Tribes then has apparently transitioned to a more sophisticated operation, known as Wayumi (as in Why/You/Me) Missions or Ethnos360. In recent years, they were reportedly operating in several countries and were outed by NBC News in 2019 for incidents of child sexual abuse in mission schools outside of the United States. Their calling then, as now at last report, are mission trips known as "church plantings." Joe Hubbard was eager to plant churches among primitive tribes and to bring his family with him, including a nine-year-old son and infant daughter, on this journey of atonement. Alcohol was no longer a part of his life, with prayer and Bible study consuming his abundant energy and inquisitive mind that, a decade later, would be consumed more by criminal justice and jurisprudence than theology and Christian ministry.

While Joe memorized large sections of scripture and whetted his zeal to introduce heathens to Christianity, Dorisann was becoming increasingly uncomfortable with the radical change in the direction their lives had taken. Though grateful for the transformation of her husband, a newfound humility and genuine caring and forgiving attitude toward others, she was becoming increasingly miserable with each passing day as a missionary trainee.

"Joe was so happy and truly believed he had found his calling," Dorisann told me almost two decades later. "He would have been wonderful, and it was as if he was reborn. I was so happy for him, but I just couldn't do it. It wasn't right for me and I was worried about the children."

That chapter ended when Joe had to make a choice. He had lost a son, a daughter at birth, and almost lost the love of his life in the birthing process. He wasn't going to lose anyone in his family again—even with his wife's blessing to pursue his journey of renewal.

It meant a return to the secular life. They would live for a number of years in the Brandon Park area of Williamsport, and Kim, small for his age but a natural athlete, would wrestle at Curtin Junior High School in that part of town. Their neighborhood on Brandon Place was bordered by a green and woodsy park, with a bandshell and tennis courts and Little League fields along its perimeter. The former steeplejack was making a decent income repairing slate roofs and chimneys. His side job as a chimney sweep was featured in area newspapers during the Christmas holidays.

If he harbored regrets about having to abort his mission, he never expressed them. Daughter, Ruth, recalls that, if anything, her parents became closer. Family life was finally happy, even serene for her as a young child, and Ruthie relished memories of the affection her father showered on her.

They had moved across the river to South Williamsport to a home at 1030 West Central Avenue adjacent to Dorisann's widowed mother's home that she shared with Dorisann's sister and her family. Joe had transitioned into a busy life as a roofing contractor and as an ambulance volunteer with an EMT certification. He did enjoy stops at local taverns, playing pool and darts. He was an excellent pool player, but tempers sometimes clash when alcohol mixes with gamesmanship. He was probably doing too much drinking and pool playing in the spring of 1971.

"Dad wasn't a drinker drinker," his daughter explains. "He was a binger. He would go weeks without drinking, fall off the wagon and binge. He was on medication too, and you couldn't mix that."

Not only had he lost his youngest son in a gruesome accident just nine years before, but now his eldest son, Kim, had dropped out of school and joined the Army. Joe had reluctantly surrendered his parental permission and would later confess that mourning the death of his other son—first by a radical turn to religion and, after that, failing miserably in connecting with Kim—had led to approving his son's military service. After all, it had worked for him.

Kim was far from dumb, but, upon reflection, may have had a learning disability or an attention deficit disorder that made academics a challenge for him. Joe had to think about what was right for Kim, and the US Army may have been just what he needed. His son enlisted in June of 1970 at the tender age of seventeen and several semesters short of a high school degree. It was a new start, but, as it turned out, there wasn't really enough time for him to assess what kind of military career he might have had or where it would have taken him.

That career path ended in a South Williamsport bar one night in the spring of 1971. Joe, a certified EMT who had been making ambulance runs for years, had just ended a shift assisting in his second job in the emergency room that night. He had only been in the establishment a few minutes when he found it difficult to ignore a drunken patron bullying an elderly man at the bar. The bully was imposing and menacing. Others in the establishment were abstaining from involvement. Joe, despite his diminutive size, chose to get involved. He could, after all, take care of himself and he had a way of defusing volatile situations fueled by alcohol. Joe with his crooked grin and raspy voice could talk a lion out of releasing a man's head from its clenched jaws. Getting through to a mean drunk was another thing.

Before he could react, a beer bottle came crashing down, literally caving in the left side of his face.

The sole provider for his family was now hospitalized and would be unable to work for some time while recovering. Pain killers and other medications would trespass into his existence. This led to Kim, who had recently turned eighteen, receiving a hardship discharge from the Army in May of 1971 so he could return home to work and help pay the bills. He dedicated himself to his role as provider while his father healed from his injuries—going back to school by day at South Williamsport High School and working part-time nights. He ultimately landed a job at the Stroehmann's bakery plant on the Williamsport side of the Susquehanna River.

By the time he secured that job in the last week of October 1973, his father had been back on his feet for months, drawing a paycheck himself in the hospital emergency room. Kim remembers life was as sweet as it had ever been. He was receiving $425 a month through the GI Bill, plus a few bucks here and there on other jobs. A job at the Stroehmann's plant seemed to cap a comeback. Even a high school diploma was now within reach.

"I know a lot of people thought I was a bum because I drove a ratty-looking car. What they didn't know is that I could have been driving a new car," he recalled. "But that wasn't my purpose for getting out of the military. It was to support my family."

Because of his military service, he was older than most of his classmates, and that only made him seem more mature to friends. By the time he turned twenty in March of 1973, he was pretty sure he was in love with eighteen-year-old Colleen Whitenight, and she seemed to feel the same about him. The two had dated before he went in the Army. Not that there were any wedding plans, but their romance was hot and heavy, something Colleen's parents, especially her father, Kenneth, had forbade her to continue. That, of course, only fueled the passions of Kim and Colleen.

October of 1973 would be a life changer for all the Hubbards. Yes, life was good for Kim, but landing the job at Stroehmann's had been preceded a few days before by something unsettling—the disappearance of Jennifer Hill, who would never arrive home in what should have been no more than a fifteen-minute walk from the Hubbard house.

When they came after Kim, it was in full force. Joe had wanted everyone in his family to cooperate, tell the police and the prosecutor what they knew, because the more they cooperated the sooner they would leave them all alone and go after the real killer. Why Jennifer's point of departure became more significant to police in their search for suspects than her route or destination has never been fully explained.

But they didn't go away, and Joe, drinking more and mixing with prescription meds, felt himself slipping way. He ended up in the psych unit the day they took Kim's car for an evidence search, and suddenly Dorisann was alone. She knew Kim was their prime suspect, but Kim wasn't taking it all that seriously. It didn't make sense, he would tell her. They would all go away eventually. His father's attitude had been that the truth would eventually prevail. It seemed father and son, who hadn't agreed on much the previous few years, agreed that the truth, a.k.a. Kim's innocence, would set all of them free from police attention verging on obsession.

Kim, meanwhile, tersely answered their questions, showing little emotion. He was what you might call stoically polite. He'd just say, firmly but respectfully, "No sir. That is not true, sir." The cops, Joe would learn later, didn't like Kim calling them "sir." They thought he was being a smartass, but he'd been taught to respect his elders, and his time in the Army made the words "sir" and "ma'am" almost automatic when conversing with authority figures.

His father was amicable at first, especially with South Williamsport Police Chief Charles "Smitty" Smith and the Mayor R. David Frey, both of whom he'd known for years. The state cops, however, seemed almost menacing at times. It got worse with the district attorney, Allen Ertel, sitting in on the interviews. That in itself was not standard procedure. Prosecutors were rarely that deeply imbedded in criminal investigations and interrogations of suspects. This, however, was a career make-or-break case for a man who would prove to have lofty aspirations.

They'd split them up. Joe and Dorisann in the kitchen and Kim on the other side of the door at the dining room table fielding questions from Ertel and the cops, Sgt. Edward Peterson and Lt. Steven Hynick.

Joe was losing control, and he could feel the enmity when they looked at Kim. Their regard toward him and Dorisann was as if anything they said didn't matter. He had felt this all of his life—the boy who was shipped out to the poorhouse—that he was some kind of a low-life in the eyes of educated people or those who regarded their status as somehow superior to his.

That's why he had been his own boss most of his life, replacing and repairing roofs and chimneys. Then, as an ambulance volunteer, it allowed him to fill a slot on the emergency room team at Williamsport Hospital. His roofing customers were occasionally doctors, lawyers, and prominent professionals, and to most of the people who hired him he was kind and affable, as they were to him.

Hynick, Peterson and Ertel didn't scare Joe, or so he wanted his family to believe. He tried to break through their dark detachment with forced affability because this would all be over soon when they got on the trail of a more likely suspect. That's what he kept telling himself and his family.

"Bugs, they've got to talk to everyone who saw her or was with her that day," he'd reassure her as well as he could with feigned nonchalance. But Dorisann, nicknamed Bugs because of her aversion to insects, couldn't stop the fear from welling up inside. They were clearly after Kim, and he hadn't even been around when the girl left and began her walk down West Central Avenue to her home on Hastings Street. Why did the cops have to take him aside and talk to him alone, his parents wondered? Kim, meanwhile, couldn't understand why they would think he'd give a kid that age a ride out of the blue. What was the point? He initially thought she had just run off. Hell, she'd be back, and he was trying to ignore the panic around him while her disappearance was grabbing headlines in a growing number of newspapers in the region. There was even a sentence in one of the articles in the Williamsport *Sun-Gazette* about her last being seen leaving a home on West Central Avenue where she had spent the previous night and most of the day of her disappearance with a friend. That friend was Ruthie Hubbard, which was not reported at that time, but it was unsettling, for sure. Still, they figured it would all be over soon.

Finding Jennifer Hill's body in a cornfield deflated and then punctured that optimism.

Then Joe was in the hospital in a matter of days—a patient not an employee—and he was really out of it. Ruthie remembered how scared she had been seeing him like that. She was only twelve, but she knew they weren't really trying to help her father. Her later training and career as a nurse would reaffirm those perceptions as she looked back years later. She often thought she went into nursing, especially caring for elderly convalescents, so nobody would take advantage of them when they were so vulnerable. Not with her around.

Ruth remembered the helplessness, the hopelessness: "Dad was in and out. Two or three times he was in the psych ward, and they kept coming to the house and talking to us. The one time he disappeared. They couldn't find him. He took off walking."

Her father had all kinds of prescription bottles in their house during the autumn of 1973, and one day they were gone. Nobody seemed to know what happened to them. Did her father toss out all those pills out of frustration? She was certain he hadn't, but, then again, he was not of sound mind by then. The cops had the run of the house in the days leading up to Kim's arrest on November 16th. Sgt. Peterson always seemed to be excusing himself for trips to the bathroom upstairs, which, at the time, seemed merely odd. In retrospect, it was suspicious, especially discovering items moved in closets and bedrooms.

Of one thing Ruth was certain: "Whatever they had him on in the hospital, it was killing him slowly. He would have gone into a coma eventually."

Joe would have only murky memories of those days in the hospital—the unrecoverable time when he wasn't there to help his son. He suspected someone at the Williamsport Hospital had allowed police access to him in his fragile state. Murky memories of his time there supported that suspicion. They had a murder case to solve, and the answer might lie with a man in a hospital bed, heavily sedated and recovering from emotional collapse.

He had been working in the emergency room there when all of this buried his whole family like an avalanche, squeezing the life out of them under its unyielding weight. As a patient, they had allowed criminal investigators access to him when he was at his most vulnerable. Nevertheless, they apparently never reaped any evidence from this hospital-sanctioned intimacy, or even as much as a lead resulting in any viable evidential grist for a case they were building against Kim.

Joe knew he had been a suspect before Kim, but too many people had seen him that afternoon and evening. His alibi was solid. It was one of the few times in his life when stopping for a few beers at a local tavern had worked to his advantage. Within forty-eight hours after the body was discovered, they had been swarming around Joe's pickup truck, like ants on a melting chocolate bar, paying particular attention to the tires. He sensed something serious was about to transpire, and he would come to regret it would be his son, not him, they'd brand as the killer.

Had he read the article that appeared in the *Sun-Gazette* on November 15, 1973—eighteen days after the discovery of Jennifer's body had transposed her from a missing person to a homicide—he might have been optimistic that the investigation would lead them away from his son.

In a four-paragraph front page article headlined "Murder Probe Continues," Captain William I. Banzhaf, Commander of Troop F, the Pennsylvania State Police barracks in Montoursville, reported that "we just need one eyewitness." They were awaiting evidentiary results from the state police crime lab in Harrisburg, he said, "before we can go much further."

The investigation seemed to have stalled, but Joe, were he not on the threshold of comatose in a hospital bed, would have assured his family that they were at last relying on real and physical evidence instead of focusing on his family.

The next day, November 16, Kim Lee Hubbard was arrested for the murder of Jennifer Hill.

The arrest warrant was quoted in the newspaper and it included the phrase "or attempting to commit rape, deviate sexual intercourse." That part would never be established as physical evidence at the trial but was wielded liberally as a motive that led to "a willful, deliberate and premeditated killing." Charges are often listed in these documents to cover the gamut of possibilities and are also helpful in the event of plea agreements where some may be dropped in the bargaining process.

Joe Hubbard had been someone people could count on when they needed a volunteer or a helping hand. He had become a dedicated congregant in the Emmanuel Baptist Church just a block away from his home on West Central Avenue. Jennifer Hill had walked past the church that day. In a matter of weeks, the church would turn its collective back on the Hubbards.

That church had been very important to Joe. His religious conversion, spurred by family tragedy, had changed his life years before. But his church friends backed off after his son's arrest. He thought the world of the pastor, but he found out he was human, unwilling to get involved or offer emotional support, and that subsequently turned him off to church and religion.

Ruthie, though just a child, witnessed this hypocrisy at the trial when one of the church's lay leaders rejected her mom by walking away whenever she saw her approaching. She felt her mother's pain and isolation and would follow his father's path by abstaining from church and organized religion throughout her adult life. Like her mother she believed in God and the teachings of the Bible but not the people who professed to be pious. Not anymore. Meanwhile, Joe's grasp on reality had returned even as all those prescribed pills dissipated. He appeared more than ready to do battle to save his son.

Appearances, as it is often said, can be deceiving.

CHAPTER 3: GRIT

A "Phantom" Weekly Intervenes...

On Sunday, October 28, 1973, *Grit*, a Sunday weekly newspaper out of Williamsport, missed out on a scoop. A front-page photo the next Sunday, November 4, presented a scene looking up the narrow, grassy farm lane cut through a cornfield. It was reported that the body of Jennifer May Hill had been found adjacent to that lane. Crumpled plastic sheeting and discarded plastic pails seemingly used in pouring casts littered the scene. She had been discovered late on the afternoon of the 28th, but *Grit* had gone to press Saturday night and would have to wait a week to provide its own coverage of what would become one of Lycoming County's most controversial murder cases.

That was the first time the readers of Grit's Williamsport edition would be informed that Jennifer Hill, reported as missing in its October 21st edition, had been found murdered after being the subject of a massive search concluding nine days and 216 hours later. About 42,000 people read *Grit* at the time, but it was the *Sun-Gazette*, then an afternoon daily published Monday through Saturday, that reported the progress of the search for the girl day after day, and then broke the news of her body being found on Monday, October 29. Most everyone who read the *Sun-Gazette* during the week bought or subscribed to *Grit* on Sundays, so very few locals didn't know it was a homicide case by the time *Grit* published that front-page photo and reported it as murder a full week after the day the body was found. (The *Sun-Gazette*, one of oldest newspapers in the country stemming from the *Lycoming Gazette*, didn't publish a Sunday edition until 1991.)

The October 29th issue of the *Sun-Gazette* displayed a front-page photo of key figures in the investigation and eventual prosecution of the case against Kim Lee Hubbard under the banner headline: "Body of Missing Girl Found in Field." Under the banner was a deck, or secondary two-line headline, stating: "Police Suspect Homicide; Autopsy to Be Performed." Perhaps the most intriguing element of the page layout was the somewhat eerie photo taken after dark of an artificially lighted scene of men huddled together under a plastic covering protecting them from steady rain and described as "looking for evidence." They form a semi-circle around the spot "where the body of Jennifer Hill was found," indicating the body had recently been moved before the photo was taken. According to one of the two men who transported the body from the body scene to the morgue, they had performed that somber task in gathering darkness and rain sometime after 6:00 p.m.

Most impressive for any journalist who has responded to a murder/death scene was the access the photographer, later identified as *Sun-Gazette* Editor John Beague, must have been given by the man in charge, District Attorney Allen E. Ertel. Access to a murder investigation is a gift for any journalist, and the principals in the crime scene investigation were all there for a group photo. Ertel was there, as were Coroner Earl R. Miller, South Williamsport Police Chief Charles E. Smith, Pennsylvania State Police Lt. Steven Hynick, administrative head of the investigation; Cpl. Ronald K. Barto, who would be the arresting officer of the suspected killer eighteen days later, and Trooper Joseph Keppick, chief processor of the crime scene. All were key figures in the investigation and trial. Newspaper reporters and photographers are usually kept at arm's length from a probable murder scene so as not to disturb any evidence. The press can be helpful when seeking potential witnesses, but *The Sun-Gazette* seemed to enjoy extraordinary access in breaking the news of the murder. The bottom line, which is nothing new in small town journalism, is that the public learned what the police and prosecutors wanted them to learn in the three months leading up to the trial.

The photo of the twelve-year-old girl in the football jersey she had been wearing the day she was last seen had appeared in the Sunday *Grit* on October 21st along with an article that search parties of volunteers were being coordinated by the hosting Civil Air Patrol Group. Weekly newspapers were not built for breaking news in pre-internet days, and *Grit* was no exception. Its only advantage was initial coverage of any news and sporting events that occurred on Saturdays, but for many the Sunday *Grit* provided the opportunity to catch up on the previous week's news on an unhurried Sunday.

There were two versions of *Grit*. The best-known was a weekly tabloid distributed nationally, with a circulation peaking at 1.5 million in 1969 and self-proclaimed as "America's Greatest Family Newspaper." It was a unique publication that chose to reach out to small-town and rural America with adolescent news carriers selling and delivering the papers for a few cents each, as well as pursuing the incentive of winning prizes for their efforts. An ad in a 1975 issue of the *Grit* displayed a photo of a boy with the distinct "Grit" cloth delivery bag and the heading: "I became $5.22 richer in less than 2 hours," referring to the time he spent on his weekly route. In another half-dozen years, six decades of Grit carrier boys and girls would come to an end.

Grit Carriers over the years included the likes of Astronaut John Glenn, "Singing Cowboy" Gene Autry, Colonel Harlan Sanders, the fried chicken mogul, and even country music icon and Kentucky coal miner's daughter, Loretta Lynn. Several generations of youngsters delivered the *Grit* until it was sold in 1981 and eventually transplanted to Kansas with a new brand under the same name and a continuing appeal to a rural audience as a bimonthly magazine catering to farmers, agronomists, and gardeners. A typical cover teaser of the successor was "Use Reclaimed Materials to Build a Chicken Coop" enhanced, of course, by chickens in vibrant color.

During the heyday of the national tabloid, credited as the first newsprint publication to include processed color photos and ads, there was only one other product for which Williamsport was better known: Little League Baseball. It started there, and the Little League World Series continues to be played and telecast nationwide in nearby South Williamsport on acreage donated to the world's most popular youth sports organization in 1958 by the founding family of the Grit Publishing Company.

Indeed, its readers did love this tabloid which provided front-page news coverage brimming with optimism, entertaining down-home columns, cartoons, puzzles, pulp fiction pieces and a wide variety of feature articles with a positive human-interest slant. Even the news accented the positive and was comprised of rewrites of dispatches from the Associated Press wire and clippings from newspapers all over the country. One full-time newsroom position was allocated for scouring subscribed newspapers from all over the country and clipping out articles with an eye toward items that would remain timely for at least another week. They would be meted out to writers who performed what we jokingly called "editorial renovation" to produce a rewrite in the upbeat *Grit* style.

The words of German immigrant Dietrich Lamade, who founded the *Grit* in December 1882, tellingly define the philosophy behind the publication: "Let us avoid showing the wrong side of things and making people feel discontented. Let us do nothing that will encourage fear, worry, temptations, or other forms of weakness." The motto of the *Grit* was "Ring the Joy Bells of Life," and we could turn bad news into better news even during the beleaguered waning and troubled weeks of the Nixon administration.

As in the case of the Hubbards, the Lamades are proof that every family, no matter how successful or respected, experiences tragedy somewhere along the way. The founder's son, George R. Lamade, on a hot August night in 1965, died by his own hand of a gunshot wound in his Williamsport home, as Little Leaguers vied in bracketed play for a world title on the field named after his late brother, Howard F. Lamade. The seventy-one-year-old *Grit* publisher, who had been with the family business for about forty-eight years, was reported to be "in ill health at the time," the only explanation for the tragedy posited by the county coroner. A few years later, the same coroner, Dr. Earl R. Miller, would play a key role in the investigation and trial of Kim Hubbard.

The ownership continued through several generations of the Lamade family, which had donated the land and lent its family name to the stadium where twelve-year-old boys from all over the world vie to be world champions of Little League Baseball. But Little League was changing too, and it wouldn't be just for twelve-year-old boys anymore. On Nov. 7, 1973, just ten days after Jennifer Hill, twelve, was found murdered, a court ruling cleared the way for girls to compete under the Little League banner.

The national edition was also known by some back in the day as "The Pennsylvania Liar," probably due to its rosy outlook and its propensity for telling tall tales. Many who remember the *Grit* and lived elsewhere in the United States were no doubt unaware that there was another Grit which, with a few exceptions, has vanished from existence, if not from the memory of those who relied on it for local news coverage.

The national and Williamsport editions were separate publications, although the editorial staff worked on both and, as one of them from 1972 into 1979, I can attest that we regarded the latter as legitimate journalism and a source of pride. After the national Grit was sold and moved, the local edition continued as Williamsport's Sunday newspaper until it stopped publishing in 1993. The local edition covered the events and government of Lycoming County, municipalities, and school districts, as well as the courts, crimes, fires, accidents, high school and college sports and, of course, feature reporting that didn't necessarily require a positive spin. The local Sunday weekly had become a legitimate newspaper which included news analysis and investigative reporting and, in its last decade at least, was truer to the tenets of journalism than many regional daily newspapers.

At *Grit*, management, encouraged by Executive Editor Terry Ziegler and Managing Editor Mike Cummings, was belatedly starting to recognize that real news reporting went beyond reprinting press releases and accepting without question official versions from elected officials, law enforcement and even prosecutors. Bylines were handed out for exemplary news stories and feature articles, which dissolved the anonymity of reporters and made us personally responsible for our reporting. Each of us had a pen name, because they didn't want us to go overboard with more than one byline. If I had two articles deemed worthy of bylines, I got to choose which was bylined with my real name and the other credited to my pen name, Harvey Schoonover. That byline policy was also adapted for full-length original features in the national edition, but otherwise its formula for content remained basically unchanged— except for a belated attempt to entice younger adherents. It was too little too late as its circulation continued to plummet throughout the 1970s due to its reliance on older readers. The circulation of the national edition was still at 1,300,000 in 1979, the year I left for an editor's job at a daily newspaper. The number dropped dramatically in the early 1980s under new ownership. The readership of the nationally circulated *Grit* was literally dying off.

The Williamsport edition was different, thanks to this change in philosophy and a team of young journalists who relished the opportunity for real reporting and writing.

One of our reporters covered the murder trial of Kim Hubbard in February of 1974, but it consisted mainly of weekly recaps of testimony that had already been reported in the Associated Press, the *Sun-Gazette* and on radio and television. For example, the trial started on Wednesday, February 20, and by the time the *Grit* came out on Sunday, there had been four days of trial testimony other media outlets had covered. The trial ended with the jury verdict on the afternoon of Friday, March 1, and when the Grit came out two days later, it was old news.

As for hard news, notably the elements of crime and punishment, local news reporters relied on gaining the confidence of police and prosecutors and the "tips" they might toss to us, like breadcrumbs to pigeons, as a reward. Pissing off our best sources wasn't recommended.

I confess I had paid little attention to the Hubbard case as it played out in the midst of my second year on the job. Reporters who covered the trial seemed convinced of his guilt. Regional news media provided the blow-by-blow coverage each day, and there were few details indicating any reasonable doubt about Hubbard's guilt in its pedantic reporting. The *Sun-Gazette*, for example, mentioned District Attorney Allen Ertel often but tended to label Patrick Fierro, the defense attorney, more generically as "Hubbard's lawyer" or simply "the defense."

The most dramatic reporting included an account of the father of the defendant's girlfriend standing up during her alibi-confirming testimony and calling her a liar—an event that threatened a mistrial. There were unflattering descriptions of the young people, mostly teens, testifying on Hubbard's behalf or attending to show their support. The term "young people" almost became an insult. There was even a sidebar article blaming them for the messy restrooms off the hallway outside the courtroom where there was always an overflow of people, including adults who apparently utilized the restrooms without contributing to the mess.

Barely three years after Hubbard was convicted, I was assigned to take a closer look at the case when new evidence not explored in his defense, as well as questionable evidence used by the prosecution, was brought to our attention. City Editor Alvin "Al" Elmer could have ignored it, as other news media outlets apparently had, but I got the word to "check it out." Such an assignment would have been unimaginable at the *Grit* even two years before.

My series ran for several weeks, highlighting discrepancies in the case, as well as new evidence. It raised all kinds of questions about the investigation and subsequent prosecution. It suggested that some protectors of law and order were willing to not just bend the rules but perhaps break a few to gain a conviction. A number of flaws in the case were obvious, but few could bring themselves to believe that there could be as much manipulation verging on corruption as was reflected in this compendium of contradictory evidence. Even those who agreed that Hubbard did not receive a fair trial could not believe it was a result of a conspiracy that would have to involve multiple people.

The what and the where have always been easier to prove that Hubbard may have been unfairly or sloppily prosecuted, but the why has always been a sticking point. Even people who have stood up to denounce the evidence used to gain a conviction were not 100 percent certain of his innocence. Those who justified unfair prosecution for their unwillingness to voice criticism were essentially playing the same game as any criminal investigator engaged in "testilying"—giving false or misleading testimony because you're sure you've got the right guy.

The *Grit*'s investigative series would be cut short when it became too uncomfortable for the continued support of upper management over and above my editors. There was admittedly pressure from Ertel, then a congressman, who prosecuted the case and was a hands-on participant in the investigation. I remember the final articles of the series being literally pulled off the layout boards by compositors when the word came down. There were no reprimands to me or my editors but just a general attitude that enough was enough and what we had reported was admirable and journalistically sound. We had opened the door for further journalistic involvement in the case.

When it came to refrigerated bodies being removed then returned to a crime scene, evidence being manipulated and clandestinely hypnotized eyewitnesses, it was time to move on before the extraterrestrials showed up. It was disappointing, if not devastating, for the series to come to such an untimely end before the big payoff, but it was only the beginning of news media interest in this case.

There had also been case analysis critiquing some of the evidence and testimony in the wake of the trial by Dick Sarge writing for the Harrisburg *Patriot-News*. After the *Grit* series, it prompted another wave of interest in the case by other news media. By that time, I had moved on the position of News Editor for *The Daily Review* in Towanda, Pennsylvania, in the county where I was born and raised.

In a case that thrived on too many evidentiary coincidences, with various experts in forensic medicine, crime scene investigation, DNA and other specialties adding their input to a long list of discrepancies in this case, there are several reasons why there has been no urgency in pursuing the truth in the Commonwealth versus Kim Lee Hubbard.

For starters, it is not a cold case, and Kim served his time long ago. He has lived an exemplary life since returning to society in 1984, as a husband, father, and hardworking business owner.

He had experienced many disappointments while in prison, as appeals for new trials were turned down time and again. New evidence and shining a light on the illegitimacy of convicting evidence added an increasing legion of believers in his innocence, but it didn't change the fact that he was a convicted murderer.

Joe Hubbard was the force behind exposing a case that might have otherwise been forgotten years before. He never gave up on his exhaustive campaign to clear his son, bringing the case to the attention of the news media, including the *Harrisburg Patriot-News*, *Philadelphia Inquirer*, *Grit* and the *Weekender*, a weekly news tabloid no longer published which ran a multi-part series on the many flaws in the case three years after mine. Others contacted included the Phil Donahue Show, CBS, NBC and even *Life* Magazine, whose heyday was between 1936 and 1972, and, along with the others, politely begged off.

Joe also secured the interest of a David Meyers, a producer for ABC's *20/20*. The *Philadelphia Inquirer* sent a reporter who devoted several months looking into the case. The former ultimately felt that although Kim may not have received a fair trial or competent legal representation, it was an issue for the appeals process which, at the time, had not yet been exhausted. The *Inquirer* assigned reporter Ed Schumacher, covering the higher education beat for them at the time, to look into the case.

In both cases, they or their superiors were not interested in cataloguing errors and discrepancies in the Commonwealth's evidence if it failed to exonerate Kim Hubbard of the crime. Had he been on death row or serving a life sentence, that may have been incentive to proceed with an investigative series. They knew Kim would be in his early thirties when he got out of prison. Despite strong suspicions, they could not state with certainty who the killer was without making the same kind of unfounded allegations that had convicted Kim. Both news agencies pulled out with apologies.

It is an old case, its investigation and trial evidence filled with discrepancies, questions, crime scene photos that don't mesh and easily challenged physical evidence. The victim, were she alive today, would be in her early sixties. Hubbard himself finished serving his time barely ten years after his Nov. 16, 1973, arrest, which in itself evokes questions, considering the age of the victim and how the crime was portrayed as a violent, sexually motivated attack with premeditation.

As one of the first to publicly question whether Kim Lee Hubbard was fairly tried and convicted for the murder of Jennifer May Hill on October 19, 1973, I am not here to solve this case. That opportunity may be lost forever, and the real evidence indicates her death may have been unintentional, possibly spurred by a burst of anger and a single blow to her larynx. There were no distinctive defensive wounds, trying to fight off a sexual predator as the Commonwealth maintained. Manual strangulation was the official cause of death, but markings on the neck supposedly indicating this were barely visible, even in enhanced color photos, and did not verify either strangling by ligature or with bare hands. One of the more distinct marks on her neck matched the fabric pattern on the neckline of the jersey she wore but in no way qualified as a ligature.

I believe I know where twelve-year-old Jennifer was killed and by whom. My version, without naming a suspect, would have been more convincing than the case presented in the Commonwealth versus Kim Lee Hubbard in at the Lycoming County Courthouse in Williamsport, Pennsylvania, in February of 1974, just three months after Hubbard's arrest. The Hubbards have always been convinced that Jennifer made it home that day.

So much for the wheels of justice grinding exceedingly slow. It required a tidy time frame of 125 days for a body to be discovered, crime investigated and, in short order, suspect arrested, tried, and convicted. Jennifer Hill's murder was probably not premeditated or at the hands of a predator as promulgated in the prosecutor's original and unlikely scenario. It is not even likely, based on evidence, that a foiled attempt at sexual assault preceded the homicide.

The *Grit*, as a local Sunday newspaper, has, in many ways, become a phantom newspaper that has essentially disappeared from public scrutiny. There is no internet niche for it, but there will be a complete archive on microfilm at the James V. Brown Library in Williamsport, which, at last report, was digitizing decades of those records for resurrection. There are also references to it in the records of the Library of

Congress, and that is reassuring. I have also learned that there are attics and basements all over the country with stacks of old Grits.

In many ways, 1973 was still a time of innocence. Despite the taint of Vietnam and how it had divided a nation, politically and generationally, in small-town America, they still believed in the justice system. Crime didn't pay. Police and prosecutors focused on making sure the guilty paid for their crimes. Innocent people didn't get arrested and convicted to bolster electability or to appease a clamoring public.

Of course, all the preceding were deemed true then, if not now, but back in the seventies nationwide cynicism was embryonic. Many of our television heroes were cops and cowboy lawmen. Looking back, this absence of skepticism toward law enforcement and our courts of law could have allowed the fabric of this fiction to flourish. That's pretty much how people in the heartland of Pennsylvania, hours away from Philadelphia, Pittsburgh, and New York City in opposing directions, viewed crime and punishment in the 1970s. This was the "silent majority" Nixon counted on, gaining re-election from it, and many of the children and grandchildren of those conservative Americans have veered even further right and had come to vocally question the fundamentals of American democracy. The age of innocence was nearing its end. The nation was being jolted by the Watergate scandal at the same time the Jennifer Hill murder investigation and Kim Hubbard's trial were playing themselves out, eventually driving Nixon out of office in August 1974.

This is not about crime and punishment as much as it is about a family who finally seemed on the verge of sharing in the vaunted American dream. In many ways, they too were victims, and, for unknown reasons, there is no record in trial transcripts or other court and case documents in which serious consideration was given to other suspects. Other than a brief mention in news articles of trying to track down known sexual predators while the girl was still missing, the investigation seemed to lack any peripheral vision from the start.

When it came to violent crime, especially the murder of a child, sympathy, not suspicion, was more likely to be extended to the grieving family—blood kin like parents, siblings, and other family members. We mourned their losses along with them, inserting ourselves in their stead. We had not yet accepted that death at the hands of a stranger or someone on the fringe of the victim's life was as much of a rarity then as now. Probably more so.

Only one of every four murder victims, according to the Bureau of Justice, is killed randomly by a stranger or someone who is only a passing acquaintance. The bureau's statistics on homicide trends started in 1980, but it seems logical that the same would have been true in the seventies.

Now even the most casual follower of crime literature and drama, whether real-life or fiction, knows suspicion starts with those closest to the victim. The murderers we came to know in the late sixties and early seventies were creepy-crawly visitors in the night like the Manson family and the first of the high-volume mass murderers, stalkers of the unknown and unwanted like John Wayne Gacy and Juan Corona.

John List, who meticulously massacred his whole family in November 1971, under the ruse that he was guaranteeing them a shortcut to Heaven, was an aberration who fooled everyone around him. He was a fugitive murder suspect for the rest of the seventies and most of the eighties. The public perception of murderers would roost on names like Ted Bundy and Son of Sam, among the serial killers who preyed on strangers. They became media stars while their victims are seldom remembered.

Susan Smith, born just two months before List killed his wife, mother, two sons and daughter in their scantily furbished Victorian mansion, would put a passive, wholesome face on evil in 1994, killing her two young sons and then blaming a fictional duo of dark-skinned carjackers.

At first the object of wholesale sympathy, she reinforced what the statistics told us all along about who our most likely murderers are. They had been known throughout history and literature as crimes of passion or abandonment of hope by the perpetrators. The lesson was not lost on criminal investigators in a murder case. You pick the fruit that hangs the lowest first—those closest to the victim—before you bring out the ladders to reach for the outer branches.

Thus arose the new millennium and, by now, it seemed that people killing lovers and former lovers, spouses, and ex-spouses and, yes, even parents and progeny, are the ones we suspect first.

Back on October 19, 1973, however, children were not supposed to be murdered in a place like South Williamsport, Pennsylvania. Their deaths came from accident or illness. It was Americana itself as the home of Little League Baseball—or at least the location of its World Series playing field, Lamade Stadium. Home plate is a mile at the most, as the crow flies, to the field where Jennifer Hill's body was found two months after a team from Taiwan beat the US Champions from Tucson, Arizona, for the 1973 Little League World Championship.

In a place like South Williamsport in October of 1973, should the unimaginable happen, the murder of a child—and a twelve-year-old girl described as "half nude" when they found her at that—it must be a pervert lurking out there on the fringes, waiting to fulfill unspeakable desires. If not, perhaps it was a total stranger with no motive other than blood lust. It might be someone known to the victim—a neighbor or, perhaps, a family acquaintance waiting for access, a chance. That was where they found Kim Hubbard, and the job of investigators and prosecutors at some point was to strengthen his tenuous link to the victim.

The first targets of the investigation, reported police in initial newspaper articles proclaiming Jennifer Hill a murder victim, were known sex offenders. The lead article in the *Sun-Gazette* dated October 29 reported the discovery of the dead girl in a cornfield just two miles east of her home. In the second paragraph, readers learned that "the body was half nude when she was discovered, but there has been no medical determination as yet as to whether the girl was sexually assaulted."

Immediately with the finding of the body of this child, the seed of a sexual assault, possibly a violent rape, had been planted, as it had in the arrest warrant. Arrest warrants have to cover all the bases, all the possibilities, but such public pronouncements should not fuel the public imagination with observations that prove to be unfounded—the same public from which the jurors would emerge.

Today they solve murder cases by clearing suspects one at a time, outward from immediate family, friends, and lovers to acquaintances, moving from the most intimate to the most remote. Back in South Williamsport, Pennsylvania, during a sparkling stream of Indian summer days in October 1973, Kim Lee Hubbard, twenty, was on the fringe of the life of Jennifer Hill even if they did spend the night prior to her disappearance in the same domicile. That, it seems, came to be of great importance to the police and prosecutor.

The girl fails to reach her home on Hastings Street in South Williamsport on the nineteenth of October, a Friday and a day off from school, vanishing somewhere on what should have been a walk measuring seven-tenths of a mile past dozens of homes in a residential area. It was late afternoon. The starting point was the home of her best friend, Ruthie Hubbard, where she had stayed overnight as a prelude to a day of play.

Even as the girl remains missing, the object of an exhaustive search and speculative newspaper headlines, official suspicion quickly falls on the family from whose home the young girl departed, never to make it home.

CHAPTER 4: KIM

"Run If You Want!"

The search for Jennifer Hill, starting the afternoon and evening she went missing, had little impact on Kim Hubbard. He felt, at first anyway, that she had just run away to piss off her parents and was probably hanging out with a friend. He had never paid much attention to her. She was this chubby little friend of his sister's. He had no memory of her on that particular day, October 19, 1973.

Things got more serious as soon as they found the body on a Sunday. He was called out of school for questioning later that week. It was the first indication that he may be a suspect, but he figured they had to check everybody out who knew the girl. He remembers being at his house on West Central Avenue and sitting across the dining room table from a pair of intimidating cops and a pasty-faced guy in glasses. The latter was Lycoming County District Attorney Allen Ertel, as he would subsequently learn much to his regret.

Always more of a visual person than into books and words, he could still see them as they faced him. Lt. Stephen Hynick, the titular head of the investigation, as it turned out, was on the left; Sgt. Edward Peterson in the middle, and Ertel on the right.

The two cops were peppering him with questions, with Ertel occasionally intervening. They persisted in getting him to remember the times of where he was and what he did that day when Jennifer started her walk from there and never made it home. No question they were trying to cross him up. That was their job, he supposed. At that point it had been, what, maybe two weeks? Did they really expect him to recall specific times on a day almost two weeks ago that was like many others to him?

They wanted times for everything, and they were writing everything down. He kept telling them he was guessing at some of this stuff. He figured they were talking to his mother, and that made him feel better. She'd remember.

Still, he wasn't all that concerned. He was thinking there were people around pretty much wherever he went, or so it seemed, and he surely had no contact with Jennifer Hill that day. They asked him something about waving at some kids down at the lot by the Super Duper. He remembered driving by his sister and some of her friends playing in the lot down there. Jennifer Hill was one of them, but he only came to know that after the fact.

"They were a bunch of kids playing and Ertel would try to make it like there was some secret signal between us," Kim recalled in a 1983 interview after he had been released from prison and so-called rehab in a halfway house in Johnstown. "It would have been almost comical if it wasn't a way to make me look like some kind of pervert."

It was the only connection they could make between the two that day. The implication, as presented by the prosecution in the trial, was that there must have been some tacit understanding between them of where and when to meet. There was a big deal made when one of those children testified that Kim had waved at them when he drove by.

"I can't say that I didn't wave. Kids in the neighborhood would wave when I drove by and sometimes I'd wave back. Did I that day? I don't know, but what difference would it have made either way?"

There was no evidence or testimony from any of her playmates that the incident made any impression on Jennifer herself. It was just one of a number of awkward attempts to link Kim and Jennifer in some way, beyond the fact that she had stayed at the Hubbard home with Ruth, as she had apparently done a number of times, and it was erroneously and repeatedly reported in the press as the last place she had been seen alive. Their one so-called eyewitness said she had seen her alive, as had the witnesses to her walk along the way.

There was testimony from a woman named Mary Mundrick who lived along Jennifer's route toward home that accurately described her.

There was also Jimmy Clabaugh, a neighbor who knew her, and another kid. They all saw her on that sidewalk headed home. She was wearing that football jersey with the number 33 on it, the bell-bottom jeans with red hearts on the knees and a strip of patterned red cloth sewn at the bottom of each leg to lengthen a pair of hand-me-downs for a growing girl. She was carrying a pink Glick (a Williamsport shoe store) bag in which she had stuffed the clothing she wore to school the day before. She started the walk wearing an old dark blue school letter jacket, but soon removed it and tied it around her waist, exposing the memorable 33 football jersey.

When she went missing, they put a recent photo of her in the newspaper wearing that same jersey. There would also be testimony from a man named Joe Mendez, virtually ignored, as it turned out, placing Jennifer—the girl in the number 33 jersey he had seen in the newspaper. She was standing on a corner at the probable time it would have taken her to walk that far, a block or two from her home.

I've stood on the corner where Mendez still insisted years later that he saw her as he waited at the traffic light. The Hill house, Jennifer's destination, is in view from that intersection. This could have been significant had Patrick Fierro, the defense attorney, recognized the value of the testimony of his own witness. In retrospect, it's difficult to understand how he missed it.

Meanwhile, the prosecution's "eyewitness," Betty Jane Nevel, placed a girl identified as Jennifer getting into a car resembling Kim's in front of her home on Howard Street. That was about three blocks in another direction from the corner where Mendez saw her and thirty minutes after Mendez's sighting.

That meant that Jennifer Hill would have been within 100 yards of her home on Hastings Street, only to turn back, retrace her steps for about a block and then veer off to walk a block-and-a-half in another direction south on Howard Street. Even more improbably, she was unseen by anyone else for a considerable amount of time until, conveniently, Mrs. Nevel spotted her at the alleged dramatic rendezvous with her killer.

Nevel, it would be discovered in Fierro's case records after the trial, was hypnotized to "assist her recollection," according to an explanatory note from Ertel. The bottom line is that there is no indication that anyone knew from the trial. The defendant and his family were not aware of the hypnosis until they picked up the case files after the trial when they had been assigned a new attorney, Public Defender John "Jack" Felix, to appeal the conviction.

Kim didn't have much of a memory of Ertel before the arrest and trial, except as a cold, hostile presence. Ertel would sit back and look him over while Hynick and Peterson asked him questions, occasionally interjecting one of his own. He was surprised during jury selection for the trial when he realized that Ertel was actually the main man, as some were wont to say in the 1970s, in the camp of the enemy. He, to this day, marvels at how naïve he was during the investigation, trial and well beyond.

His strongest memory was of Hynick, the highest-ranking cop in the investigation and Administrator of the Criminal Division at the Montoursville State Police Barracks at the time. Even though Hynick, then in in his late fifties, was viewed by Dorisann Hubbard as a menacing presence, Kim didn't see him that way. Not until that day at the Humdinger when he pointed a handgun within inches of his face.

"I think he was just playing one of a number of roles and not pulling the strings in any frame-up," he explained. Hynick himself, during the trial described his role as "administrator to see that the proper persons were doing their jobs." It was, I would later learn, something of a demotion presaging his own career ending run-in with the law in general and Ertel in particular.

Some fifteen months after his involvement in that investigation, Hynick would be accused of tampering with a witness in another case, warning another of impending apprehension and blackmailing the District Attorney to dissuade him from continuing with a wiretapping investigation against city officials in Williamsport. The DA was Allen E. Ertel. What he was "blackmailing" Ertel about was never specified due to a plea agreement that kept him out of jail and allowed him to retire with thirty-eight years of pension.

Returning to October of 1973, Kim was realizing things were getting serious in the wake of Jennifer Hill's disappearance: "Talk would come back... stuff would get back."

He was going to school and working nights. Friends would come to him at school. The gist was the cops were asking a lot of questions about him and his car. Then it started getting back to him that he was somehow a suspect. (A suspect in what? The girl was supposedly missing, a likely runaway who had argued with her mother on the phone less than an hour before she disappeared.) It was all about her being at the Hubbard house and that he resided there.

"That stuff started bothering me."

He remembered his parents talking about it, trying to understand where she might have gone. His father had been actively involved in some of the early searching activity for the girl. Kim, meanwhile, was thinking she was just a brat kid who took off. To him it seemed they were making too big a deal about it at first. Then it started getting strange as the days went by.

The mayor and police chief were nosing around a lot, sniffing out information in conjunction with the state police. In fact, the state police had set up headquarters at the South Williamsport Borough Hall. They were acting as if the girl was dead long before she was found murdered. Both Chief Smith and Mayor Frey came nosing around asking weird questions about Jennifer's activities and dietary choices before she embarked on her fatal journey from their home.

On October 28th—nine days to the hour after she went missing between 4:00 and 5:00 p.m.—Jennifer's body was discovered by a Civil Air Patrol searcher in a cornfield on Sylvan Dell Road barely a mile away from her home.

Kim was working his second-shift job (10:00 p.m. to 2:00 a.m.) at the Stroehmann's plant when the word got out. They were on break and it came over the radio. That's all everyone talked about until the end of the shift. It was the first time he really felt a sense of foreboding, because of all the things that had come back to him. He became genuinely worried, remembering how a couple of nights before two guys who had obviously been drinking, came to their home at a late hour, bringing accusations of murder. They told a story about Kim being seen throwing a body into the trunk of a red sports car.

One of them was Carl "Puff" Pfirman who they learned was some kind of big shot at Williamsport Hospital. Why was Pfirman, who was supposed to be a local high school football hero back in the day, so sure Jennifer had been murdered? It was getting crazy and now, several days later, she was a murder victim instead of a missing person. Kim knew things were getting serious. Obviously, word was out that he was suspected of something before there was something to be suspected of.

"It shook me up, but it wasn't fear. I couldn't figure out why they're wasting all of their time looking at us. I figured they were probably playing games with others like they were with me."

There was obviously a killer out there and it didn't seem they had their act together. The turning point in his life came on Nov. 3, 1973—just six days after the body was found. There were the interrogations by police and the talk was getting louder about him being the killer. Chief Smith came to their house that day and told Dorisann that they knew Kim did it. She called Kim and told him what Smith had said and Kim was, in his words, "sick of all this." They weren't going to leave him alone, and they were only wasting their time while the real killer was out there. Smith asked him if he would take a lie detector test. Why not? He had watched enough cop shows to know that this was one way to get them off his back.

Kim remembers Smith driving him and his mother to the state police barracks in Montoursville. The place was overflowing with police.

"They kept saying, 'We know you did this.' I'd just tell them to arrest me if they had all this evidence. Probably wasn't smart of me, but it was getting weird."

They kept coming at him in teams of two. When he asked if he could take a break and go to the restroom "I think I counted eight staties escorting me." After he took the test, the place was virtually deserted. "I know I passed that test. There's no doubt in my mind that they were ready to arrest me then and there if I flunked that test. They said they had all this evidence and casts and it was like everybody was there figuring on me flunking or giving them a confession."

Even Smith, who drove them back from the barracks, seemed friendlier and Kim said he felt a sense of relief. Maybe it was over and they could move on. He and his mother had a laugh about them claiming they had casts of the prints of his boots at the body scene. Both knew he had worn his sneakers all that day. They also knew they had taken his boots to compare, which seemed like a good thing at the time.

"Smitty didn't seem to find it that funny, though."

Both Kim and Dorisann always maintained that Smith, who she chose to address as Charles, had stopped at the airport in Montoursville on the way back and suggested they could buy plane tickets and that perhaps "the best thing for both of you is to get away from this whole mess." His mother reminded the chief that she had a twelve-year-old daughter at home and a husband in the hospital recovering from a nervous breakdown due to this "whole mess."

Smith has never admitted what would have been a clumsy attempt to encourage Kim to flee from potential prosecution. For Dorisann it was frightening. None of it made sense. Why would he even think they would run away? Had someone higher up in the investigation told Chief Smith to make that suggestion or was it a spontaneous display of compassion? Had he been sent there as a sympathetic figure to encourage Kim to agree to a lie detector test at the barracks? He is said to have commented about his role in the case in casual conversation with people he knew. However, he preferred not to talk about it to the press—even some 45 years later. It seemed to Dorisann Hubbard back then as if everyone around her had gone crazy. Who were their friends and who were their enemies? Joe was in the hospital now. She needed him back desperately.

Kim had to quit the Stroehmann's job after they impounded his car on October 31 and didn't return it until November 7. They even kept his Stroehmann safety helmet. Plus, there was too much drama with the police on the home front. His father was out of commission in the hospital.

Everything seemed to be falling apart. The complete collapse came on Friday, November 16. He stopped at the local fast-food hangout, the Humdinger, where his girlfriend, Colleen Whitenight, was waiting for him. The place was crawling with cops when he got out of his car, but he could see Colleen sitting by a window. He walked inside and before the door closed behind him, his erstwhile interrogator, Hynick, was standing in front of him, his arm extended and a gun barrel almost touching the tip of his nose.

All he said was, "Run if you want."

They put him in the backseat of a police car with five cops in it. He was sitting between two of them, each with a leg over one of his. "I was scared to death." It was a surreal ride. There was a factory burning across the river on Third Street in Williamsport. He remembered that. Returning to the barracks, where he had been almost two weeks before, he was fingerprinted and grilled with more questions. Most of them he'd heard before.

He remembers Hynick asking tiredly, "Why don't you just confess?" Hynick seemed to be the point man in all of this, but when they got to the trial, Kim accurately recalled him describing his job as "some kind of evidence custodian."

Kim would spend his first night in the county jail in a screened cell and the next day he was taken to the second floor in what they called the federal cell, which was isolated from other prisoners. That walk across the parking lot at the Humdinger would be his last taste of freedom for more than a decade. He did get to call home and tell his mother he'd been arrested for Jennifer's murder.

A guy he knew in jail, another prisoner, brought him the local newspaper, the *Sun-Gazette*. It brought home that this was all too real. To this day he can't really explain the feeling of being in jail for the first time. He felt he would be getting out, even if it meant waiting for the trial and acquittal. In the meantime, his parents had found a lawyer, Patrick Fierro.

"Fierro kept telling me, 'Don't worry about nothing.' He told me that throughout the whole trial and everything. He always had something that would blow them out of the water."

The preliminary hearing turned out to be one of waiving and stipulating from Fierro to Ertel. There was no transcript of that hearing, but those who attended remarked that there was no physical evidence introduced in this stage of the process, which is basically for the District Magistrate—in this case Richard T. Eisenbeis—to confirm there seemed to be enough evidence or a prima facie (presumed to be true) case to bind it over for trial.

"I will stipulate to that," Kim remembered Fierro saying several times to Ertel's requests. The prosecution's key eyewitness was Betty Jane Nevel. There was testimony from Chief Smith and Trooper Joseph Keppick. His sister, Ruthie, also testified about what she and Jennifer did that day. The testimony of another of the victim's friends, Linda Peck, was disallowed as not relevant.

They called Pat Fierro the one-arm bandit. He was missing an arm and reputedly known for getting his clients off or cases dismissed altogether. Kim had been pulled aside by one of his teachers at South Williamsport High School before his arrest recommending Fierro as an attorney if it ever got to that point. Kim passed that on to his parents.

There was a report in the newspaper weeks prior to the trial that he was engaged in combative behavior with other prisoners at the county jail. At the end of the article, the warden dismissed it as an argument with another prisoner and of no great consequence.

"County jail was like basic training. You don't take a lot of shit, because these guys want to see what you can take, you know?" Kim explained. "Mostly, I played a lot of cards and learned a lot about the dos and don'ts in jail."

It's the type of stuff that helps you survive. Surprisingly, he got virtually no flak, either in county jail or state prison, from all the negative publicity—before the trial at least—about it being portrayed as a child-sex crime. As it turned out, the physical evidence in the trial proved there was no molestation or typical injuries indicating attempts at sexual molestation. Her cricoid cartilage, fractured, had collapsed her airway resulting in death by manual strangulation. And yet many people in the

Williamsport area carried the belief for years that Kim Hubbard was a pervert who killed a twelve-year old girl in a sexually fueled attack. That was a motive provided by the DA with no physical evidence corroborating such a storyline. Years later, this storyline would be resurrected in a one-sided account in a book that included his case.

Then came the trial, starting on Feb. 20, 1974, fewer than four months after the body of Jennifer Hill was officially discovered and three months after Kim's arrest. Most of the trial was a blur to him, and he has no clear memories of many of the witnesses, with the exceptions of his girl, Colleen, and Mrs. Nevel, the so-called key prosecution witness.

"She (Nevel) acted like she was drunk up there. She was like mumbling and all slouched over." He vaguely recalls Ertel trying to cross him up and how he sucked it up to remain calm and courteous in his response. "It was like, 'I didn't say that. You did,' and then he'd try to put words in my mouth again."

What else? "I remember people with bag lunches. I remember the judge asking me if I had anything to say." That, of course, was immediately following the guilty verdict.

"I remember testifying. It reminded me when they were questioning me before they had me write everything down. It was about times and when I was here or there that day. Like I said, I was guessing, estimating, a lot of the time. So, a few things in my testimony conflicted with that. So, he keeps saying I'm a liar and if I lied about little things, I'd have to lie about murdering somebody. Stuff like that."

It was that very issue, labeling Kim a liar whenever he'd make a statement, that came closest to the state Supreme Court granting him a new trial a few years later, with one of the two dissenting judges assertively recommending that recourse.

At the trial, Kim got a lot of support from high school classmates, and a loyal group of them were there in the gallery every day. Several, of course, testified for both the defense and the prosecution, mostly about whether they did or did not see a white helmet on the backseat ledge of his car when riding with him.

They behaved themselves better than many of the adults who would boo or laugh at defense witnesses. The judge had to lecture them to quiet down and behave several times. Others were faithful attendees, and one of those who encouraged them was Bill "Buck" Byham, a teacher and coach who was something of a local radio personality as a sports commentator. Byham was supportive of Kim after he became a suspect and the one who had recommended Pat Fierro as their attorney.

However, Byham apparently changed his mind about Kim's innocence on the day the guilty verdict was rendered, Friday, March 1, 1974. The next week on Tuesday, March 5, he called the senior Vo-Tech class together, apologizing to them for giving them "false hope in Kim's case."

"I will simply tell you this," he told them in a mimeographed statement of the speech that he advised they pass around to others. "That afternoon (March 1) I talked with Allen Ertel for about forty-five minutes and got the education I should have had before I ever opened my mouth in a classroom."

Byham praised them for their loyalty to Kim and advised them not to be bitter, but implied that his conversation with Ertel convinced him they should be assured of their classmate's guilt and reminded them of "a hard fact (that) the law has found him guilty." He offered to "explain what happened" for any interested in learning more. Byham later passed on to students that Kim had become something of a troublemaker in the state prison in Rockville when, in truth, he had been a model prisoner there and, after that, at Chase Correctional Facility. Had his former teacher been educated by Ertel on this fact as well, or did someone else relay this tidbit of erroneous information?

CHAPTER 5: UNINVITED GUESTS

"Lynch Party from the Central Grille"

It didn't take much to awaken Dorisann Hubbard in the early morning hours of Friday, October 26, 1973. She had been sleeping restlessly—more like resting sleeplessly—for a week now, and Joe was on the overnight emergency room shift at Williamsport Hospital. She could hear a lot of banging and yelling outside. And it wasn't just anywhere outside.

It was on the front porch at the door!

The kids—Kim and Ruthie—were in bed in their rooms. She had heard Kim come in maybe an hour before and had dozed off a bit surrendering to the relief of mothers knowing their kids are safely home. She looked at the clock at her bedside. It was 2:15 in the morning. Even if Kim somehow locked himself out, he wouldn't have made a racket like that. There were multiple voices. It sounded like a mob, and her heart sank. What else could happen this week?

She cautiously opened her bedroom window, feeling the refreshing coolness at the end of a warm autumn day invade the bedroom. She shouted to whoever was out there. "What is it? What do you want?"

An imposing figure, silhouetted in the dim lighting from the street, had stepped out from the porch and emerged onto the sidewalk. The voice was threatening, and his speech slurred. "We want to talk to you people," he barked maliciously. "Let us in or you're going to be in a lot of trouble!" Then he said, as if as an afterthought, "It's Carl Pfirman."

Strange and a bit scary. She recognized the name. Joe mentioned it at one time or another. Somebody at the hospital, an administrator or something. Had something happened to Joe? Was he in some kind of trouble? She yelled back that she couldn't let them in because her husband was working, but that only seemed to make them angrier. They started yelling and pounding again. She had seen two of them, but there seemed to be others standing in the darkness on the back fringe out of range of the street light.

She genuinely feared they would break in. Who knew what their intentions were? Panicking, she called Joe at the hospital and, with little explanation, told him with great urgency that he had to get home right of way. People were trying to break in!

She then realized that Kim had emerged from his room and was already downstairs. It was the last thing he needed with all that was going on.

Before she could react, Kim had opened the door to the porch. Then, instead of letting them in, he stepped out onto the porch itself and latched the door behind him. By this time, she was downstairs herself and Kim was clearly being verbally accosted. The voices grew in both volume and rising pitch of accusation. After interminable minutes of anxiety, she realized Joe had pulled up at the curb in front of the house, and that, in itself, eased her concern. Joe had a way of calming people down. At least that evened the odds, because she could now discern through a downstairs window two men confronting Kim. The man calling himself Pfirman was larger than Joe and Kim put together, but she recognized the other as Bob Shoalts who had to be close to fifty and not in the best of shape. She then realized that the two had Kim against the wall. Joe told her later that Pfirman was jabbing a finger into Kim's bare chest when he arrived.

Joe talked to him like you might to a drunk on a window ledge ten stories above the street. That seemed to calm things down. He called him by his first name calmly and firmly. "What's the problem, Carl?... What are you doing here, Carl?" It was the answer that revived the surge of panic she had felt when summoning Joe from the hospital.

"We know that little girl was killed here, and you better talk to us!" Pfirman, clearly irate, challenged.

Kim had no shirt on, and Joe told him he had better get into the house. Then instead of ordering the two bullies off the porch as she had hoped, he murmured something to their uninvited guests, and they all ended up in their dining room. Pfirman, still speaking loudly despite their close quarters, continued to carry on about Kim murdering the girl.

"You're drunk, Carl," Joe finally said, turning to Dorisann and gesturing toward the adjacent kitchen: "Bugs, can you make us some coffee?" he asked quietly. She gave him a what-are-you-doing look, but decided he felt he had everything under control.

Pfirman had moderated his voice by this time, but he was acting as if it was his house and he was in charge as he advised Kim and Joe to sit down. After the four sat at the table, Shoalts told them something so astonishing that Dorisann could not believe he was actually saying it. He explained that the previous Friday, October 19, at "exactly 4:30," someone driving by their house had seen Kim loading a large bundle into the trunk of a "sporty" red Chevy and, as he put it, "drive off a hellin'." (Had that allegation been true it would have been an alibi to exclude Kim from the crime him for which he would subsequently be accused.)

He said, with great certainty, that he knew the bundle was the body of Jennifer Hill, who was still the object of a massive search after turning up missing the day of this alleged sighting, and he somehow knew Kim was disposing of her body. This inspired Pfirman to renew his accusations, which included a stream of foul language.

Now it was Dorisann's turn to lose her temper, ordering the uninvited pair to get out. Joe had tolerated their rude, threatening behavior, perhaps to learn all he could about what was going on. In response to her command, Pfirman stated that he did not intend to leave.

With that, Dorisann ran upstairs, phoned South Williamsport Police Chief Charles Smith and told him about the trespassing pair, who they were and that she was fearful of what might happen next.

"Hell, Dorisann, I'm so goddamned tired now, if I come down there, I'll just get tied up," he told her. "Call the state police if you think you need help." He then volunteered to provide their phone number, which she quickly turned down, and hung up. She remembered telling him without rancor, "Thanks," as if he had done her some kind of favor. They needed all the friends they could get, and Smith had seemed more supportive than the state cops.

When she returned downstairs, they were still at it, and she could see that Kim was so upset he was visibly shaking. He continued to be the target of derision from Pfirman who was making fun of his "hippie hair" and telling him he was "no damn good." That made her angry. Kim's hair was actually shorter than most of his friends, the comment momentarily distracting her from the seriousness of their allegations.

Joe calmly advised Kim to go to bed, nodding toward the stairs, and Kim, now totally befuddled, complied. It was then that Joe became the target. Now he was the one being accused of murdering Jennifer. It was Joe's turn to order them out and literally pushed them toward the door. If the drunken pair had come there as rogue investigators to extract some kind of confession, they must have realized by then it wasn't going to happen. They departed mumbling with halfhearted resistance.

Joe watched them leave the premises, proceed down the sidewalk and get into a truck about 50 yards away around the corner on Clinton Street and drive off. He was surprisingly composed, almost nonchalant, after the encounter and, once the stumbling duo left, assured his wife with a kiss on the cheek that they would bother her no more. And yet she also sensed a tenseness about him that told her he was desperately weighing the seriousness of what just happened. He returned to his own pickup parked in front of the house and drove away to resume the remainder of his emergency room shift.

A few minutes after he left, Dorisann heard noises outside and suspected there were others who might have come with Pfirman and Shoalts. She proceeded to call the police as she started to boil a large pot of water in case further protection was warranted from intruders. It was the only deterrent she could think of. Patrolman Ken Balliet, who was on call at the borough police station, belatedly responded and assured her he'd keep an eye on the house. Then he left. She turned off all the lights, then fielded a call from Joe who was making sure all was well in a weary and muted monotone that alarmed her. It was at that time, some twenty-five to thirty minutes after it had departed, she observed from the eastern kitchen window the truck slowly returning to the spot where it had parked before on Clinton Street. It sat there for a few minutes in the dark. She waited expectantly for figures to emerge, but then it drove off, as deliberately as it had arrived, and turned onto a nearby alley that bordered the rear of their property. By that time, it was at least 4:30 a.m.— two hours and fifteen minutes after the whole episode began. Dorisann was certain the truck had returned to pick up or confer with two or three more people. There had seemed to be movement in the darkness outside the truck, though the interior lights of the pickup never came on.

She waited another hour or so until shortly after dawn's early light to check with her nearest neighbor to the west, Lois Johns. She confirmed she had heard all the commotion and was admittedly "frightened to death." She also stated that she was sure there had been someone in the Hubbards' backyard. Lois had sensed motion in the dark, perhaps voices, and her dog had carried on accordingly.

After Joe returned from work as the sun edged upward above the tree line, they patrolled the perimeter of the house and found signs of disturbance at several locations, including fresh scuffed dirt and imprints and one fresh large footprint in a freshly dug flower bed in front of their dining room window. Someone had stood there.

Perhaps the most jarring part of this encounter was the horrible talk about murder. As she learned later that morning, Jennifer Hill was still a missing person. Her body would not be found for two-and-a-half more days, or about sixty hours, after the two men made their accusations.

Even more puzzling, as it turned out, there was never any mention throughout the investigation and Kim's trial of a red car or any further mention of Shoalts and Pfirman in connection with the case.

Pfirman, after a night of drinking and alcohol-inspirited imaginings, may have made a mistake of believing Shoalts's so-called eyewitness account of body snatching. They may have been running a total bluff on the Hubbards, but why were they so sure there was a murder at that early date and that Kim Hubbard would be the appointed killer?

Carl Pfirman's brief, mysterious and distressing appearance before a missing girl became a murder victim would remain of interest because he was one of a number of connections to the Williamsport Hospital as the case played itself toward Kim's conviction four months later. Pfirman might have been in a position to garner inside information from colleagues, including Dr. Earl Miller, the county coroner and a prominent member of the hospital's medical staff. The hospital housed a secure cooler where a body could be securely preserved and where the autopsy was ultimately conducted. And then there was the Way Unit, a psyche ward where a heavily sedated Joe Hubbard would end up five days after that early-morning confrontation.

Two years after "the lynch party from the Central Grille," as Joe Hubbard would later label their uninvited guests, a criminal complaint was filed by the Hubbards against Pfirman, mainly because Joe hoped they might gain more insight into the Hill homicide investigation that might be helpful in his crusade to prove his son's innocence.

What had triggered this early-morning assault on the Hubbard residence?

The hearing established for the record that indeed Carl Pfirman, Director of the Rehabilitation Services Department, and founder of the Sports Medicine Program at Williamsport Hospital, was making a scene at the Hubbard residence between 2:15 and 4:00 a.m. on the morning on October 26, 1973. District Magistrate Ronald Blackburn determined that he was guilty of being drunk and disorderly. The penalty was a fine. For Joe Hubbard, however, it raised another of many questions about the death of Jennifer Hill and the ensuing investigation.

Two state policemen, Trooper Leon Whipple and Corporal Donald Houser, a member of the criminal investigative team testifying at Kim Hubbard's murder trial, appeared at the Pfirman hearing. Only Whipple testified, with Houser apparently there as an observer at a hearing for a misdemeanor case that had not directly involved the state police at the time it occurred. Whipple had basic knowledge of the disturbing incident, it seemed, but did not seem to be a factor.

"The purpose in the Hubbards bringing charges against him at such a late date was to see if he knew anything about the death of Jennifer Hill prior to the 28th," Charles King, who attended that hearing, has stated.

It didn't necessarily shed new light on the crime itself, but it was another piece of information indicative of a murder investigation going on before there was an acknowledged murder. It was what Trooper Whipple said when asked by Blackburn why he, as a state policeman, had appeared at the Hubbard home in response to the allegations against Pfirman:

"He said he was there into the official investigation of the death of Jennifer Hill," recalled King, who made his observations in detailed serial coverage of the Hubbard murder case in the *Weekender* newspaper.

The death of Jennifer Hill did not become a murder case until her body was officially discovered at approximately 4:00 p.m. on October 28, 1973. As for Whipple's involvement in the case against Pfirman, he conceded that he had not been asked by either the plaintiff or defendant to testify at the hearing. The only person who had asked him to attend the hearing was Houser, he explained to the District Judge.

Following is how King described what happened next when Whipple took the stand:

"Blackburn asked Trooper Leon Whipple if either the prosecutor or the defense had asked him to be there that day. He said no. The Magistrate asked him why he was there. He said Cpl. Houser told him to be there. Trooper Whipple had a book with him which evidently was the State Police records. He indicated he interviewed the Hubbards separately about the Carl Pfirman affair. (He said that) none of the Hubbards' testimony conflicted or contradicted itself."

> Note: Because King was a friend of the Hubbards, closely tied
> to Joe Hubbard in particular as they strove to exonerate Kim or
> secure a new trial, some might question his objectivity. I spent
> hours with King and, as was the case with Joe Hubbard, I never
> caught him in a lie or exaggeration when it came to evidence
> and information they gathered. Their speculation about the

why's and how's behind their findings could be subjective, sometimes highly so, as has often been the case for those trying to solve a mystery and the motives behind Kim Hubbard becoming a sacrificial lamb.

Carl L. "Puff" Pfirman was a hometown boy and South Williamsport High School football star who, after his graduation in 1946, earned a football scholarship to Penn State. He had a distinguished career after graduating from Penn State, serving in the US Air Force in the Korean War as a 2nd Lieutenant. It was this military commitment that reportedly forced him to turn down an offer to play professionally with the Philadelphia Eagles. He returned to civilian life and earned a degree in physical therapy from the University of Pennsylvania. From there he embarked on a three-decade career at Williamsport Hospital and was a notable advisor to nursing homes and other providers of physical rehabilitation.

Pfirman died at the age of eighty-one at his Williamsport home on October 19, 2010—forty-seven years to the day from the disappearance and probable death of Jennifer Hill. What instigated his appearance on the evening and early morning of October 25-26 at the Hubbard home will probably never been known.

CHAPTER 6: DECOMPOSITION

What Really Happened to the Body?

She is dead, and there is no memory here of what happened before she, as a corpse, was deposited in this field. Her body may have to provide the clues that will reveal her murderer, the sole living possessor of the memory of those last few minutes of her life.

She had been young and healthy, only twelve years old, and now time passes, not with growth but with decay.

It is a pleasant October afternoon when she is lain here, apparently quite carefully, in this field among withering stalks bearing the weight of tasseled ears of corn. Her trousers and panties are pulled down to her ankles. A jacket is thrown across much of her torso, leaving only part of the abdomen and the tan line crossing just beneath an exposed right hip. You might call it a partial cover-up or limited exposure. Underneath the covering garment, a dark blue football jersey and bra are pulled up, almost cautiously, to expose part of a pubescent breast. Only photos taken after the body is discovered, with the jacket pulled down, reveal this. Perhaps the killer intended to convey the impression of a sex crime without being too revealing.

It is harvest time, perhaps a bit late. Harvesting of field corn has already begun in nearby fields in northeastern Pennsylvania when her lifeless body arrives here. She lay here nine full days amid these stalks, which provide little cover from the warming sun, constant from dawn 'til dusk, and a daily span of about eleven hours of direct sunlight this time of year.

Temperatures hang at just above fifty degrees that first evening, remaining there even after darkness falls before dropping slightly into the upper forties throughout the morning hours of the next day. Temperatures climb steadily into the sixties the next day and, again, there is little to shade the body from the ever-present sun. Clear blue sky prevails, with only wispy clouds dotting the sky. And so it goes, repeating for the next twenty-four hours, and then the next and the next. Then, as you might expect even in a mild October, the temperatures become a little crisper in the early morning hours, though never within six degrees of freezing, climbing back up into the fifties and sixties in the sunny afternoons and early evenings. Wind speeds, which could have provided some cooling and inhibited the invasion of flying and crawling insects, are negligible, certainly unremarkable.

The National Weather Service, with a station just across the river from the cornfield, recorded higher temperatures on the afternoons of the sixth and seventh days her body lay there with hourly readings between 64 and 68, almost mirroring each other. Again, nothing approaches freezing in the early morning hours. Dew points are generally in the thirties and forties, limiting formation of ground moisture. Dry conditions usually mean more rapid decomposition of the body, though some moisture from scant dew on the grassy ground activates bacteria like coliforms and clostridia that have by now spread through and from the gut to elsewhere in the body as putrefaction accelerates. The final forty-eight hours in that field narrow the gap between high and low temperatures, staying generally between the mid-forties and mid-fifties.

The girl may be dead, but, from the very onset, countless tiny organisms in her body are still alive and teeming in the gut, or gastrointestinal tract. They start to break down the cells in the intestines within hours, literally eating through the gut and toward the extremities. It is a short trip up to the mouth and into the head where the tongue thickens and protrudes. A thick mucus-like liquid escapes from her mouth. Simultaneously there is the brain where the cells that once produced thought and sensations like pleasure and pain perish within the first hours after death. This, too, liquefies within two or three days. The body stiffens in two to six hours with the advent of rigor mortis, the contraction of bodily muscles, starting with the smaller ones, that may last up to twelve hours.

This may be seen initially in the facial muscles, which may be locked into a grimace or even a look of horror. Some would have misinterpreted this as reaction to the last thing she saw as she was being murdered, but that phase passes and the face softens to resemble untroubled sleep.

Her corpse probably looked normal for the first day or two, the period of initial decay. Decomposing tissues produce a green slime, if you will, and the brain turns to mush within a few days. Yet any dead body lying above ground in a place such as this in a field with nearby woods, wetlands, and a river, will be violated by insects and animals, which include bluebottle flies laying eggs on the decaying corpse. These eggs hatch maggots that start feeding on the human carcass in four days, possibly three. The body may be literally covered by maggots by now. Assorted flies, ants, beetles, and other creepy-crawlies and flying creatures are drawn to the distinctive odor of decomposition as the putrefaction process speeds up in the third, fourth and fifth days.

Heavy bloating is imminent unless delayed by continual exposure to cold temperatures at or close to freezing. This is known as refrigeration and may be either natural or artificial. With refrigeration, a body found in moderate temperatures within forty-eight hours, may be kept for multiple days and look much the same as when found. If maintained in cold morgue conditions, it could be autopsied in optimal condition.

Followers of murder mysteries know that turning up the air conditioner or opening windows to allow the invasion of outside cold weather in a room where there is a dead body can fool investigators into prolonging the time of death to accommodate an alibi. There is no air conditioner or refrigerator in this field, out in the open and hundreds of yards from the closest human habitation. The Susquehanna River is at most fifty yards on the other side of a paved road at the edge of the field serving as a barrier between of weeds, brush, muck, and thick clumps of trees. Birds patrol from those trees. Various varmints thrive there.

Then at about 4:00 p.m. on October 28, her body is discovered. Shortly after crime scene investigators arrive at the scene, there is a cloudburst, a hard rain lasting between twenty minutes and a half hour with a drizzle following. The body, reportedly covered from the rain, is finally removed from the field shortly thereafter under wet and muddy conditions.

The body that is found should be bloated and discolored. It should be difficult to recognize at first even by loved ones. The odor of decomposition or "decomp" would be strong enough to attract the attention of any person searching nearby, especially beyond four or five days following the girl's disappearance.

This is how they should have found the body of Jennifer Hill between four and five o'clock on October 28, 1973, after allegedly lying in the cornfield as described after nine days, 216 hours, in the cornfield along Sylvan Dell Road just outside the borough of South Williamsport. Instead, one of the men called from a local mortuary to transfer the girl's body from the field that night admitted being shocked at seeing a corpse that looked as if it had been dead for only twenty-four hours, forty-eight at the most. He concluded she hadn't been dead all that long and, knowing she had been missing more than a week, assumed she must have been held captive for most of the time they were searching for her and then killed. The other option was storage in a refrigeration unit before bringing the body here. He was accustomed to picking up bodies within hours after death, and this one seemed much like the rest of them, except it was an otherwise healthy child.

"The skin would have torn right off if you touched it (if it had been on the field that long)," Steven McCune, the funeral home employee and embalmer, told me several years later from a funeral home he was then managing in Wilkes-Barre. The news coverage of the trial raised some questions, but he didn't recall much being reported about time of death and body condition. Darkness was falling by the time McCune and manager of the Noll Funeral Home, Steve Shaler, arrived at the field that night.

Upon finding the body, which was the top story in the October 29th issue of the *Williamsport Sun-Gazette*, state police made it a point to report the body was "partially decomposed." This would be the only reference to the condition of the body from the acknowledged start of the murder investigation throughout the suspect's trial and conviction. Was this meant to establish that decomposition was obvious and advanced? And what exactly is "partially decomposed?" Virtually every stage of decomposition from the first twenty-four hours, through the first few days and first few weeks could be described as partial.

Even the pathologist who performed the autopsy refrained from mentioning decomp in his testimony or, perhaps, was asked nothing by either the prosecution or defense that would elicit any attention to that process. Now knowing what the body should have looked like from the mouths of experts of body condition and decomposition, one wonders why the person who conducted the autopsy did not report this in a postmortem report that was never entered into evidence.

Clearly the body extricated from the field had been preserved, halting decomposition, if death had indeed occurred on the afternoon or evening of October 19th, a critical date in the Commonwealth's case against the defendant at the trial in February 1974.

The condition of the body was not deemed remarkable or even addressed in trial testimony by Dr. Robert L. Catherman, the forensic pathologist called in from Philadelphia to perform the autopsy on October 29th. That was an additional 24–26 hours after the finding of the body. Apparently Catherman was the only forensics expert who viewed the body directly or via photos over the years who was not amazed at its splendid condition. By the time he saw it, the stretch of time the dumped body was dead was now over 10 full days, but of course the cooling morgue McCune observed that evening had provided the only attested refrigeration, whether artificial or natural, before the autopsy.

Then again decay or putrefaction was not brought up in his testimony or questioned by the defense or prosecution. It was mentioned quite casually in the Postmortem Report as "early slight postmortem decomposition of the body." Three years later, after the trial, Dr. Catherman would agree that the body had been refrigerated but was quick to point out to this reporter who brought up the body condition that it didn't mean it was by artificial means. He speculated that natural refrigeration could be one explanation and cited "cooling breezes" as an example of that effect. He could not cite any meteorological records that corroborated this. There weren't any. Quite the opposite. The man convicted of her murder had been sitting in a prison cell for months stretching into years before body condition was questioned in the news media.

The postmortem or autopsy report signed by Catherman, Deputy Philadelphia Medical Examiner at the time and former Williamsport resident, was, as previously noted, never entered into evidence. Dr. Catherman had done his residency at Williamsport Hospital and had been called upon to perform the autopsy by Lycoming County Coroner Earl Miller, a friend and former colleague. Miller, an M.D. for almost twenty-eight years at that time, also served as a senior member of the medical staff at the Williamsport Hospital with access to its facilities.

The autopsy, as well as any information and data reported from it, is not to be regarded as evidence in and of itself. As an expert witness, a medical examiner, coroner, or forensic pathologist testifies as to the facts of the autopsy as he interprets them. The higher courts have affirmed "there is no irrefutable assumption that a doctor is always a witness of truth."

It would seem that such documentation, entered for jurors to examine and consider, would be essential with manual strangulation being proclaimed the cause of death and it being depicted, despite no evidence of molestation, as a sexually motivated assault. Perhaps it was conspicuous lack of injury exemplified by a body that could have passed for a young girl, eyes closed, soundly sleeping.

Most critically, there was no evidence of sexual molestation despite pre-trial publicity suggesting otherwise. Only the disturbed clothing called out to the viewer that this may have been a sex crime. This is a common tactic when someone close to the victim wants to detour the cops into seeking out known sex offenders. When there are no injuries indicating a violent assault, no defensive injuries and less than convincing proof of strangulation by hands or ligature, it diminishes the probability that it was as portrayed by the prosecution in the trial of Kim Lee Hubbard.

Dr. Catherman was able to say that time of death most likely occurred on October 19, 1973, the day she was reported missing, due to stomach contents which were recognizable and indicated foodstuff, including grapes and a hoagie the girl had eaten earlier that same day. However, two of the most respected forensic pathologists of their time, Dr. Floyd C. Coles and Dr. Glenn M. Larkin, concluded in a 1980 recorded and transcribed interview, that the girl could not have been dead more than a couple of days. *(See Chapter 13.)* They reviewed all the evidence and body photos right down to slides of the intact brain.

Based on the temperatures over those nine days, both experts agreed that Jennifer Hill was either not killed when the prosecution said she was or she was taken from the field earlier, refrigerated and placed to be officially discovered minutes before the search was to be called off.

CHAPTER 7: RUTH

Little Sister: A Childhood Abandoned

There is a pain so utter that it swallows substance up
Then covers the abyss with trance —
So memory can step around — across — upon it
As one within a swoon goes safely where an open-eye would drop him —
bone by bone **– Emily Dickinson**

Ruth Marie Day still lives in South Williamsport in the pleasant house on West Central where she grew up through adolescence and where her friend, Jennifer Hill, spent her last night alive on October 18, 1973, the eve of her disappearance. Even as she approaches the age of sixty, a sadness and sense of loss emanates from her that comes across as stoicism, not self-pity. It seems tragedy has long been a part of her life, with brief reprieves, even as an adult. Going through the trauma of her older brother being accused and then convicted of killing her best friend, as well as testifying at his murder trial—all within five months during an impressionable time in her life—was only part of it.

Her dark, expressive eyes, reminiscent of her mother, Dorisann, who died on July 14, 2011, seem to stare fixedly toward some distant place where she has returned too many times to recount the death and tragedy in her life. She does so with a passiveness of a woman with a lifetime of oppressive memories. She has contemplated suicide more than once, and even made one failed attempt, but she is mourning other losses than her falsely tried and convicted brother. He got to turn the page and start a new life. He was able to walk away from the prisons in which he spent a decade of his life, but she can't seem to escape the confinement she has inhabited, with sporadic relief and bursts of happiness, for her entire life.

She lost her childhood when Jenny left her house to walk home that day. They were both twelve and life was still fun and carefree. In a matter of weeks, as the little sister of an accused and then convicted murderer, she was taunted, teased, and bullied. At one point, her mental state was so fragile she took the advice of a court-approved psychologist and her parents to be tutored at home until she was ready to return to the occasional cruelty experienced inside and outside of the classroom.

Ruthie was born between two tragic events, perhaps a portent of what was to come after some semblance of a normal childhood.

There was Ruth Elizabeth, who never had a chance to escape the birth canal, dying gruesomely when the doctors had to crush her oversized skull to save the dying mother and avert a double tragedy. Ruth Elizabeth remains just a name, never to be seen alive outside the womb. She was a water head baby, a coarse name for hydrocephalus. Her head was so engorged with fluid overflowing the cavities and recesses of her brain that she was literally trapped inside her mother's body. The mother would likely have died from the trauma of birthing this child whose chances of survival were negligible and, at best, would be severely brain damaged. The baby's head, to be blunt, was too large to squeeze through the birth canal. The child was lost, but the name Ruth, after the mother's mother, would get new life.

It was a name she shared with a tragedy, and Ruthie, as everyone called her, probably did not dwell on this until she reached middle age and started looking back on her life. Ruth was still an infant when a brother she never got to know died at the age of six when he slipped under the wheels of a school bus backing up outside an elementary school just blocks away from home on a snowy day. His name was Donald, named after their maternal grandfather, Donald Forsburg, who himself had died suddenly and unexpectedly eight months after Ruthie was born.

So, it seemed there was a miasma of deep mourning and sadness throughout her infancy, but who could know the impact on her psyche, a brain too undeveloped to comprehend what was going on around her? Or was it?

Now we meet Ruth Marie Day, age fifty-four, on a summer day in 2014 when we talked in depth about her life until then. Not only were both of her parents gone, but she lost a husband, Dennis "Denny" Day, father of her two daughters, Amber and Autumn. She remarried and soon lost her second husband to heart disease. It is no exaggeration to say that she lost all the important men in her life, including her big brother, Kim, who was out of her life from the ages of twelve to twenty-three before being released from prison, and her father, Joseph Riley Hubbard, barely six years after they had all been reunited as a family.

Ruthie had no contacts with the Hills after Kim's arrest, and the last time she talked to Jackie Hill, Jenny's older sister, was in the library right before she was taken out of school.

"I guess I was going through a lot of flak and they sent me to a psychologist to see if it was messing me up psychologically." The shrink advised her parents to have her tutored at home. They would never have to send her back, they were told, because she had already been subjected to traumatic experiences, including loss of friends whose parents forbade them to associate with her. "I don't remember much of what took place back then, but the psychologist asked me ten questions. I wish I could remember what those questions were."

Additional trauma had the potential of destroying what was left of her self-esteem. "I did go back on my own. I told Mom and Dad I have to go back. I couldn't stand staying home and going through what happened to Kim over and over…" She wanted a return to a normal childhood, thinking that she could magically recapture the pleasant times she'd had before the death of her best friend. She insisted on "going back" to a time she so desperately missed, and it seemed school had to be part of it.

"I was so apprehensive about going back and at the door (of the school) was this great big girl. They named her Bubbles. And I thought, 'Oh, here we go,' and I thought, 'I'm gonna get it now.' She says, 'Hey, Hub, if anybody says one word to you, touches you or anything, I'll take care of them.'" Ruth smiles, those expressive eyes lighting up at the memory. "We're still friends on Facebook." It was no accident that she carried on her brother's nickname.

"I never got much out of school," she confesses. There was an understanding among the teachers that once she started looking out the window "my mind was gone." One time a girl spit "a great big goob" on her back... "She sat through English class seething and we had gym the next class.... She was one of the two bad girls in school, mean. I picked her up and threw her against the locker. I held onto her and told her that if you ever do that to me again...." Her voice trails off and her mouth widens into a brief grin. And then she shrugs. "Well, she became my friend after that. Funny how things happen."

The mistreatment continued into senior high school: "A kid, John (last name omitted), grabbed my books and art project and threw them down over the bank. I remember that. I was so proud of my art project too. He turned out to be a preacher. I already knew from the way church treated my parents that religion doesn't make you a good person."

"I never fit in with anybody, and when Kim went away, the only friends I had were classmates of his." That's when she started smoking, hanging with the older kids. She remembers that any time Elton John's "Benny and the Jets" came on the radio they'd light up a cigarette. None of the kids who were her friends and playmates in October 1973 when Jennifer Hill's death turned her world upside down, came around anymore. Parents wouldn't allow them to play with her. She had a birthday party when she was thirteen or fourteen and nobody came "because of who I was," she recalled numbly. It hurt a lot at the time, but she came to realize it wasn't about anything she had done and that adults could be just as cruel as kids. Two of her closest friends, twins who were tight with her and Jenny back then, weren't around for a few years but they reconnected later.

"I went from the highest to the lowest. Tech rats. You name it... I was always the class clown. That's how I dealt with things too. Everything was a big joke. Just a big joke. I got locked in the closet one time by a teacher..." Tech rats were basically in the nonacademic courses. She wasn't a tech rat herself. She could hang with anyone, but she felt most comfortable with them. They were the ones who seemed to genuinely accept her company.

Her mother kept her life, especially her behavior, from careening off the rails. "I got in with the wrong crowd for a while and Mom put a stop to that immediately... I never had a reputation. I was only known to be crazy. I was into cars, with a Charger with mag wheels. Into motorcycles—a 650 Midnight Special. I was a tomboy."

By that time, it wasn't so much teasing by the other kids. More like a cold shoulder. "The boys wouldn't date me because of who I was. I was a Hubbard."

She did eventually manage to have a social life in her adolescence, but it required taking a detour from the path she seemed to be on before everything collapsed in the autumn of 1973. "I never dated anybody from South Side. I never ran with a group of girls. All my friends were primarily guys."

She was basically a loner, usually by herself, she said. One time some guy in a car looking really pissed off pulled up beside her. She sensed imminent danger and took off running to her grandmother's house on the next block. They had been receiving threats too. She remembers when they had to put a "rat trap" (recording device) on their phone after some girl called, unleashing a hateful rant. "I guess I cried about it. She said some pretty horrible things." They were able to trace the call and the father of the girl made her apologize. Ruthie knew her parents were probably being ostracized and threatened too.

While she was dealing with her own adversities, life at home was also a challenge. Everything was about the case, getting Kim exonerated, a new trial or another journalist interested in the story. Her father was obsessed by it and, when he wasn't working, buried himself in the evidence they used to convict her brother. She was really bothered by continual discussions about "the case." It wasn't that she didn't believe in her brother's innocence. She always has and knows, as her mother testified, that Kim was at the house when they said Jennifer was getting into that car—if there was any car—in front of Mrs. Nevel's house. It's just that it seemed like such a lost cause, and she didn't like what it was doing to both of her parents. Everyone was so sad and upset. She had little faith in the justice system, loyalty of friends and organized religion. For years after the trial, there were media people interested, legal channels open for appeal and reporters fascinated by the crazy-quilt evidence. Maybe it was just a thrill thing for them, getting inside information on a murder case. When that all dried up, her father was pretty much using her mom, who had heard and seen all of this over and over, as his sounding board. Or he'd go down to the bar to relieve the self-imposed stress.

"The times when he would go off on a binge, I'd be the one to go down and get him," she said, shrugging her shoulder resignedly. "I wasn't even fifteen."

"I've always been a caregiver, and I think it was my calling—32 years' worth so far." Ruthie took care of everyone in her family, including her first husband, Denny, who she calls the one love of her life. Colon cancer claimed Denny, a physical, powerfully built but gentle man who became close to Kim after he returned home from prison. They played softball together, and Joe was their coach. It was a male bonding thing. Denny came across as kind and caring man, and he brought some balance and stability to Ruthie's life.

I'm sure there were a lot of stressors in their marriage, which produced daughters, Amber and Autumn, but Denny became part of the Hubbard family. When Denny got "the cancer," he, like Joe almost a dozen years before him, spent his final days in the house on West Central Avenue, weak, emaciated, and enduring pain like the tough guy he was. Ruthie nursed him through his final hours, as she ended up doing with everyone close to her. Ruth Hubbard Day buried her husband and first love the day after she turned forty.

Five years later, she married Dave, twelve years her senior. She doesn't mention his last name but has nothing either positive or negative to say about him. It is telling that she goes by the last name of her first love. About two years after their marriage, Dave died suddenly in his sleep of a massive heart attack. "It sounds stupid, but I married him because he needed me." Little did she know how much he'd need her and how soon.

"Denny's the only one I ever fell in love with. We went through Hell in the marriage, a roller coaster ride, and I held on because I remembered the person I fell in love with. I remembered how my knees shook when he kissed me."

Their love was reignited not long before Denny was diagnosed with the cancer that killed him. "I never forgave God for that one. I was finally where I needed to be and then it was gone."

She felt that, just like her mother, she was inside this overturned glass bowl, unable to get out but sensing everyone was looking in at her and seeing the friendless tech rat from her dismal school days.

"I take care of all the death"

"In twelve years, I lost Denny, Dave, a grandchild, Connor, who died at birth." Three months before Connor, she tried to commit suicide. "A lot of anger, frustration, hurt..." she said, her voice barely audible. I suspect it was the nurse in her—the healer and caretaker—who, ultimately, would not allow her to die by her own hand. She sees herself as an angel of death, her real calling, because she nursed both of her husbands and both of her parents. She was there, with them, bringing them comfort and loving reassurance, in their final days, hours and minutes.

As a nurse, she had worked nine years in a psyche ward, but it was her time nursing the elderly in the final months of their lives that she regarded as her true calling. It was as if she had been placed on this earth to serve these people who were often set aside, out of the way, by their families and handed over to the care of strangers. Nursing them in their final years you become like family. She was, in a way, their protector and she knew that came from what she had endured and from watching helplessly as others took advantage of the vulnerable. She had been one of the vulnerable herself, as had her parents and brother, and she found that empowering others did the same for her.

She has learned that the process of dying can be a beautiful thing and a life's lesson. She was with her mother constantly at the end of her life. "The day before she died it was called a gift day. Anyone in hospice knows what a gift day is. It's almost as if God gives you a gift. You perk up. You make sense." It happened to Dorisann on the day before her death. She remembered people and events again—pieces of her life that seemed to have been lost to her in the preceding months—and started talking. "She recognized the beauty of the day. Mom could always see the beauty in everything."

"Mom was my best friend. She was all I had. I told her everything, and she told me everything about her life."

Where her mother died as gracefully and graciously as she had lived, her father had fought his inevitable fate, as he had for Kim's exoneration. Joe Hubbard had emphysema and was dying in the hospital. Ruthie was working in the psyche ward where her dad had been "treated" sixteen years before and keeping close tabs on him. He was in steroid psychosis, saying a lot of weird things and desperately proclaiming that he had to get out of there. It wasn't fear as much as anger that he was ending up at a place which he believed housed conspirators in the framing of his son. Ruth, the anointed caretaker, got him out of there.

"We brought him home and he eventually died because his bowels blew up. He was on Prednisone drip and they were treating him for pseudomembranous colitis. His bowel was paper thin, and he died a slow death from peritonitis over eighteen hours."

The end came on December 7, 1989. The beginning of the end came with a pursed-lip breath, a tear moving slowly down his cheek and, signaling the dissipation of anguish, a smile. There were several more pursed-lip breaths and then he was gone. "I think he saw Donald. I really do." Meanwhile, Kim, had a chance to spend time with his father before he died and told him, perhaps for the first time since childhood, that he loved him.

Joe Hubbard was only sixty.

It was within a few days of Joe's death, upon a rare visit to the attic, that Dorisann noticed a photo of Donald that they hadn't seen for years sitting out in plain sight. Miracles have happened in her life, she concedes, and it has to be God who is doing it.

"I believe in Heaven and I believe in Hell," Ruth states. "I believe I'm a hypocrite."

One incident that affected her and her beliefs was when her father was in the hospital around the time Kim was arrested in November 1973. Financial stress was also bearing interminably down on her mother, who still believed God would come to her aid. The Lord helps those who help themselves and they were doing the best they could. She had compiled a list of the bills that had to be paid, placed it in her Bible and prayed for God to provide.

"She literally stood on her Bible and she told God straight out, 'I'm standing on your word!'" Ruthie recalled of that horrible time. Shortly thereafter, they discovered a letter in the mailbox postmarked outside the area. There was money inside and "it was for the exact amount she had prayed for." Even with miracles like that, the faithful daughter was reluctant to redirect it to some kind and generous soul instead of God. Somehow God had intervened. She once suspected that it might have been recompense from someone, maybe several someones, from the church congregation that had rejected them after Kim was arrested. She would have liked to believe that it was human compassion alone but, in the end, her trust had to be in a kind and loving God who had somehow moved someone to respond to her mother's fervent prayers.

"That was no trick," she said of that miracle. "That's why I had to believe."

Dorisann had told me years ago of times when these little miracles happened at low points in their lives. There would be food left on the porch when the cupboards were bare, an envelope with cash in the mail slot when the fuel bill needed to be paid during a cold winter. A job that paid particularly well would come up out of the blue for Joe at a time when it was desperately needed. Ruthie remembers they were really hurting for money the first Christmas after Kim went to jail. "I remember onion sandwiches, mayonnaise sandwiches, as our big meal, but we got through it."

Kim was in prison during that time, and he wasn't counting on God for any breaks. Of course, he didn't know of the sacrifices being made by his parents on his behalf. That's another thing he regrets. He should have known, but maybe that's what drew him back to South Williamsport again.

"Kim fronts a lot. I can't believe he doesn't want to believe in God. He doesn't want to believe in God because if he believes in God, he'll want to know why he was sitting in a cell and why Dad died the way he did."

Ruth tries not to dwell on the memories of Jenny and the innocence of childhood that was literally destroyed on a single afternoon. All was right then. Her father was back working. Kim was bringing in money from working too, and, at the same time, finishing his high school education and going with one of the best-looking girls in town.

Ruthie and Jenny spent a lot of time together. Neither of the girls were into boys yet. Their friends and playmates were a mixed group, as was the case on the last day they were together.

"She always played the boy, and I always played the girl. We'd go to the amusement park, get on the ride and it had to be boy-girl. She was husky with shorter hair and I always had the long hair…. The only way she got to Knoebel's, Hershey Park or the Bloomsburg Fair was because of Mom and Dad. Her parents never took them."

Jenny didn't have many restrictions, Ruthie recalled. She basically ran free, which contrasted with Ruthie's stricter oversight on her home front. Jenny always had a place to go, and if her parents couldn't find her, they'd call the Hubbards and she'd usually be there or close by. "Mom lost a child on the street. I wasn't allowed to cross streets. I was overly protected. Jennifer was the other way around." Virtually no supervision, even with an older brother and sister at home. When Jenny was missing, she remembered there was an article in the paper about her parents not letting her do this or do that, like they were really strict. It would have been funny if what happened next hadn't happened.

Then Jenny was no longer missing. She was found dead. They arrested Kim barely a week before Thanksgiving. Then he was sitting in jail for a couple of months, and then, in the dead of winter, there was the trial. By that time, people were paying a lot of attention to Ruthie, but it was as if they were looking her over like she was some kind of alien.

"People gawking at you and that. I could never eat in front of people until my mid-twenties… What turned me off to eating was going to the Humdinger with a group of Kim's friends and I was so hungry for a cheese steak. I sat down to eat, and something just dawned on me. It was during the trial. I looked up and everybody was staring at me. Everybody! I couldn't eat in front of people for the longest time."

She wasn't ashamed of anything she or her family had done, but there were some things best left unsaid. "I like to talk to people. I'd talk to anybody, even after what happened to Kim, but I'd never tell them my last name. That I remember. When they asked me my name, I'd say Ruthie and I'd just turn my head."

One thing that stood out in her mind, and later made more sense when she went into nursing, was her father having the breakdown and being hospitalized in the Way Unit at Williamsport Hospital. There were cops all around, and it was just Kim and her mother. They didn't pay a lot of attention to her at that time except wanting to know Jenny's activities the day before she disappeared. Chief Smith was around a lot and acting like he was there to help her mother, with Joe recovering in the hospital. He would try to pry information out of her—and this was while Jennifer was still considered a missing person. For one thing, he seemed very interested in whether Jennifer had a "bowel movement" before she went home that day. He asked several times. Ruthie, being just a kid, thought that was sort of a sick question for a man to ask kid.

It wasn't until after the trial, after her father was told about it, that the questions about what Jennifer ate and if she went to the bathroom made sense. Ruthie learned that it had to be with stomach contents, which helps determine the day and time of death. So, if a kid goes missing, is this something that is helpful in finding her? It was another indication that they may have already had a body—unless the chief had some kind of feces fetish.

Ruthie was taking medication for depression when interviewed. If she doesn't take it, she said she can get "ugly mean." She isn't one to hide either her strengths or her flaws. "I carry a lot of anger in me—a lot of anger." She says it's not about one particular thing. It probably starts with Kim and then to Denny dying and the other losses. She started experiencing anxiety attacks after Kim went to prison. High anxiety could probably be blamed for Joe's so-called nervous breakdown when they were investigating Kim and the growing perception that they were looking at him for the murder.

She was no juvenile savant at the time, but looking back with the benefit of her years of experience caring for such patients, she came to recognize what was happening to her father as disassociation. When he had his breakdown, "he threw his hands up over his eyes. He could not rationalize. He could not comprehend... He was overwhelmed... He did not want to associate in his mind what was going on. It made no sense to him." It was a mental departure from reality. It can't be healthily processed and happens during or near the time of the event, according to psychologists.

Ruth lives in the house on West Central Avenue from which Jenny departed all those years before, but she says she is not haunted by memories of the tragedy that emanated from there. Most people with whom she associates and works with have forgotten about "the case," and many aren't old enough to know about it anyway. It seemed to encircle her like a vulture over a corpse for so long, but she has at last outlasted the predators.

CHAPTER 8: MENDEZ

"That Girl's Wearing My Old Jersey Number!"

Forty-one-year-old Joe Mendez was right on schedule to get to wife Dorothy's four o'clock appointment with her chiropractor when he stopped at a red light on Market Street where it intersects with West Central Avenue in South Williamsport. The chiropractor's office was about three blocks away off the same street.

As he waited for the light to turn green, he spotted a young girl coming to a halt at the corner sidewalk waiting to cross. He initially noticed her approaching on West Central to his right, glancing at her as she stood no more than ten feet from his car.

In the fleeting seconds before the light changed, Mendez would find himself focusing on something about the otherwise ordinary girl that grabbed his attention. It was an image that would remain fixed in his mind.

"Hey, that girl's wearing my old jersey number," he remembered saying to Dorothy who offered no comment or even bothered to look. It would undoubtedly have faded from his memory had he not seen the girl in the same jersey a few days later in both the local afternoon paper, the *Williamsport Sun-Gazette,* and the Sunday *Grit.*

Indeed, the girl was in an oversized dark blue football jersey with the number "33" prominent in white. It was October 19, 1973, and the time, date and the girl in the South Williamsport High School colors would eventually converge, resulting in Joseph A. Mendez testifying in a murder trial.

Mendez loved sports, especially football which he played in high school where he grew up in Brooklyn, NY. He was in his early forties and still had the solid build of a fullback or a linebacker, carrying maybe 25 pounds above his high school days. In later years, he officiated the game on the side when he wasn't punching a clock at the Bethlehem Steel plant in Williamsport where he was active with the local chapter of the United Steelworkers of America, eventually presiding as chapter president over several hundred members. The US Army veteran would go on to play an active role on the transition team when the company made the corporate transformation to Williamsport Wirerope Works, Inc., in 1989, a few years before retiring after twenty-eight years with the company.

The Joe Mendez with whom I became acquainted obviously had leadership qualities and was respected by his peers, but he wasn't the type to call attention to himself or become involved in anything controversial. There was always some potential for the latter as a union leader, but that was as close as the Williamsport resident would come to a high public profile. And yet he was one of those guys who believed in doing his civic duty with a minimum of drama.

He certainly wasn't anxious to take the stand in a highly publicized trial in which the girl in the jersey was the murder victim. A cop had talked to him about the sighting, but it was about a week after she was no longer missing. Her body had been found in a field not so far from where he saw her that day. They were still investigating the murder, and he supposed they were trying to figure out her movements that day.

Mendez would later learn that Jennifer May Hill was believed to have been murdered that same day, perhaps within an hour or so after he saw her. She had been killed that same afternoon or early evening, one news article reported.

He remembered telling the cop that he didn't know who Jennifer Hill was, but he recognized that jersey and her general features matched. The hair seemed different in the photo he was shown, but his first impression when he saw that picture in the paper was definitive: "That's the girl!"

An article in the *Sun-Gazette* on October 26 described the parents, Norma and Jack Hill, as hopeful but upset enough to be relying on sedatives to keep them going most days. The admittedly distraught father said he hadn't been able to go to work at the Avco Lycoming plant but chose to stay close to the American Legion Post on Market Street where some 100 Civil Air Patrol members and other volunteers had set up headquarters to coordinate search efforts. The legion post was just a few blocks away from where Mendez sat at the light that day when he spotted the girl.

Market and Hastings, opposing one-way two-lane thoroughfares cutting a swath through South Williamsport Borough, run parallel to each other and separated by a wide median strip of houses, with Market southbound in its alternate identity as US Route 15 winding out of town and up the mountain toward Harrisburg. Hastings is two lanes northbound toward the river bridge where it merges with Market to cross the Susquehanna River into Williamsport. Mendez, when he spotted the girl bearing his old high school number, was barely more than a block away in the opposing direction from the Hills' home. The girl, if it was Jennifer Hill, was that close to home if she crossed the intersection, took a left and proceeded north on the sidewalk for about a block.

Mendez would later concede that he probably wouldn't have noticed the girl had it not been for that numbered jersey. But notice he did. He didn't get a close look at her face nor did he have reason or time to study her facial features. He remembered she appeared to be a little chubby in the loose-fitting jersey, not necessarily fat, with straight brown hair of undeterminable length. It seemed to hang straight along her face, maybe pushed back so the length was tough to determine.

Just a few days later he saw the girl in the jersey again. This time in the local daily newspaper, the *Williamsport Sun-Gazette*. She was missing and police were seeking information that might lead to her whereabouts. A week or so after that he learned from the same source that the missing girl was now a murder victim.

"Police are asking that anyone who recalls seeing her on Oct. 19 to contact them at the South Williamsport Borough Hall," the caption under that photo stated. The newspaper reported that the girl had been seen walking along West Central Avenue "at about 4:00 p.m." It had to be the girl, he realized, because the time was right, and she had approached him from West Central Avenue. It would have been a few minutes before four. And then there was that jersey. It would have to be the hugest coincidence ever if it were not her!

Reinforcing his certainty, the caption under that photo described her as "wearing the shirt she was wearing at the time of her disappearance."

State police investigators were headquartered in the borough hall following her disappearance and throughout most of the brief murder investigation. The Pennsylvania State Police barracks was in Montoursville some five miles away. Mendez hadn't been sure whether the information he had would be helpful in finding the missing girl until the October 29th issue of the afternoon daily. Then he learned Jennifer Hill's body had been found the previous evening, nine days after her disappearance, in a cornfield on Sylvan Dell Road just east of the borough and some two miles from where he had seen her. Now he just might have something helpful to share in the murder investigation. He didn't know. If not, he would at least be doing his civic duty.

The photo accompanying the article reporting the discovery of her body showed a younger Jennifer in a collared blouse. Her hair was neatly styled and swooped demurely upward at the shoulders, possibly an elementary school portrait photo from an earlier grade. He had probably seen that photo too, but it rang no bell of recognition. Jennifer was a seventh grader when she disappeared. The other photo in the football jersey showed a more mature girl making the early transition into adolescence. The height (five feet) and weight (120 pounds) seemed right too. No question it was her. He wouldn't have contacted the police otherwise. He wasn't one to jump to conclusions.

One thing bothered Mendez. When he first talked to a police official at the South Williamsport Borough Hall on October 26 about sighting the missing girl, he was assured a criminal investigator would contact him. It was what that official said at the end of the conversation that he found disturbing: "You might have pertinent information into the death of Jennifer Hill." He assumed her body had been discovered and not yet reported in the newspaper. No such report in the next day's newspaper, which would have been a Saturday. It wasn't until Sunday, two days later, that her body was found, as reported on Monday, October 29, in the newspaper. Mendez wasn't sure what to make of the aforementioned comment. Had the official merely misspoken or perhaps just convinced her demise was inevitable?

As it turned out, the cop who came to his house a week and a half later, on November 6, didn't act like anything he said was pertinent. The photo Mendez was shown on that visit was the front-page photo of Jennifer in the October 29th issue, as he would subsequently learn. It wasn't the photo of her in the football jersey. That threw him off. This girl was clearly younger, dressed in dark clothing and with well-coiffed hair caressing each side of her face. Little girls change a lot between the ages of nine and twelve.

Mendez remembered telling the cop that the hair of the girl seemed longer, fuller than that of the girl with the "33" jersey which he recalled as being stringy.

Joseph A. Mendez came to realize that his testimony was important to the boy's defense—though how important wouldn't dawn on him until after the trial concluded on the first day of March 1974 after eight days of testimony, including his as the first defense witness on February 26th. The jury hadn't taken long to render their verdict, the paper reported.

Jennifer would have traveled ten blocks straight down West Central to where he saw her that day. (The entire distance from the Hubbard home to the Hill home measured three-fourth of a mile—or .75—and .71 of that was between the Hubbard's home and the spot she was seen by Mendez.) That seemed to correspond with the time it would have taken her to walk that distance.

That initial photo had appeared in newspapers on two days, perhaps three, following her October 19th disappearance. It was the first photo released of Jennifer by her family for publication. The caption of the photo stated that she had been seen on West Central Avenue walking toward her home shortly before four o'clock. That was precisely the time reported by Mendez, but the prosecution didn't call him to testify. The witnesses they chose as among the last to see her that afternoon described her clothing, including the football jersey, a jacket tied around her waist and blue jeans and were all within three blocks of the Hubbard home. Dorisann Hubbard and daughter, Ruth, told police Jennifer had left their home at about 3:45, and Mary Mundrick, who lived a block closer to Jennifer's destination, confirmed it was "about quarter of four" when she saw the girl, reinforcing Mendez's time estimate of when he saw her eight or nine blocks later. It didn't fit quite as comfortably with the time the Commonwealth's "eyewitness" said she saw Jennifer in front of her house forty-five minutes later. Mendez did not know any of this until after the trial when he made the acquaintance of Joe Hubbard and looked more closely into the case.

Mendez's testimony would be elicited in Kim Hubbard's defense during his murder trial three months after his arrest and four months after Jennifer's disappearance. It wouldn't have been much of a plus for the Commonwealth's case, which would have had to explain why the girl was not seen again, by anybody, for another thirty to thirty-five minutes after being within sight of her home.

Joe Hubbard would come to wonder the same thing in a letter to the Department of Justice's Chief of Public Integrity Gerald McDowell after his son was convicted: "Is that why Joe Mendez, who could have shed some light on the movement of Jennifer Hill the last day she was seen alive, was virtually ignored by the police and the prosecutor?"

The Commonwealth's chosen eyewitness, Betty Jane Nevel, testified she saw Jennifer Hill get into a car resembling Kim Hubbard's at 4:30 p.m. barely three blocks away in the opposite direction. A four o'clock half hour soap opera, "The Secret Storm" she had been watching on television had just ended and the next, "The Flintstones," was just starting, she explained in the trial so there was no question about the time. Mendez was sure the time he saw her too. He knew it was accurate within a minute or so because he arrived at the office of Chiropractor Norman Wengert in time for his wife's 4:00 p.m. appointment. Wengert's office at that time was on South Market just before it veered sharply left into US Route 15, called the Montgomery Pike by locals, less than a half mile from that intersection.

Mrs. Nevel would testify that she saw a girl her daughter identified as Jennifer Hill get into a car that resembled Kim Hubbard's more than a half hour later in front of her residence on Howard Street.

84

Had Jennifer turned around after being so close to home? Where was she for those missing thirty or more minutes? If you just go by the sightings of her walking down West Central and disregard Mendez, there are forty-five minutes where Jennifer Hill was wandering around, or possibly in hiding, until allegedly being spotted by Nevel.

Mrs. Nevel would be regarded as the "key eyewitness for the prosecution" in news reports and her testimony spanned fifty pages of trial transcript. More of it came from cross-examination by defense attorney, Patrick Fierro, than the direct examination by District Attorney Allen Ertel.

Mendez would be subpoenaed to testify as a defense witness, something he found puzzling at the time, because he thought it would be the prosecution who would want to reconstruct her whereabouts that day. He knew that much about murder cases from watching *Dragnet*, *Kojack*, and *Columbo*.

What he saw might not have mattered at all had he not later confided in Dr. Wengert, who had followed the case closely through the arrest of Kim Hubbard on November 16, 1973. Wengert was surprised that the state police hadn't regarded Mendez's information as important. He had read that the girl had vanished along the walking route home on October 19 and found it compelling she had wandered off in another direction from her home. The chiropractor felt that the place and time of the sighting should have been of interest to somebody.

Wengert contacted Joe Hubbard, father of the murder suspect. He knew the young man and had found him polite and respectful. He had mentioned to his father that Mendez had contacted the state police about seeing the girl after her photo, wearing the same jersey, appeared in the newspaper. Apparently, his information didn't fit within the parameters of their case, and they seemed somewhat skeptical that the girl he had seen was Jennifer Hill. Who else could it have been? Joe Hubbard was clearly excited about the information the chiropractor provided.

Dr. Wengert would become an avid defender of Hubbard and a strong believer in the unfairness of the investigation and trial. After the trial, he wrote letters to various state and federal officials on behalf of the

Hubbards and was involved in a citizens group that held rallies and petitions for a new trial signed by several hundred people.

Was he certain that Kim Hubbard, who he described as "a typical youth of our times, not atypical," did not kill Jennifer Hill? His take on that in a letter to me in late July of 1977 was typical of the attitude of others, originally convinced of his guilt until they looked into his case:

"I don't know, certainly and absolutely, that Kim didn't commit the crime, though I consider it highly unlikely. My wife is convinced of his innocence. Was he capable of it? Most of us are capable of violent crimes, given the right juxtaposition of moment, setting, emotion and other factors."

Like Mendez he came to judge what happened to Kim Hubbard by what was on the record and all the conflicts therein.

Despite the potential of Mendez's testimony—at the very least to create reasonable doubt—it seemed that Hubbard's attorney, Patrick Fierro, after calling upon Mendez to testify, had made only a half-hearted effort in his direct examination. Fierro asked only fifteen questions of his witness, other than name, address, marital status, and place of employment. He established the date and time Mendez saw the girl, that she was wearing the number 33, his old football jersey number, and that Mendez got his wife to her four o'clock appointment on time. However, he failed to follow up in establishing Mendez's credibility as a witness and clarifying the importance of his testimony, even to indicate that it would be unusual for her to be there based on other time references in the case. As a result, the jurors may have deemed it as superfluous.

Ertel, however, was clearly anxious to devalue him as a witness of any importance. He was well aware that Mendez had been questioned by a state police criminal investigator eleven days prior to November 16, the date of Kim Hubbard's arrest. The DA started his questioning with the well-worn tactic of deprecating Mendez's powers of observation and, other than not remembering the name of the state trooper, the witness seemed comfortable with describing his questioner until Fierro objected and the judge sustained that objection.

He was there to identify the girl he saw on the corner, but Ertel got him to concede that he was not certain of the girl's hair and that it seemed to be shorter than in the photo shown to him by the police investigator on November 5. The problem was that Ertel never showed Mendez a photo or asked if it was the same one shown to him by the state trooper. Nor had Fierro. Remember there were two photos of Jennifer Hill that the police used—both of which were published in regional newspapers.

Mendez was being truthful, though perhaps not helpful to the defense, in this exchange with Ertel during cross-examination:

> Ertel: After that, were you shown a picture of Jennifer Hill?
>
> Mendez: He showed me a picture.
>
> Ertel: You could not identify that. Is that right?
>
> Mendez: Not by face. No sir.
>
> Ertel: You said you did not, you could not identify it?
>
> Mendez: Right.
>
> Ertel: And your comment was that the girl had shorter hair than the one in the photograph?
>
> Mendez: What I thought...
>
> Ertel: And isn't it also true, Mr. Mendez, that is all you knew concerning this, that you could not identify Jennifer Hill at that point?
>
> Mendez: No, I never said I could identify Jennifer Hill.

Mendez would later concede that he was shocked that Fierro had no follow-up questions to clarify the obvious. He didn't know Jennifer and could not identify her as such. What he could identify was the girl in the football jersey with his old number on it was the one he saw on the day of her reputed death. That girl was Jennifer Hill.

Joe Hubbard recognized that placing Jennifer Hill at that corner at that time by a very credible witness ran contrary to the Commonwealth's scenario that there was a clandestinely arranged meeting between the twelve-year-old tomboy and the 20-year-old defendant. Fierro chose not to take that opportunity to create more reasonable doubt.

"It was like he (Fierro) just wanted to get me on and off the stand," Mendez complained in 1976 when quizzed about his role in the trial. "I was told to just answer the questions straight-up. Not to add anything."

That he did.

"He questioned me like he wasn't interested in what I had to say,"

Again, Ertel did not show Mendez the photo of the girl in the jersey that he would have seen in the newspaper and asked if this was the girl he saw. Instead, he conveniently limited it to Mendez's recollection of what he said to the state trooper about "the photograph." For his part, Fierro should have shown Mendez that photo in re-direct—if not a copy of the original at least as it appeared in the newspaper. Instead, he had "no further questions" after Ertel's cross-examination.

Mendez would not learn about contradictory evidence used to convict Kim Hubbard until after the trial. He hadn't been sure it really mattered whether it was Jennifer he saw at that intersection until he met Joe Hubbard several months later. It subsequently occurred to him that the state police had homed in on their suspect, as well as an eyewitness who could get them a conviction, and his testimony would only complicate their trial strategy. Why Fierro seemed so oblivious, even unwilling, to further discredit Mrs. Nevel's tattered recall of a girl whose description fit that of Jennifer Hill, puzzled Mendez. The same girl got into a car resembling Kim Hubbard's 1967 green Oldsmobile Cutlass at 4:30 p.m. on October 19, 1973, but there was no identification of the driver because she only saw a beckoning hand that she believed belonged to a man.

Joe Mendez, as is the case with so many key figures in the crime, investigation, and trial of Kim Lee Hubbard, is no longer with us. He died at an inpatient hospice facility in Williamsport on July 14, 2018, at the age of eighty-six.

Jennifer Hill, the girl wearing Joe's number 33, would have been fifty-nine in late December 2020 as I write this chapter. Kim Hubbard is sixty-seven and still calling for justice. As for me, the twenty-nine-year-old reporter who wrote a series of articles about the flawed case that convicted Hubbard for the murder of Jennifer in 1977, I turned seventy-four in October 2021.

CHAPTER 9:
MRS. NEVEL AND HYPNOSIS

What the Eyewitness Really Saw

Joe Hubbard realized too late that he had made a huge mistake in hiring Pat Fierro as his son's defense attorney. He felt responsible, because he wasn't there for Kim again. Guilt weighed heavily, a knapsack filled with bricks, on his already stooped shoulders, stifling the chances of redeeming Kim and bringing him back home. It was going to be a steep climb and Fierro had made it even more precipitous.

He had started out so well at the preliminary hearing where Fierro had their precious eyewitness mumbling and bumbling, contradicting the very piece of evidence that could make or break Ertel's case. It had been typical Fierro—flamboyant and bombastic with some sleight-of-hand thrown in.

Had it been the trial itself, it might have been a game changer, but, then again, he had a few shining moments before it all came apart.

Betty Jane Nevel was the witness in question, and much of the Commonwealth's case resided with her credibility in the eyes of the jury. They hadn't reached that point on December 7, 1973, because Ertel had to present the foundation of his case in a preliminary hearing before District Justice Richard T. Eisenbeis. In Pennsylvania, the prosecution still has to show it is probable that a defendant has committed the crime for which he or she had been arrested and charged. It is a significantly lower hurdle than the reasonable doubt premise of a trial itself. It requires convincing the judge that a prima facie case has been established, that it could be "presumed to be true" and justifies trying him before a jury of his peers.

For Ertel, or any District Attorney prosecuting a high-profile murder case, it requires a legal strategy so the defense can't anticipate all your moves at trial. It comes down to revealing enough of your hand to show you have a reasonable chance of convicting the defendant but, at the same time, not giving away more than you have to. The defense attorney uses testimony and physical evidence submitted at this hearing—and what he can learn from the arrest complaint and even news media coverage—to plot his own strategy for an impending trial when everything is on the line.

District Judges, known commonly as District Magistrates in those days because they preside over one of several Magisterial Districts in a typical Pennsylvania county, seldom rule against the Commonwealth in a preliminary hearing, and the defense, as often as not, does not present its own witnesses. At the trial, both sides must make the other aware who their witnesses will be and the gist of their testimony. Defense attorneys do get to cross-examine the DA's chosen witnesses at the preliminary hearing, perhaps exposing weaknesses in the case that may be pursued later. Pat Fierro must have felt he's been handed a gift when he interrogated Betty Jane Nevel that day. For starters, she clearly wasn't happy to be there. Yet sometimes reluctant witnesses, rather than eager ones, make a better impression on judges and juries.

Also testifying at the mid-morning hearing was one of the state police investigators, Trooper Joseph Keppick; South Williamsport Police Chief Charles Smith; the sister of the defendant, twelve-year-old Ruth Hubbard, and a girl who Ertel intended to show that Kim Hubbard occasionally gave kids and teens rides in his car. Eisenbeis struck the latter testimony from the record as being superfluous to the charges being considered. The excluded girl did not testify at the murder trial, as it turned out, but Ertel would find several other young people to drive home that point.

With that, they laid the essential groundwork for the evidence Ertel reportedly had at his disposal that would make it at least possible, if not likely, that the defendant had the opportunity and motive to commit the crime.

Then Mrs. Nevel took the stand. She would testify that she had seen Jennifer Hill walk in front of her house the day of her disappearance, October 19, 1973, and then get into a car that stopped further up the street. After she described the preceding, Ertel showed her a photo of Kim

Hubbard's 1967 Oldsmobile and asked if it was the car that picked up Jennifer that day.

"Yes, I'm positive," she responded with little hesitation.

When it was Fierro's turn to question her, he engaged her in some routine questions and then seemed to reach for another photo and hold it at his side as he led her through her narrative about the girl running up the street to what was assumed to be the killer's car. Raising his voice accusingly, Fierro asked her if she was sure of the previous identification of the car and, theatrically showing her the same picture, asked, "How about this one?"

"Positively not!" she responded.

Fierro then faced his small audience in the hearing room, holding it up for them to see and mutely calling to everyone's attention the import of what she had said. Then he returned to face her, showed her the photo again and asked whether it was the car she saw Jennifer enter. Amazingly, Mrs. Nevel repeated her assertion that it was "absolutely not" the same car.

> Charles King, who was among those at the hearing, remembered Ertel jumping up, perhaps fearful that Eisenbeis wouldn't bind the case over for trial, saying: "But we have tire casts and boot prints ... that are Kim's down to the nail holes..."
>
> According to the scanty record of that hearing included with the original complaint in the arrest warrant: "At the conclusion of the testimony, the court ruled that a prima facie case had been established and the defendant was bound over for the court."

At that point, there was reason for optimism among the Hubbards, but they knew that repeating that contradictory, and perhaps discrediting, testimony was not about to happen again. It was like the tree falling in the forest with no one there to hear it. The most Fierro got out of that incident at the February 1974 trial was the admission from Nevel that "I seen the car again in the garage," referring to the borough garage where it was still impounded at the time. The relevance of that will be explained later on.

When she was asked by Fierro at the trial about her confusion in recognizing the car at the preliminary hearing, she said, "Some things about it, but the damage confused me." (The front fender on the driver's side was significantly damaged, but she never mentioned that in either the hearing or the trial in describing the car that allegedly picked up Jennifer.)

There were no newspaper articles about the preliminary hearing itself, first assigned to District Judge Ronald Blackburn and then switched to Eisenbeis, who was also an attorney, or at least testimony induced there. Most District Judges in Pennsylvania do not have law degrees and have to be certified in a week-long course consisting of lectures about the Judicial and Crime Codes. At its end, they were required to pass a lengthy essay test to confirm that they retained information provided in lectures. The main challenge was to take extensive notes of the repetitive lectures and then regurgitate them in the final test. To discourage cheating, the budding citizen judges were required to write their essays by hand. Computers and laptops were not allowed (at least through 1999) because of the potential of cheating by storing previously composed essays within.

Oddly enough, there was a brief newspaper article that a grand jury had indicted Kim for the homicide and attendant charges filed against him, with the indictment concluding that the accused "did feloniously kill and slay another." The is the only known mention of a grand jury, either in newspaper coverage or court records. This is unusual even today because a preliminary hearing is preferred in binding a defendant over to trial, with a grand jury a recourse if the Commonwealth's case is rebuffed by the District Judge. The previous grand jury option with testimony presented behind closed doors was abolished as unnecessary in 1976. Then, in 2012, it was reinstated by the Pennsylvania Supreme Court for specified cases and for fact-finding. The preliminary hearing remains the preferred method to bind a case over for trial. A state-prosecuted felony case through the office of the Attorney General, however, often relies on a grand jury.

Moving on to the Murder Trial

The next and final step toward the conviction of Kim Lee Hubbard was the trial itself, required to get underway within sixty days after being bound over by the magisterial court. The juggling of judges continued there too. News articles reported the case would go to trial with Dauphin County Visiting Judge Richard B. Wickersham presiding. However, not long before jury selection in February, it was reported that Lycoming County President Judge Charles F. Greevy would preside instead in his own courtroom.

"No reason was given by the court for the change," the *Sun-Gazette* added.

Joe Hubbard admitted that Fierro had his moments during the trial in the main courtroom of the modern, rectangular Lycoming County Courthouse dedicated just two-and-a-half years before. He was an experienced interrogator known for his colorful summations in jury trials, and he and law partner, Anthony Miele, were highly sought in working divorce and family law cases.

And yet he was a seat-of-the-pants lawyer who seldom relied on notes. His greatest talent was finding weaknesses in the credibility of a witness and exploiting them. However, he wasn't particularly organized when it came to tying the various testimonies together, and, as became evident in his questioning of Joe Mendez, he occasionally underestimated or misunderstood the relevance of his own witnesses. Joe Hubbard discovered that Fierro wasn't all that efficient in mustering and prepping his own witnesses, and he had a tendency to bully and threaten when things didn't seem to be going his way.

Although Miele would assist him when available, Fierro relied mostly on the person who hired him to essentially play the role of his chief investigator. That meant Joe was running down leads, gophering for this or that, and rounding up potential defense witnesses as he had done with Mendez and others. Joe once joked to Fierro that maybe he could get a refund after the trial to make up for the hours he put in.

"Hell, Hubbard," the lawyer lashed back, failing to appreciate the joke, "you wouldn't be able to afford me if I had to bill you for an investigator."

He was probably right, but, looking back, Joe realized how much of the testimony he had missed over those eight days of the trial because he was in and out of the courtroom at Fierro's bidding.

If there was upside to all of this, it gave Joe a quick, condensed lesson in criminal law that would later serve him well in solving some of the mysteries of the criminal justice system and the fine points of how a case is constructed against a defendant in a murder trial.

Joe and Dorisann had to take out a second mortgage on their home on West Central Avenue to pay for Fierro's services but, being financially strapped, they had to rely on the Lycoming County Public Defender John A. "Jack" Felix when the case went to appeal. That's how they ended up in Fierro's office to retrieve his case file. Fierro wasn't there, or so they were told, but his secretary seemed relieved to hand it over. Things had become quite intense there during the last few days of the trial.

There was very little there that would be helpful to them—with one exception that was astonishing, totally unexpected.

In the file was a brief letter dated January 28, 1974, from Allen Ertel which stated:

> *In accordance with our oral conversation on the date of the preliminary hearing, this letter is to confirm that Mrs. Nevel was hypnotized to assist her recollection. We will have available to you the doctor who hypnotized her so that you can be assured that no suggestion was implanted in Mrs. Nevel's mind.*
>
> *Only very small portions of her testimony were recalled through hypnosis.*

The use of hypnotism to improve the memory of the only witness who put Jennifer Hill in contact with Kim Hubbard—more precisely a car identified as his via a photo—was never brought up at the preliminary hearing or the trial. A copy (cc) of the letter should have been sent to the Office of the Prothonotary, repository of county court records, but it appears that Ertel and Fierro were the only officers of the court and trial participants who were aware this memory inducing procedure was used.

Judge Greevy would have obviously had access to it, and if he wasn't aware of it at the trial, he clearly was a year later at an evidentiary hearing on February 19, 1975, when he placed the onus on Fierro for not stating an objection to the utilization of hypnosis.

The hypnotist, it turned out, was Dr. LaRue Pepperman, MD, Family Medicine Specialist. This in itself is unusual, because hypnotists typically used in criminal investigations are psychologists, but a Medical Doctor and other health care professionals with a Master's Degree or higher can become certified as practitioners through testing, course work and a rigorous application process, with a state medical license often required.

Since the Hubbards no longer retained Fierro at this point, their former attorney never made himself available to explain this. In fact, Joe never saw Fierro, at least to talk to, after his closing summation to the jury. Fierro hadn't been there for the verdict, with Miele, his law partner, there in his stead. He was out of town on business, the judge explained.

Four years to the month after Kim's murder trial, and during the period when the news media first started reporting on the discrepancies in the case, the colorful attorney died suddenly on February 18, 1978. It was never known for certain whether he was aware of the hypnotism when he questioned Mrs. Nevel at the preliminary hearing on December 7, 1973. Ertel's letter was dated almost two months after the preliminary hearing, but it stated they had an "oral conversation" about it that day.

There were apparently no reporters at that hearing, perhaps because it was continued (rescheduled) from November 26, 1973, due to the illness of the District Attorney. The DA's office simply informed the press that Kim Hubbard had been bound over for trial. There were, however, a few people in attendance. Among them was Charlie King, who later joined an effort to prove Kim's innocence after his conviction more than three months later, partly because of what he observed at that preliminary hearing.

A copy of the preliminary hearing transcript was requested after the trial by Felix on the defendant's behalf. He was informed there was no transcript made, other than notations on who testified. There weren't even general notes or an outline of witness testimony. It appeared during the hearing, however, that a woman was speaking into a recording device during the proceedings.

Using hypnosis to refresh a victim's memory is admissible, but the jury should be able to consider its credibility, and the defense should be able to cross-examine the witness as well as those who conducted the session about the process used, surroundings and relevant circumstances. There is a danger of false recall if, for instance, a witness is shown something she is supposed to identify from an earlier experience prior to trial testimony. The jury, in considering the merits of such testimony during deliberations, typically has access to recordings, transcripts or videos if available.

The court, or presiding judge, has the authority to determine the admissibility and appropriateness of using this tool, whose results, according to law, are not necessarily regarded as truth. He or she has the authority to deny the testimony of the witness. We don't know where this hypnotism took place, or how often, but we do know that Nevel was taken to see the impounded car twice before the trial and that she was originally, in the preliminary hearing, not sure if the car could have been Kim Hubbard's. She was certain at the trial itself where she professed a clear memory of the vehicle, if not who was in it.

One of the dangers to the defense if the prosecution informs the court that hypnotism has been used to refresh a witness's memory is a historic belief that it acts as a truth serum. On the other hand, there are suggestibility and propriety issues that might have to be addressed for admissibility.

Courts have been advised to give cautionary instruction that hypnosis was used, placing no greater weight on that testimony than any other. This was standard handling of such testimony at that time, but Judge Greevy apparently chose not to do this—if he even knew that hypnosis had been used at the time of the trial. He did have an opportunity to offer an opinion when the case was brought back to him on appeal. He then discounted it as immaterial and stated in his opinion overturning an appeal for a new trial based on newly discovered evidence that "hypnotism was used only as a recall stimulus prior to the defendant's arrest." It was up to the defense attorney, not the court, to challenge this, he concluded eleven months later after an evidentiary hearing.

It has also been the case that the defense is allowed to question the hypnotist about procedure and questions asked. For instance, could the witness be programmed with known details of the crime or, in this case, visual details? As for Nevel, how much of what she described in testimony was of the impounded car and how much of the car Jennifer Hill allegedly got into on October 19, 1973?

At the trial, Fierro, aware hypnosis was used on Mrs. Nevel, raises the question of whether she was remembering the car Jennifer Hill entered or the vehicle impounded in the borough garage. But this line of questioning stopped there. Raising even more questions, considering what Fierro knew about the hypnosis that his clients didn't, was a comment he made about the value of Mrs. Nevel's testimony: "Tire casts and footprints can be manufactured, but a witness was a hard obstacle for us to discredit."

Why was the utilization of hypnotism as an investigative tool to refresh memory not introduced then and there? Was it a mistake, a failure, incompetency, or a strategic decision based on Fierro's concern the jury might be influenced by the so-called "truth serum" repute of hypnosis? He opted to keep this from his client. Had it not been included in the case file picked up from Fierro's secretary it would have never been known that hypnosis had been used on the witness during the sixteen days between the impoundment of Kim's car and his arrest. Ertel had protected himself by putting the hypnotism on record for the defense, if not the defendant himself.

The bottom line is that the credibility of the witness is for the jury to decide, but they should be aware when hypnosis is used, how it was used and when it was used. This is applicable to witnesses being hypnotized before a trial as part of the investigative process and on the rare occasions when a witness is under hypnosis while testifying.

Underlining the acceptance of hypnosis of witnesses in a court of the law during the 1970s was the precept that "hypnosis affects credibility but not admissibility." It also raised a concern that this tool can be abused and that all its circumstances should be explored by both the prosecution and the defense in a criminal trial. In the 1980s and 1990s hypnotism was challenged more frequently, with more decisions overturned because of its accumulating implementation in cases where it was used to refresh memories of alleged child sexual abuse victims.

> *In United States v. Adams, (1978) the Ninth Circuit of the US Court of Appeals upheld the admissibility of hypnotically refreshed testimony, but the court expressed concern "that investigatory use of hypnosis on persons who may later be called upon to testify in court carries a dangerous potential for abuse. Great care must be exercised to ensure that statements after hypnosis are the production of the subject's own recollection, rather than of recall tainted by suggestions received while under hypnosis."* – **US Department of Justice Archives**

Fierro quizzed Mrs. Nevel about why it took her so long to come forward about her alleged sighting of Jennifer and, again, there were conflicting responses. She said she knew there had been a search going on for Jennifer Hill from the day she turned up missing—"I think everybody did"—but she seemed to have little curiosity beyond that.

"I just didn't bother reading it until Sunday morning when I picked up the Grit on Sunday, October 28, and saw that photo of Jennifer 'and it all came back to me,'" she testified. That issue of the weekly took the case right up to the date the body was found. The report of the body being found dominated the front page of the Monday *Sun-Gazette* (October 29).

However, she didn't continue reading about it in the daily paper. She indicated that even though she heard about it, "I didn't pay any attention to it." She was too wrapped in her cat dying and some sewing she had to do.

It was her husband who eventually went to police about it on either October 29 or 30. She said it was because she was afraid to get involved in all of this, "having to go through this." For what it's worth, Ertel confirmed there had been a reward offered "at the discretion of his office and police." The DA also alluded to a reward offer in the newspaper.

These were the only mentions of any reward, how much was offered or whether Mrs. Nevel or anyone else received it.

"I didn't have any idea any reward would have anything to do with me. I didn't find her." she said. "The only reward I knew when they found her body looking for her." This either means she thought the award was for someone who found the girl (her body?) or that she didn't know about the reward until the body was found.

Also testifying at the trial was Mrs. Nevel's eleven-year-old daughter, Beth, who affirmed that she was with her mother that day watching television and identified the girl walking up the sidewalk as "Jenny Hill" after her mother asked who it was. Mrs. Nevel said she was curious because "it is unusual for her to be walking up Howard Street."

Beth said she saw the girl get into a "pale color car," but could provide no more description because "I turned my head" and had no further description of the alleged encounter. Aside from recognizing the girl as Jennifer Hill, Beth's description was: "She had a Glick shoe bag. She was wearing slacks." Her mother identified all the clothing: the jacket, jersey and even "black and white sneakers," but said nothing about the pants, which should have been the jeans with the brightly colored band of red hearts at the bottom of each leg if they hadn't been changed elsewhere by then. When asked again on cross, she repeated her description word for word.

She seemed to indicate that the girl she saw get into that car was excited to see whoever was inside: "Well, the car pulled up and she took a little skip before she started to run, and she went across the back of the car and into the opposite (of?) the driver's side."

Fierro did ask her if it was true that she couldn't identify the car at first when taken to where the defendant's car was impounded in the Borough Garage and she responded affirmatively, adding "the damage was (what) confused me." She confirmed that Lt. Hynick and Francis Ross, a South Williamsport Policeman, took her to see the car at the garage and that she was shown the impounded car twice. The damage was extensive to the front driver's side of the car, but she added, "I just seen the hand," and not the damage which should have been visible just below the hand in the driver's window. She adjudged the driver to be a male because the knuckles of the hand were larger than a female's. When pressed by Fierro on her powers of observation about the hand, she added that she saw the head but was fuzzy about hair length and the line of questioning dissipated after objections by Ertel were sustained.

Despite the confusion, the need to make visits to see the impounded car and relying on hypnosis to refresh her recollection, Mrs. Nevil's description was crisp and certain when questioned by Ertel shortly after taking the stand: "Well, it was light green and it was metallic and had a helmet on the back, on the back ledge, and a Pennsylvania license number." When asked if she remembered the number, she said there was either a 1, 9 or 7 and believed it was the first number.

Indeed, the license number was 9U4995 as seen in photos of the car in the garage where she viewed it.

Even though prosecutors love to dramatize the reliability of having an eyewitness to any element of a crime, we have come to realize that eyewitness testimony is not always reliable. In fact, "mistaken eyewitness testimony" has been a factor in an estimated one third of wrongful convictions.

Judge Alex Kozinski, a conservative federal appeals court judge appointed by President Ronald Reagan with more than three decades of presiding over criminal trials and appeals, is among those who have taken issue with eyewitness testimony and the human dilemma of false memories. Judge Kozinski has stated that findings about false memories by cognitive psychologists raise "troubling implications for criminal trials where witnesses are questioned long and hard by police and prosecutors before the defense gets to do so—if ever. There is thus plenty of opportunity to shape and augment a witness's memory to bring it into line with the prosecutor's theory of what happened. Yet with rare exceptions, courts do not permit expert testimony on human memory." *(Note: Kozinski stepped down in 2017 after allegations of sexual harassment outside of the courtroom.)*

The Commonwealth's key eyewitness supposedly saw the victim get into the car she identified as belonging to Kim Hubbard either before or after being shown a photo of Hubbard's car or before or after being shown the car in impoundment. But it was the drama of the helmet on the window ledge that seemed to seal the deal in the trial, and it required two different helmets to up the ante.

CHAPTER 10: HELMETS AND LIARS

"How Can You Sit There and Lie?"

... and once he started to lie to cover it up, they kept getting bigger and bigger and he kept getting enmeshed in his own lies.
– Lycoming County (PA) District Attorney Allen E. Ertel describing the defendant, Kim Lee Hubbard, in his closing argument to the jury on February 28, 1974.

The preceding statement, as it turns out, may have been a more apt description of the Commonwealth's evidence against Kim Hubbard, reflecting a patchwork case shuffled together like a dog-eared deck of cards to convince an overwhelmed jury of the defendant's guilt in the murder of twelve-year-old Jennifer Hill. And yet the jury was able to deliver its verdict so quickly that they literally changed the meaning of deliberation, the process they were directed to perform by Judge Charles F. Greevy after charging them to decide Kim Hubbard's fate on that Friday morning—the first day of March 1974.

Considering the complexity of the case and the evidence that had to be digested, the jury returned quickly—three hours maximum to discuss and debate the evidence and then tally their votes. Having been on a couple of juries in criminal trials for what were far from capital offenses, I know that it can be an hour or more before you settle in and even start to discuss the case after a long trial. There is time required to catch up with all that testimony, because you aren't supposed to discuss trial evidence until deliberating. The more evidence both ways, the more reason for debate.

In the Lycoming County Courthouse on March 1, 1974, the jury only required about four-and-a-half hours between being dismissed to deliberate and returning to the courtroom to render their verdict.

The foreperson of the jury is usually chosen in seclusion before testimony begins, but most of his or her duties come after the panel is charged and dismissed to deliberate. He or she decides how the evidence is reviewed and may seek input and recommendations from others, to assure that all evidence and arguments made during the trial are considered.

Then comes the matter of settling the voting procedure and any other evidentiary points they want to discuss or argue. Studies of jury behavior tell us that if a majority of the jurors vote one way or another in the initial poll, that will most likely be the verdict at the end. It is then most likely that it will not take as long to convince dissenting jurors, if there are any, to agree with the majority. Jurors didn't need to admit that it didn't take much discussion or debate. It usually takes time to move toward a consensus and then unanimity, especially in a murder case.

After conducting their vote and agreeing on a verdict, they alert the tipstaff, the courthouse staffer in charge of the jury throughout the trial, who, in turn, notifies the judge so they could alert all the principals that a verdict had been reached. Then came the logistics of reconvening. This jury returned to render their verdict at 2:40 p.m. Plenty of time to get home on a Friday for long weekend, a relaxing dinner and settling in for a normal routine.

If the news media covering the trial were expecting it to at least extend into the evening, possibly the next day, they were pleasantly surprised to find the jury in place and the judge gaveling the court back in session so soon. In fact, such a quick response after nine full days of trial and more than 93 witnesses, elicited this comment in the ensuing issue of the *Sun-Gazette*: "The jury surprised many of the veteran courthouse personnel and lawyers by their swiftness in reaching a verdict."

The evidence, as laid out in a hodgepodge of the physical and the circumstantial, must have been almost impossible for the jurors to follow in real time from photos presented out of sequence in making divergent evidentiary points. Whether you believed in Kim Hubbard's guilt or innocence, there was a general expectation that the deliberation would be, well, deliberate. Deliberations are by definition, after all, "discussion and consideration" of all aspects of an issue. Of course, the trial itself did not reveal many things we came to learn about the evidence that most influenced the jurors. Otherwise, they may have paused and reflected for a few more hours.

And what evidence impressed jurors so much in spurring them to return with such a minimally deliberated verdict? Again, reported the *Sun-Gazette*: "Most of those (jurors) conceded the most damning evidence during the case was the boot prints found under the body and the tire tracks found in the cornfield off the Sylvan Dell Road, along with a white helmet found in Hubbard's car."

The *Sun-Gazette* of the 1970s took the quaint view about bylines for reporters. It was an old-school approach to journalism and bylines were deemed a bit audacious and unnecessary because they detracted from team spirit of the news staff. Furthermore, it would be just another reason for reporters to ask for raises. The best-known names in the paper were syndicated columnists like Paul Harvey and "Dear Abby" Van Buren.

Such was the case in the trial coverage. Most of the testimony was paraphrased with few direct quotations. Testimony of witnesses for the defense were rattled off with basically one-paragraph summations, and it was typical to label a defense witness as "a friend of Hubbard." Some were even lumped together as "Hubbard's witnesses," which, in a way, they were, but it suggests they might be dissembling to help out a friend.

One of those rare quotations could have easily led to a mistrial, and the *Sun-Gazette* devoted a separate story to the incident which occurred when Kim's girlfriend, Colleen Whitenight, was on the stand with alibi-confirming testimony. She disputed her father's testimony about the time of a phone call which supported Kim's alibi. The opening paragraph of that article reported that while his daughter was testifying as a rebuttal witness for the defense, Kenneth Whitenight, stole the show as elicited in the lead paragraph:

> ... the father of Hubbard's girlfriend jumped to his feet in the back of the courtroom and shouted: "Colleen, how can you sit there and lie? For God's sake," he continued, "you've lied enough already."

The story went on to report that the judge ordered the apparently distraught father removed from the courtroom and, as Whitenight was being escorted out, he apologized to the judge, with the article continuing the account. "As he was leaving, Whitenight said: 'God forgive her. She doesn't know what she's doing.'" The last quotation was not included in the trial transcript, though the first one was.

It was almost Biblical and certainly prejudicial, reminiscent of the dying request of Jesus, "My God forgive them. They know not what they do." It must have had quite an impact on a jury of mostly parents who could commiserate with a father's anguish over a child led astray by an amoral lover.

Another example of picking and choosing quotes by a reporter came during the testimony of Cpl. Ronald Barto, the arresting officer, who stated that when he arrested Hubbard on November 16, he asked him if he wanted to give "a statement or confession" on what happened on Oct. 19 between him and "the Hill girl." (quotations as paraphrased in the article). Then the article stated:

Cpl. Barto testified that Hubbard replied, "Yeah, you blew it."… Cpl. Barto said Hubbard "laughed and walked away" after making the statement.

Let's hope he didn't walk too far away. He'd just been arrested. He could have been charged for resisting arrest.

Kim freely admits telling Barto "you blew it," because "the way I saw it was somebody was getting away with murder because they had this hard-on to go after me."

Judge Greevy, in his instructions to the jurors, advised them to rely on "common sense and human experience" in coming to their conclusions of guilt or innocence, which is standard. As "the sole judgers of fact," the judge also stressed that it was important the jurors "consider the witness truthful and accurate." Ertel had continually hammered home that Kim Hubbard was a liar. (A tactic two Pennsylvania Supreme Court Judges said should have warranted a new trial.) Hubbard admitted under cross-examination that when applying for the job at Stroehmann's he had not mentioned having worked for Eastern Wood Products because he had quit that job at the end of a shift. When asked why, Kim said perhaps too bluntly but truthfully, "I lied to get a job." It was an intentional omission, but omissions and exaggerations are commonplace on job applications but not necessarily indicative of a criminal mind.

In his summation, Ertel got as much mileage as you could get from such an admission: "The defendant said, 'I lied to get a job.' He said that sort of proud. 'Would he lie if he murdered? Certainly.'"

Finally, Ertel offered his final thoughts on Kim Hubbard the liar and, therefore, the murderer:

And when you conclude it didn't happen in that cornfield, where did it occur? Only two people know. One of them is Jennifer Hill. She will never tell you, and the killer... What we do know is that the defendant has consistently fabricated in this case. Does he know?

When taken before the Supreme Court of Pennsylvania, Justice Samiel J. Roberts, who would later become Chief Justice, took exception to this tactic by declaring in an opinion filed January 28, 1977:

> *This was an unprofessional expression of the prosecutor's personal opinion regarding the appellant's guilt and credibility. These remarks far exceeded the bounds of propriety.*

Roberts, whose opinion did not prevail, concluded that Hubbard's sentence should be vacated and he "would remand for a new trial" as, he added, should have been done twenty-nine months before at the evidentiary hearing before Judges Charles Greevy and Thomas Raup. We'll get to that later.

Roberts was joined in dissenting by Judge Louis Manderino, a strong Civil Rights advocate. Although other appeals followed, with other minority opinions favoring a new trial, this was as close as Kim Hubbard would come to another chance with another attorney before another jury.

Ertel had also gone after the defendant's alibi witnesses: Dorisann Hubbard, his mother, and Colleen Whitenight, his girlfriend. Both were labeled as liars because they were trying to protect Kim. Ertel was basically dismissive of everything Dorisann said, including her recalling that Chief Charles Smith had suggested prior to Kim's arrest that she might want to purchase a plane ticket for the two of them to get away from it all. It came down to who would be the most likely liar, an officer of the law or a mother desperate to save her son from being arrested for murder.

Other things she stated in her testimony really had more to do with the events leading up to finding Jennifer's body and very little to do with guilt, innocence, or the crime itself. She testified that when Jennifer left her house that afternoon, she had her jacket on and it was "closed" (buttoned up). Ertel made a point of dismissing this as "ridiculous" for such a warm day, but it explains why, after Jennifer started walking, she removed the jacket and tied it around her waist. It was clearly an attack on the credibility of the person who would attest to Kim being in the Hubbard house buffing a floor at the same time the prosecution had him spiriting the girl away to her death.

As for Colleen, her credibility took a big hit from her father's emotional outburst during her testimony. Perhaps he was more upset about other testimony, another truthful admission, in this exchange during Ertel's questioning of his daughter:

> Ertel: Have you been having sexual intercourse with him
> during that period of time?
> Colleen: Yes.

Colleen was subsequently asked how long she had been dating Kim, and she estimated almost three years, including before he enlisted in the Army and again after his return to South Williamsport due to a hardship discharge. She also confessed that her parents didn't know she was seeing Kim for much of that time, and when they found out, they forbade her to continue the relationship. Nevertheless, Colleen and Kim continued dating and spending time with each other.

It was more than a credibility issue. It was about morality, an embarrassment for her church-going Methodist parents, for a high school girl to admit being sexually active. And so it went for the defendant, his mother, his girlfriend and all the young people dismissed by one courtroom observer as "long-haired gooks" who testified on his behalf.

Even though Ertel himself proclaimed circumstantial evidence as the strongest part of his case, the jurors, after their verdict, were most impressed by the so-called physical evidence. Most of all, it may have been that white helmet whose existence was blurred by mixed testimony about whether it was even in the car until after Jennifer Hill went missing. Based on contradictory testimony, it became a matter of now you see it and now you don't.

The white helmet emerged as a huge factor when identified by Betty Jane Nevel as prominently perched in the back window ledge when she saw a girl she identified as Jennifer Hill get into the car with her presumed murderer. The descriptions of the car itself were not particularly revealing, ignoring one prominent feature of the car, and could have described hundreds of cars in the Williamsport area alone. The helmet was the only notable item missing from inside the car when it was returned to Kim on November 7 nine days before his arrest. By that time, Mrs. Nevel had been taken to see the impounded car on two occasions over a span of a week starting on October 31. Lt. Hynick, the administrative coordinator of the investigation for the state police, testified that the white helmet was prominent in the back window of the car while impounded in the borough garage.

Of course, one might expect a potential eyewitness to be taken to view a suspect car for verification, or at least a photo of that car, as part of the investigation. Objective photo identifications might consist of a photo lineup of several similar cars with the witness pointing out the most probable. What one wouldn't expect, and what the jury never knew, was that the witness had been hypnotized to "refresh her memory." The white helmet was what made the car, an inconspicuous 1967 Oldsmobile Cutlass seven years out of production, unique. It certainly made an impression on the jury.

That modest white protective scalp helmet common on industrial work sites, should have been etched in the collective minds of the jury, mostly due to a courtroom drama played out in real time that triumphantly produced a second white helmet.

Ertel apparently didn't know about the origin of the helmet until Fierro cross-examined a Commonwealth witness to elicit that information. It required Ertel to scramble to find somebody, anybody, any reason, why Kim would be driving around with a helmet on October 19, 1973.

The helmet had been elevated to huge importance.

It looked as if Ertel's case had taken a big hit when Fierro triumphantly produced a witness who stated conclusively and with documentation that Kim was not even issued the white helmet from the Stroehmann's Roll Plant until October 24th—five days after Jennifer Hill went missing and five days after Nevel said she saw the girl get into that car. Ertel would be able to dramatically pull a rabbit out of the hat and save the day, turning the helmet into the most incriminating piece of evidence since the ladder that ultimately convicted Bruno Hauptmann with the kidnapping and murder of the Lindbergh baby.

Ertel took great pride in what he described as setting the trap for Kim Hubbard that made the white helmet so significant. In fact, it was the evidence the DA stressed in remarks to the press after the verdict, reinforcing its importance but, at the same time, underlining how fortuitous it had been to keep the helmet in play.

In the March 2, 1974, issue of the *Sun-Gazette*, was the following report:

> *After the trial the DA said when he learned in the courtroom that Hubbard was going to claim he didn't get a white helmet until Oct. 24, he had police investigators do some further work to find out about the possibility of Hubbard acquiring a helmet before that date. He said it was then a matter of waiting for Hubbard "to go out on a limb" during his testimony and state he didn't have any white helmets in his possession until Oct. 24."*

It started with three witnesses from Stroehmann's plant who testified that Kim was issued a white helmet there on October 24th—his first day on the job as a baker's helper in the Sweet Rolls Department and five days after Jennifer went missing.

Carl Fenstermacher, Office Manager at the Stroehmann's plant, took the stand on the sixth day of testimony. The eighteenth witness for the defense dropped a bombshell by stating that Kim Hubbard was assigned a white helmet at 4:00 p.m. on October 24th at the start of his first eight-hour shift. Fenstermacher brought notarized copies of the work records to confirm this. He identified the "scalp cap" helmet as the same brand they issued. Work records showed that Hubbard's last day of work was the end of his shift on October 30th and that the helmet was never returned. It should be noted that Kim's car was impounded by police, along with the helmet, on the next workday, October 31st. Without a car, Kim couldn't continue his routine of driving to his evening work shift after school.

Improbably, Fenstermacher was initially called as a Commonwealth witness by Ertel to establish that Kim had applied for the job there weeks before the crime was committed. If there was a trap being set there, it seemed that the prosecutor may have unknowingly got caught in it. This was apparently what put Fierro on the scent of something critical to his case and subsequently confirmed by his client. In his cross-examination, Fierro confirmed that Fenstermacher had brought Kim's work records and then asked the following: "Will you tell the jury when Kim Hubbard went to work for your company?"

When Fenstermacher responded, "The 24th..." Ertel immediately tried to cut off the response by objecting "This is not relevant. The application is what I called him for..."

"He is still a Commonwealth witness," Fierro countered.

The judge overruled the objection and Fenstermacher stated, "October 24th." Seizing the opportunity handed to him, Fierro then started asking a string of questions about the plant and the application process there. When he got to what equipment was issued on that day, an exasperated Ertel objected again. This time the judge sustained the objection, but the can of worms had been opened and the cat was escaping from the bag. This would prove true when Fenstermacher took the stand for the defense as did two subordinates from the Stroehmann's plant to confirm that the helmet could not have been in the car that Nevel said she saw on October 19.

Both Production Manager Robert Simon and Kim's shift supervisor, Terry Andrews, confirmed that it was company policy to assign helmet and uniform on the day an employee started working there. Ertel must have assumed that the helmet was given to Kim when he was hired earlier instead of when he actually reported to work, if he had considered either until that critical juncture. He responded with aggressive cross-examination, intent on getting both Simon and Fenstermacher to say that it was at least possible that the defendant may have been driving around with that helmet earlier. Neither was willing to do that, and they had the documentation to corroborate their denials.

Ertel's aggressiveness was subdued by the time Andrews, the shift supervisor, was called to the stand as the first witness on the following day, Wednesday, February 27, the seventh day of testimony and the eighth of the trial. After Andrews, the person who assigned that helmet, verified that it would have occurred on October 24, Ertel had no follow-up questions. It appears that was when, as he boasted to the press after the guilty verdict, he unleashed his criminal investigators "to find out about the possibility of Hubbard acquiring a helmet before that date."

There was a lot of mixed testimony from people who saw a helmet in the car or didn't see a helmet in the car and when they saw or didn't see it. Much of it on the final morning of testimony on the final day of February. Even though press coverage didn't play up the helmet drama, Ertel, and then Fierro, obviously made the helmet seem like the key to guilt or innocence to the jurors themselves. Ertel set it up in his cross-examination of Kim when he quizzed him on previously working for Eastern Wood Products in the spring of 1973 about six months before his short stint at Stroehmann's.

*Ertel: "You walked off of the job and never even picked up your
paycheck at Eastern Wood Products. Isn't that true?"*
Hubbard: "That is correct and never picked up my helmet either."
Ertel: "You had your helmet and never gave it back. Isn't that true?"
Hubbard: "That is an incorrect statement."

Hubbard worked the night shift there and still insists today that only
employees who had been working there for a year or more had their own
helmets. Others on the first shift would leave helmets at the end of their
shifts. Second-shift newcomers, himself included, would grab one of those
spare helmets left by the previous shift when they came in to work. Most
of the work he did, sweeping and janitorial duties, did not require him to
wear a helmet.

Reinforcing that the helmet in his car came from Stroehmann's, he
pointed to a red material on the helmet as the "sticky bun stuff" from his
job as baker's helper there. This would have been easy to substantiate by
testing if either the prosecution or defense had thought to do so.

The momentum changed on Wednesday evening shortly after
reconvening at 5:15 p.m. for Commonwealth rebuttal witnesses. Ertel
called Clair J. Kiper, a foreman at Eastern Wood Products, who attested
to his belief that Kim, who had been hired in March, left the job "during
the shift" on May 21, 1973, and he took his helmet with him. He
admitted to Fierro that he didn't see him leave with the helmet but
knew "it was not turned in to me." Unlike the management people from
Stroehmann's, Kiper had no documentation tying Kim to a specific
helmet and apparently didn't have records keeping track of equipment
that wasn't returned.

Ertel knew he had to account for the red-colored smear that Kim
called "sticky bun substance" and he asked Kiper if the red stuff on the
white helmet in evidence could have been contracted at his plant.

"It could have been red wax," suggested Kiper. "It is red." This was
an appropriate lead-in to a give-and-take between Ertel and Kiper suitable
for an Abbott and Costello routine.

Ertel: "What color is the red wax you have?"
Kiper: "Red wax."
Ertel: "Is it bright or white or medium?"
Kiper: "It could be bright. It could be very light."

Disregarding how red wax could be white, Ertel asks if the alleged red wax has an odor. Kiper believes it doesn't and refuses his offer to smell it.

Ertel attempts to nail the coffin of Kim's defense shut by calling a witness, David Kinney, who worked with Kim at Eastern Wood Products and left with him on the day he quit. It wasn't quite clear at first why Ertel chose this rebuttal witness based on the following question:

Ertel: "Did he take anything with him when he left?"

Kinney: "No."

What he really wanted from Kinney came later with a sequence of leading questions which drew objections from Fierro. The result was that Kinney said he recalled seeing a helmet, maybe two of them, in Kim's car "around July," he surmised. Conflicting and inconclusive testimony about the helmet, about who saw one in the car and who didn't, dominated the last morning of testimony in the trial. How could the jury not be influenced by the importance of the helmet?

Kim still remembers the helmet drama and recaps it quite succinctly:

"Ertel tried to bully a lot of my friends into saying there was a helmet in my car. He was desperate. But to make a long story short, Allen Ertel never produced a helmet from Eastern Wood and the reason why he didn't was simple. There never was one! Ertel even tried to insinuate that the jelly on my helmet was some kind of red wax used at Eastern Wood. He knew it was jelly. That's why he never had it analyzed. Maybe he did and decided not to share that information."

Whatever effect the reincarnated helmet had on the jury, it brought out the wrath in Fierro who must have felt victory was near at hand. It seemed he had beaten Ertel at his own game, with one of his own witnesses, and then everything fell apart. Fierro ranted to Kim back at the jail, blaming him for not giving him a heads up about the job at Eastern Wood Products.

He told Kim he was "going down the river" because of his so-called omission, a conversation Sheriff L. Eugene Pauling said he overheard. The next day would be the final rebuttal witnesses and summations to the jury by both Ertel and Fierro.

Fierro blew up on Colleen in the hallway outside of the courtroom, pontificating about how "we must disprove this helmet" and ruing loudly that they had lost the case. This apparently got back to Ertel who took the opportunity to turn it against the defense when he got to cross-examine her as a rebuttal witness for the defense on the last day of testimony. He asked her about the conversation she had with Fierro the previous evening after Kiper's testimony.

> Whitenight: "Conversation about what?
>
> Ertel: "Like what he told you what had to be done about that helmet?"
>
> Fierro objects and Ertel rephrases his question.
>
> Ertel: "Did he tell you out in the hall he had problems with the helmet, and he had to get over it and he had to have you testify to it?"
>
> Whitenight: "Yes."
>
> Ertel: "He had to change the stories of the boys that testified concerning the helmet. Did he tell you that?"
>
> Whitenight: "No."

That is why jurors credited the helmet with removing all reasonable doubt (and seemingly further discussion) about Kim Hubbard being the murderer.

And yet the judge himself recognizes the inconclusiveness of all the testimony about the white helmet was, where it came from, when it was seen and who saw it or didn't see it. He even speculates about the witnesses. Some saw none. Others saw one. And then there was the guy who saw "a couple."

"Now if you, the jury, find in weighing the testimony that you can't reconcile some of the testimony, it then becomes your duty to determine which testimony you will believe," the judge assured the jury. "Whom do you think was telling the truth about what happened?"

Then there were those tire tracks and footprints providing the physical evidence that allegedly placed the defendant at the scene where the body lay in repose down at the Dell. As it turns out, there may have been more than evidence scene basics involved in the casting of those prints. And what about the timeliness of a conveniently shoveled wide band of impressionable clay across that remote cornfield lane on the same day the body of Jennifer Hill was carefully deposited in that field?

Police Report No Clues Into Whereabouts of Girl

South Williamsport police say they have no clues yet as to the whereabouts of Jenifer M. Hill, 12, of 353 Hastings Street, South Williamsport, who has been missing since Friday afternoon.

Police were joined by volunteer firemen this weekend in searching alleys and wooded areas of the borough for any possible clues. Other area police agencies have been notified to watch for the child.

The seventh grade student at South Williamsport Junior High School was last seen walking along West Central Avenue towards her home at about 4 p.m. Friday.

Police said the girl had been visiting a friend in the 1000 block of West Central Avenue.

Police Chief Charles E. Smith said there are no indications the girl might be a runaway.

When last seen, she was wearing a football jersey with number 33 on it, blue jeans, a black coat and black sneakers. She is five feet tall and weighs about 120 pounds, police said.

Chief Smith also said the girl was carrying a pink and white "Glick's" shoe bag containing a pair of blue jeans, pajamas and underclothes.

According to police the girl had stayed at her friend's home last

JENIFER M. HILL

Thursday night since South Williamsport schools were closed Friday.

STATE POLICE today released this picture of Jennifer M. Hill showing her wearing the shirt she had on at the time of her disappearance on Oct. 19. Police are asking that anyone who recalls seeing her on Oct. 19 to contact them at South Williamsport Borough Hall.

Kim Lee Hubbard

56   G R x Z *City News Section*   July 31, 1977

Mr. and Mrs. Joseph Hubbard, of South Williamsport, and Their Daughter, Ruth (Standing), Have Been Pushing for a New Trial for Convicted Son, Kim

Jenny In Jersey: *Joe Mendez saw this photo in the local newspaper and recognized the girl he later learned was murder victim, Jennifer Hill, as the one he saw on the afternoon she disappeared in October 1973. She wasn't where the prosecution claimed she should have been in their flawed murder case.*

Police Report No Clues
Into Whereabouts of Girl

South Williamsport police say they have no clues yet as to the whereabouts of Jenifer M. Hill, 12, of 353 Hastings Street, South Williamsport, who has been missing since Friday afternoon.

Police were joined by volunteer firemen this weekend in searching alleys and wooded areas of the borough for any possible clues. Other area police agencies have been notified to watch for the child.

The seventh grade student at South Williamsport Junior High School was last seen walking along West Central Avenue towards her home at about 4 p.m. Friday.

Police said the girl had been visiting a friend in the 1000 block of West Central Avenue.

Police Chief Charles E. Smith said there are no indications the girl might be a runaway.

When last seen, she was wearing a football jersey with number 33 on it, blue jeans, a black coat and black sneakers. She is five feet tall and weighs about 120 pounds, police said.

JENIFER M. HILL

Thursday night since South Williamsport schools were closed Friday.

Younger Jenny: This photo of Jennifer Hill at a much younger age also appeared in local newspapers when she was being sought as a missing person. It was the source of confusion which the prosecutor used to bewilder a defense witness who could have derailed his case.

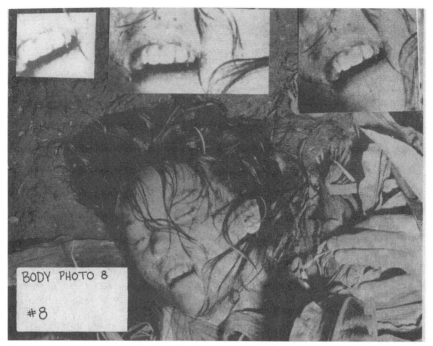

Injector Views: This evidentiary photo, a close-up view of the face of Jennifer Hill lying in the field where her body was found, was used throughout the trial and appeals before Joe Hubbard spotted something suspicious. Two funeral directors, experienced embalmers, identified it as a needle injector used in embalming. This begged the question of how a device used in embalming was in a recently discovered body.

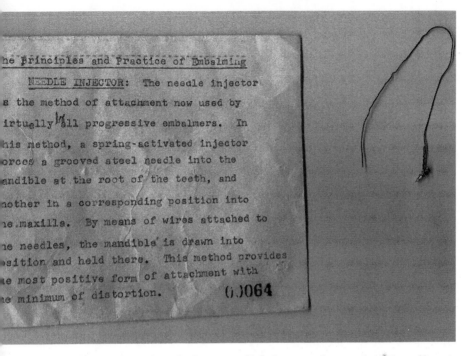

he Principles and Practice of Embalming

NEEDLE INJECTOR: The needle injector
s the method of attachment now used by
irtually all progressive embalmers. In
his method, a spring-activated injector
orces a grooved steel needle into the
andible at the root of the teeth, and
nother in a corresponding position into
ie maxilla. By means of wires attached to
ie needles, the mandible is drawn into
isition and held there. This method provides
ie most positive form of attachment with
ie minimum of distortion.   0.)064

*Needle Injector: A closer look at a needle injector and an explanation of how it
is used from The Principles and Practice of Embalming by Clarence G. Strub.*

Car in Garage: *Why was there cast-making activity in the South Williamsport Borough Garage, as attested to by an employee who was on the premises after Kim Hubbard's car was impounded on October 31, 1973, and returned a week later. Testimony stated that all tire casts were made at the Pennsylvania State Police Crime Lab in Harrisburg. The suspicious substance seen on a tire still on the car and tracks on the floor say otherwise.*

Plaster on Tire: *A closer look at white substance on the only deep-treaded tire on the car at the borough garage. This was the tire that wasn't on the car until after the body was found.*

Letters on Cast: *One of the mysteries of the case was how prints from a tire on Kim Hubbard's car could have been cast at the body scene when it hadn't yet been installed on the car. Another was how the last four letters of the tire brand "Kelly Springfield" (above) could have been cast from a moving tire.*

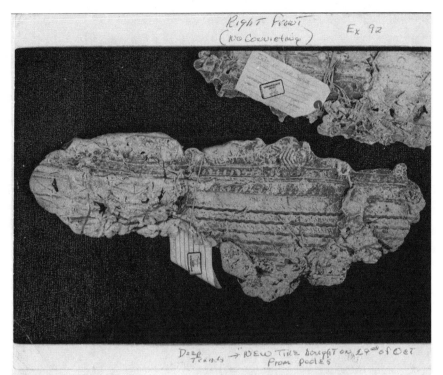

Tire RF Deep Tread: *This is a cast of a deep-treaded car identified as on the right front of Kim Hubbard's car at the state police crime lab. However, the garage owner, who described all the tires as bald or balding, installed the newer tire on the left front where it was when impounded. No wonder the tires and testimony thereof became so bewildering that Hubbard's attorney at an evidentiary hearing a year after the trial fled the courtroom and locked himself in his office.*

Morning After: *This view of the lane through a cornfield taken the morning after Jennifer Hill's body was discovered, just a few feet off the left of this roadway, shows the remnants of recent state police processing. Descriptions of just how far up the lane the body was found were conflicting in trial testimony, leading to questions about when and where in that field the body was really found.*

(Right) On Body: *These were the light blue pants found on Jennifer Hill's body as photographed in evidence. According to several witnesses, she walked to her death wearing a pair of brightly patched blue jeans, which were found in a bag a few feet from her body. This raised even more questions about the negligible amount of time the prosecution gave Kim Hubbard to commit this crime and place the body in the field unseen on a busy Friday afternoon.*

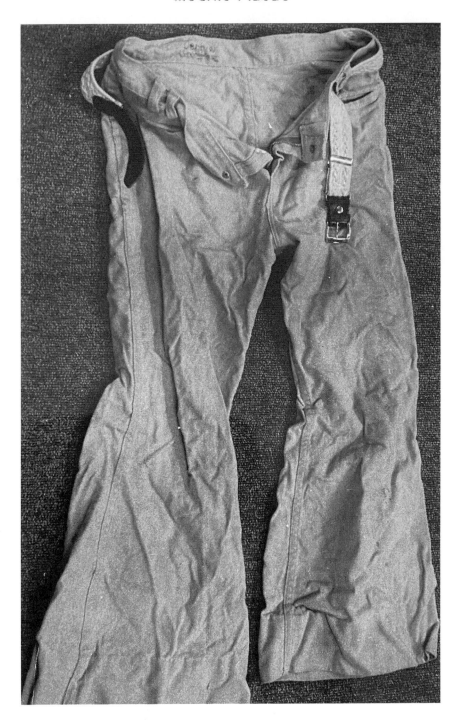

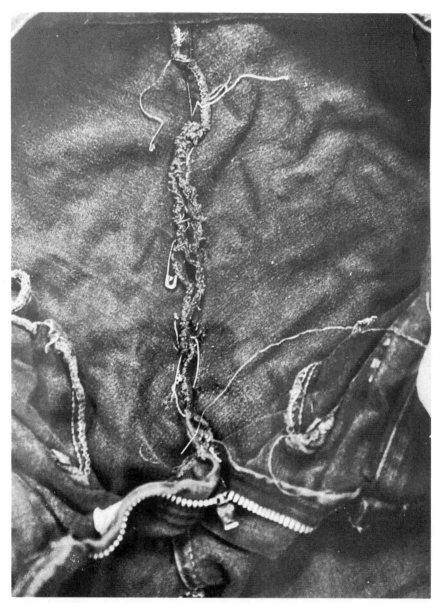

Sewn Pants: *A close-up look at the repaired rip in the seat of her blue jeans that raised speculation of how Jennifer Hill really died and what appears to be an attempt to sew up the split seam. The foreign thread clearly differs in size and texture from other material in the seam.*

CHAPTER 11: FIERRO

"You Go with What You've Got"

Remember this and things will turn out OK.
Colleen, you know, I mean I hope you know
that I didn't kill anyone.
I hope you believe me because I will kill myself
before I go to jail for something I didn't even do.
Love you always, Kim.

"Kim's going down the river!" Fierro shouted, swinging his one good arm upward in frustration. Joe Hubbard remembered that, but mostly the overwhelming, almost paralyzing, sinking sensation he felt as he watched his son's defense attorney unravel in the hallway—outside the DA's office at that. "That God damned helmet! He lied to me! It's over! That God damned helmet!"

The calvary had come to save Ertel as a rebuttal witness at the end of the next-to-last day of testimony. Final summations to the jury took place the next afternoon, February 28, 1974.

Patrick H. Fierro came oh so close to a real Perry Mason moment in his defense of Kim Lee Hubbard in February of 1974. Ertel had painted himself into a corner with his witness and that helmet. Fierro had him trapped. Or so he presumed.

Fierro was flamboyant, bombastic and, on occasion, something of a flimflammer when questioning witnesses and arguing in front of a jury. He had shown that with Mrs. Nevel at the preliminary hearing, but there was no jury to impress there and virtually no press coverage. It did give Ertel a heads-up on how to avoid future embarrassment to his only eyewitness when the trial came around.

The peppery defense attorney seemed to consider the courtroom his stage and not so interested in rounding up his own witnesses and briefing them in defense of his client. He had Joe Hubbard running around, tracking down and confirming leads and potential defense witnesses, playing the role of his chief investigator. Make that his only investigator. Truth is that Fierro was not all that familiar with some of his own witnesses before they took the stand.

One telling remark came after the testimony of Norma Hill when the judge agreed at the initial request by Ertel to sequester all witnesses from that point on. Fierro is asked if any of his witnesses are present in the courtroom. He looks around and says, "I really don't know them all that well."

His law partner, Anthony Miele, was occasionally involved in the case, but he had other obligations of the firm outside of criminal law, including divorce actions and estate settlements. It was Miele who was sitting next to Kim when the jury returned the verdict. Fierro had to leave town on business regarding some racehorses he owned. Like an actor who had played his last scene, he really had no other part to play, other than taking the final bows which he knew was unlikely. After Ertel brought another helmet into play in the dwindling final two days of testimony, Fierro seemed to shrink from the combat with Ertel that he had clearly thrived on up to that point.

And yet Fierro did have another of several moments of perceptiveness on the third day of testimony when he crisply extinguished Ertel's implausible narrative that by waving to Jennifer, Ruthie and other kids playing earlier in the day when driving by that it was some kind of signal between he and Jennifer to meet later. This time the bearer of that message was Sgt. Edward Peterson, who provided most of the testimony about the interviews of Kim by Hynick, Ertel and him three days after the discovery of Jennifer's body.

In asking Peterson whether Kim admitted ever having personal contact with Jennifer that day, he responded thusly:

Peterson: *That he saw her in a field and waved to her and the kids waved back.*

Fierro: *Did he say he waved to her alone or just waved at the kids?*

Peterson: *He said he waved to the kids in the field.*

The white helmet in the back window ledge was a major identifier of the car, a well-traveled, repainted, metallic/light green Olds with a severely damaged front fender on the driver's side. Mrs. Nevel didn't recognize the crumpled fender when she described the car. She hadn't seen the driver of the car and could only identify him as a man because the knuckles she glimpsed beckoning in the driver's window approximately fifteen to twenty yards from her vantagepoint through the slats of a window blind "were too big for a woman."

The white helmet was critical. It would be the helmet that would change the course of the trial—once and then again.

Fierro may have been quite fierce in his courtroom defense, but he wasn't exactly comforting to the Hubbards. He started nagging Kim from the eve of the trial. Colleen Whitenight's account of what they did that day had to be spot on with his, he urged his overwhelmed client. No room for discrepancies in their accounts. In retrospect, most of what Kim and Colleen did together occurred well before or after Jennifer Hill disappeared and the alleged sighting by Nevel.

To accommodate his attorney, Kim wrote his girlfriend a letter, desperately urging her to remember what they did on the afternoon and evening of October 19th, reminding her of some of the times. "Remember, remember, remember" was his entreaty. His mother subsequently delivered the letter to Colleen after enclosing it in an envelope. The letter would be construed by Ertel, who hammered Kim about it in his cross-examination, as coaching Colleen to lie. His urgency in entreating her to remember what they did, at times upon which they had to agree, had been portrayed by Fierro to both Kim and Colleen as being of critical importance.

The times that Kim begged Colleen to remember were all about what they did that evening, starting with a 4:30 phone call she made to him at his home, which was the only item in that timeline that had any relevance to the crime. It coincided with the time Mrs. Nevel said she saw Jennifer Hill rendezvousing with someone who was her probable killer. Ertel couldn't disprove that so he chose to the tactic of discrediting Colleen as a liar, as he did with the most important alibi witness, his appointed killer's mother.

Kim did not take envelopes with him to the Lycoming County Prison and was hesitant to correspond with anyone by mail. He didn't want interceptors reading his personal messages to his girl. His mother was the courier for any correspondence between the two. The envelope enclosing the crucial letter was subsequently handled by Kim before it was delivered, because Colleen's name was allegedly on the outside in his handwriting. "Allegedly" because 22 years after he was sentenced and another 22 years after that, a detective claimed he found Kim's DNA on "a second envelope" Kim sent to Colleen. He professed that he was able to confirm it as a match to a touch DNA sample on the waistband of pants in evidence worn by Jennifer Hill some four-and-a-half decades before.

You can't make this stuff up—even when it sounds like the schlock of bad fiction. The improbable DNA story will be told later.

Surprisingly, all the items and documents admitted as evidence during the trial were available for examination, even physical handling, during the appeals process by various people. That included at least two post-trial attorneys—Jack Felix and Peter Campana (and possibly Richard Watt in the final round of appeals)—as well as Joe and Dorisann Hubbard themselves. This was years before DNA was even imagined as a tool. Such random handling of the evidence, including Jennifer's clothing, the letter and other items would never be allowed today because the evidence itself would be tainted and compromised. The chain-of-custody would have been broken by who knows who looking through it over the years. Imagine how compromised it would be after sitting for at least twenty-two years after it was supposed to have been disposed of (a.k.a. approved for destruction) by court order through the Office of the Prothonotary.

One problem is that neither the letter nor any envelope was listed in the evidence in a Motion for Disposition/Destruction of Property on March 5, 1996. Nor was the helmet. Her clothing was documented right down to bra and panties and a solitary earring, as well as tires, casts, clothing, and soil samples, but both of Kim's parents handled those items multiple times prior to an evidentiary hearing and on through years of higher court appeals. They took multiple photos of the items laid out by them on a table or floor for closer examination. Several showed someone's hand literally touching items of Jennifer's clothing spread out for the photo taken by Joe Hubbard.

As for the letter and envelope, subject of testimony during the trial, they were handled by Dorisann, Colleen, and a close friend of hers who took possession so her father, Kenneth Whitenight, wouldn't see it. Whitenight, the indignant and injured father, may have had more impact on the jury with a seemingly unsolicited outburst than any testimony or evidence.

The letter that contained no provable lies was depicted by Ertel as a manipulative attempt by Kim to get his girlfriend to lie, and was, therefore, a big lie in and of itself. It was no longer listed in the evidence to be disposed of 22 years later. Kim did not contest the 1996 Motion for Disposition in the required time to respond (three work weeks) because appeals had been essentially exhausted, and his father had been gone for six and a half years. The Prothonotary's office, which had no record of what happened to that physical evidence when contacted in 2018, stated that it would be the DA's office that had removed it to an undetermined destination subject for disposal.

"I should have asked them to keep it or give it back to me, whatever they do, but I didn't want this case consuming the rest of my life," Kim said few years after the Motion for Disposition. "I wasn't thinking about exoneration then, and I knew there wasn't any chance of another trial. I was out, still young and healthy, and, hey, life was good. I should have done something. I owed that much to Pop."

Although Fierro appeared to have given up his aggressive counterattacks, he still had a trial to finish. Perhaps it was his final summation to the jury that revealed some of that lack of combativeness, with an occasional burst of feistiness and spontaneity that was his courtroom persona. He seemed almost too accepting of the jurors' human frailties for a lawyer who is supposed to be reminding them of the importance of their deliberations while trumpeting his client's innocence and, of course, reasonable doubt.

"I recognize that you and I are human beings, and I don't mind telling you that you have failings," he said in an observation that seemed to lead nowhere. Then, as if defending a weak case or its futility, he states resignedly: "You go with what you got."

Then comes the real poser that seems to let the jury off the hook: "I will tell you right now, if this boy is truly guilty, the way you see it, by all means you should find him guilty." He then goes into the typical homage to "beyond a reasonable doubt," but the judge would more effectively emphasize the importance of that in his instructions to the jury before sending them to deliberate.

Fierro reminds them, as the judge would also point out, that police testimony carries no more weight than from anyone else. He then offers that a policeman, like anyone else, might testify to what he "subconsciously wanted to see" and the truth may be colored by "who he was testifying for or against."

He meanders a bit, perhaps revealing suspicions he can't quantify: "It could happen because of corrupt prosecution. I'm not saying we have one, of course. I don't know…"

Perhaps most unbelievably, he reassures them that whatever they decide "I will sleep tonight." It almost seems as if it is not about a young man accused of murder, but about an aging lawyer, lost and beaten, who just wants everyone to know he did his best.

Fierro then touches on something that would raise questions years later about the clothing switch between Jennifer Hill walking home and the body lying in the field. It was as close as he would come to opening the proverbial can of worms. He reminds them that Wendy Shaffer, Mrs. Mundrick, and others saw the blue jeans with hearts on the knees (and the red band of fabric at the bottom of the bell bottoms to keep up with a growing girl's lengthening limbs), as did others during Jennifer's walk toward home from the Hubbards. Mrs. Nevel, however, described everything BUT the colorful jeans. The girl was found in that cornfield in a pair of light blue pants, and the other jeans, ripped at the crotch, were in the pink Glick bag she had been carrying. Jennifer's mother, Norma Hill, was insistent in her testimony that she was wearing those light blue pants when she left the Hubbards. Having not seen her daughter that day, she would have no way of knowing what pants she was wearing, but was identifying the pants found on the body in the field.

Fierro, by the way, brought none of those factors together. He mentions the mystery of the pants in passing but doesn't pursue it and how it might impact the already condensed amount of time Kim would have had to commit the crime in the sequence outlined by Ertel.

He wonders aloud why it took Mrs. Nevel eight days to report she saw Jennifer after the first article and photo reporting her missing appeared in the local newspapers. Jennifer's photo appeared in local newspapers multiple times during that span and was certainly the talk of the school her daughter, Beth, attended. It was Beth whose testimony verified she had identified the girl her mother allegedly saw get into that car as Jennifer Hill.

"The town was talking about absolutely nothing else. Kids at school were being questioned," said Dr. Norman Wengert, the South Williamsport chiropractor who convinced Joe Mendez to report his sighting of the girl with the "33 jersey" to police on the day Jennifer disappeared. "I can't believe Mrs. Nevel wouldn't have been aware of her disappearance."

Kim Hubbard's courtroom defender apparently knew at least three months before the trial that Nevel had been hypnotized to improve her recollection of what she saw. And yet he didn't bring it up when questioning her about being shown the impounded car. Again, we'll never know if the hypnotism was discussed in the judge's chamber or in a sidebar that was not transcribed, where the judge could have ruled it was information that shouldn't be presented because it might prejudice the jury. Otherwise, one might conclude that Fierro and Ertel mutually agreed to withhold this piece of information.

Mrs. Nevel was represented to the jury as eyewitness to the crime itself—the only person to physically link the victim and the accused that day. It had been revealed in news articles shortly before Kim's arrest that "an eyewitness had stepped forward" to offer conclusive evidence. To his credit, Fierro does try to discredit Mrs. Nevel through her inconsistent statements. He even gets her to state, as she did in the preliminary hearing when she first saw Kim's car impounded in the borough hall garage, that "I could not say it was and I could not say it wasn't" the vehicle that picked up Jennifer Hill. This would have been crucial had the jurors been aware hypnotism was used to refresh the recollection of the witness. For example, did they (a) hypnotize her after she failed to identify the car the first time it was shown to her, (b) then hypnotize her and (c) show it to her again? We only know the opportunity was there and may be the reason for at least two visits to see the impounded car.

If the jury was expecting Fierro to bolster the lack of evidence showing there was no violent assault preceding her death, they must have been surprised by his conflicting observations that were among the last remarks they would hear from him in his summation before the judge's charge to the jury the next morning.

Fierro ticks through most of the prosecution witnesses thusly:

√ Gleckner and Hunsinger, the body finders on October 28, 1973, "didn't say anything that helped us. They were telling the truth. There was nothing."

√ He passes casually over the extensive testimony of Dr. Earl Miller, the county coroner who testified about most of the physical evidence at the body scene. Miller identified footprints, casts and testified to the fine points of the body scene. Yet Fierro never once questioned why the coroner was offering testimony one would expect from state police criminal investigators or crime scene specialists.

For some reason, Fierro was trying to confirm nails on one of Jennifer's hands as being "torn," but neither Dr. Catherman nor state police criminal investigators would buy into that.

"I merely observed those nails on those two fingers showed an appearance different from the remaining nails...," Catherman testified, describing them as "irregular and ragged" and probably common for an active twelve-year-old girl. Even though the word "torn" was used in his report, he said they did not rise to the level of defensive injuries. Cpl. Donald Houser, custodian of the evidence, and Trooper Alfred Gomb, who was charged with a meticulous search of the interior of Kim's car on November 1 four days after the body was found, described it as "dirty" and with no evidence of it having been cleaned recently. They gathered and collected hair and dirt samples, as well as a fingernail—none of which could be linked forensically to the victim at the Pennsylvania State Police Crime Lab in Harrisburg.

"There were some paper cups there, cigarette butts, a lot of dirt, and items we talked about on the ledge of the backseat, straws, an empty soda bottle..." said Lt. Steven Hynick, who also examined the exterior of the car.

Nevertheless, Fierro persisted, without success, in asking the man who conducted the autopsy to agree that her nails were "torn off in some violent fashion." Why? It seems that his strategy was to underline the lack of any injuries observed on Kim by state police or any other witnesses who had close contact him while the girl was missing and after she was found.

Perhaps more damaging, as Fierro pursued an explanation for the lack of observable injuries to both the defendant and the victim, was his speculation in closing remarks that it may have been consensual: "or were they both doing it, because there is no damage to the clothing, and that means what? Cooperation." Apparently, realizing that a cooperative child victim wouldn't gain his client any favor with those who would soon pass judgment, he quickly retreats from that scenario: "I am talking about the time factor, not the little girl's morals."

It may have been construed by jurors as blaming the victim in some way—and a child at that. The Commonwealth had stretched the girl's involvement about as far they could go with their premise that this crime emanated from an unlikely planned rendezvous between killer and victim.

Elsewhere among his final words to the jury, Fierro makes the following points:

√ Making a valid assumption about obvious lack of injury beyond a few minor scratches to the victim and none to the alleged perpetrator: "Don't you fight back if strangled?"

√ On Catherman: "He is a forensic pathologist, and I agree with everything he said. That is the State's own witness."

√ Taking advantage of the fact that no evidence was presented of the girl ever being in that thoroughly inspected car, which was described as dirty and messy by Lt. Hynick and not cleaned for some time. "How do you find nothing in a car where this girl was killed?" asks Fierro who answers his own question. "On television. That's about the only place."

√ Making a point of reminding the jurors that Trooper Gomb interviewed 75 people on Howard Street—talked to seventy-five people—and nobody else saw Jennifer on that street, or anyone getting into a car stopped in the street in front of the Nevel home between 4:00 and 5:00 p.m.

√ Having made a passing remark about "a corrupt prosecution," he seems to indicate that he knows something that wasn't brought to light until after the trial when he asks the jurors: "Did anybody tell you when the boot prints were made? Did anybody tell you when those tire prints were made?" Affidavits were attained from witnesses after Kim was convicted and jailed who saw casts being made in the borough garage while the car was there. There are telling photos on the "Kim Hubbard Story" website that show the car jacked up with white powder on the tires and white tracks running to and from the car—one of them with clearly pronounced treads.

√ Wondering aloud to the jury why the best tire, the only one on the car with deep treads, was used for most of the comparisons. "I can't make any conclusions," he says in what must have seemed like an odd statement at the time. Of course, we would learn too late that the only tire on the car with deep treads was mounted on the car at a local garage after the body was found but shortly before Kim's car was impounded. That tire couldn't have made the prints cast in a band of clay on the cornfield lane while depositing Jennifer Hill's body, but those prints could have been cast in the borough garage after her body was found.

√ Suggesting, to his credit, that the prints on that convenient band of impressionable clay between 26 and 29 feet down the farm lane would have had to have been made by a moving car up and down the lane to the body scene another 100 feet beyond. There were clear impressions in a tire cast with deep treads of the last few letters of the brand name (Kelly Springfield) from the tire sidewall. Footprints allegedly cast in the same area would indicate that car stopped, and somebody got out at that spot. The alternative? The killer stopped the car there and then walked an additional 100 feet carrying a corpse to deposit the body at the declared body scene. (Fierro never suggested that latter part of this scenario, but it might have raised some doubts if he had.)

It is not uncommon for a convicted defendant to file an appeal declaring ineffectiveness of counsel, that his lawyer either failed in bringing out evidence favorable to his client or was essentially incompetent. This was true for Kim Hubbard, whose father was taking full advantage of the legal system and, at the same time, accumulating an amazing amount of new evidence disputing that used against his son. Their attorney at that point, Peter Campana, was forced to follow a typical path in the appeals process, including both the actions of the prosecutor and what might be described as the inaction of the defense attorney.

Ertel's inflammatory remarks, labeling Hubbard a liar on multiple occasions, were well documented when brought before the Pennsylvania Supreme Court, a seat on which he himself unsuccessfully sought in 1988 with the blessing of Gov. Robert P. Casey, a fellow Democrat. Although two of the five justices felt that Ertel had stepped over the line by exhibiting prejudicial conduct, Hubbard's conviction stood.

As for ineffectiveness of counsel, the chief charge against Fierro focused on one thing he failed to do: object to the prosecutor's inflammatory remarks.

Again, two of the five justices felt this failure alone should have vacated the judgment of sentence against Hubbard. Justice Samuel J. Roberts stated it bluntly:

Trial counsel's ineffectiveness in failing to object to the prosecutor's remarks prevented (the) appellant from receiving a fair trial.

Chief Justice Michael Eagen along with Justices Robert N.C. Nix and Rolf Larsen agreed a new trial was not warranted and that counsel's strategy in choosing not to object was effective. Fierro had argued that not objecting was a strategy that played a role in his client being convicted of second-degree murder instead of a life sentence or a cell on death row. (Capital punishment still stands in Pennsylvania, but, as of this writing, there have only been three executions since 1976.)

As for Fierro, he said he felt credibility was key to his defense and that the tactic of allowing the DA to become shrill in his attacks on his client was part of his strategy to prejudice the jurors against the prosecutor. He argued in his response to the Supreme Court that had he been granted a mistrial based on Ertel's inflammatory remarks that "we would have lost the best chance we at that point in time of ever getting whatever favorable verdict a jury might give us, and that a second go-around would have been a disaster in the view of the entire case as it finally developed."

He indicated that a second trial (at least with him as Hubbard's defender) would have been lost before it got off the ground because, essentially, his client would have had no credibility left. Even though he did not explain what would have been different in a second trial, regarding his client's credibility, he did point out that he was, in one way, victorious because the jury's verdict was a lesser murder count.

It was, in his eyes, a victory because it convinced the jury that his client's actions were not "willful, deliberate or premeditated," the standard for murder in the first degree.

It all came down to, as Fierro looked at it, whatever made Ertel look bad was good for him and his client. If Fierro was concerned about his client's credibility, which was essentially the depiction of his client as a liar, he pooh-poohed that approach in his closing to the jury.

"The State said he made some inconsistent statements," he expounded. "About what? About where he was at a certain time? Whether he paid this bill first or that bill second? You know what I think it is, ladies and gentlemen? Baloney!"

It was typical Fierro, and maybe his summation did have the effect of dissuading the jury from a verdict that might have brought life imprisonment or a death sentence. However, the evidence presented was, we now know, very fragile. The defense clearly didn't take advantage of the flaws in the Commonwealth's case, including body condition, questions about the processing of foot and tire prints reportedly cast at or near the body scene, as well as a missed opportunity to negate Betty Jane Nevel's credibility as the witness that put Kim Hubbard and Jennifer Hill together at 4:30 p.m. on October 19, 1973.

Should he have known?

I was not involved in trial coverage and only in my second year as a reporter when the murder and the trial transpired, but I communed with reporters covering the high-profile trial. Their consensus was that Fierro came across as shooting from the hip, taking delight in goading Ertel, and eliciting the DA's objections when cross examining. At the same time, nothing he did came across as being particularly passionate about his client's innocence. He could be rude to witnesses, including the mother of the victim, and regarded as a bully by the jury.

"He was recommended to us because he was known for making witnesses look bad," Joe Hubbard, sadly shaking his head, would tell me several years after his son's conviction. "Some people called him the one-armed bandit because he could steal a not-guilty verdict. He sure didn't put much effort into looking into their so-called evidence."

CHAPTER 12: GLECKNER

"The Sorriest Day of My Life!"

Search started early this day. Weather was good and the turnout was great. As for the CAP and volunteers, they searched 'til dark and at this stage the group were all tired and exhausted. But, still with hope in their heart, they tried to rest and get started for the next long, hard day.

—From handwritten notes by Major Louis Hunsinger, Mission Coordinator for the Civil Air Patrol (CAP) who oversaw the search for Jennifer May Hill on the eighth day of searching for the missing girl. The next day would prove to be the last, and the beginning of years of tribulation for the man who discovered her body.

The four short sentences above summarize the searching activity for Jennifer Hill on October 27, 1973, as documented by Lou Hunsinger, Commander of the hosting CAP unit in Williamsport. It was part of a handwritten draft of a terse Mission Coordinator's Report. As the host commander he was responsible for a hodge-podge of volunteer groups and individuals ultimately involved in trying to find the missing girl, including other CAP units, volunteer firefighters from several municipalities, a Boy Scout Troop, at least two four-wheeler clubs, a group called the Bixby Ranger Team and, something that would probably not happen today, school students released from classes to assist.

The man who discovered the body and testified to the same was Duane Gleckner. We interviewed Gleckner four years and ten months after he, as a Captain in the Civil Air Patrol and second in command to Major Hunsinger, was intimately involved in the search for the twelve-year-old. Gleckner, an insurance agent by trade, was the person credited with finding the girl's body on October 28, 1973, which, interestingly enough, was to be the last day of searching—in fact "just minutes before the search was to be called off at 4:00 p.m.," according to the October 29th *Sun-Gazette* article reporting the finding of the body.

It was August of 1978. I was assisting Edward Schumacher, a reporter for the *Philadelphia Inquirer* at the time, due to my familiarity with the case and my series for the weekly *Grit* the previous summer, reporting a conglomeration of evidentiary discrepancies. My investigative series had ended suddenly after several weeks when my publisher, Andrew Stabler, who was being pressured by then Congressman Allen E. Ertel, decided to bring it to an end. It was admittedly touchy stuff for a place like Williamsport with its conservative, family-friendly values, and I was getting into issues of potential misconduct of police and respected public officials. The *Inquirer*, however, saw the opportunity to not merely correct an injustice, if confirmed, but to follow a trail of evidence to emphatically prove Kim Hubbard's innocence and possibly implicate the real killer.

Ed and I had a lot of questions for Gleckner, because contradictions in his testimony seemed to put Jennifer's body in two different places as he described his approach to where the body lay and its location in the field. The repercussions of his testimony, photographs from the body scene and the condition of the body itself suggested more than one body scene when comparing photos and ensuing body scene testimony. Findings after the trial could lead one to conclude that the body had been preserved and then returned to the field in a different location further from the view of passersby. Not that Gleckner himself was intricately involved in some conspiracy, but his testimony started laying the groundwork of the Commonwealth's case against Kim Lee Hubbard.

Would Gleckner have had to know, or at least suspect, that all was not as it seemed for a body that had apparently been lying in a field for nine whole days? Some who have looked at this case feel he should have had his suspicions. Others feel he could have been an unwitting pawn. One thing was clear. He soon came to rue the day he got involved in that search.

Gleckner testified that he walked up the farm lane in the midst of a large cornfield off Sylvan Dell Road—about halfway by his estimation, approximately 100 feet. This would have put her at the body dumpsite identified by the Commonwealth and from which all alleged body scene testimony emanated. At that point he said he looked toward his left as he walked with his back toward Sylvan Dell Road and toward a levee and fenced-in industrial area abutting the cornfield. He saw her sneaker-clad feet barely "three or four feet" off the lane. One evidence photo, supposedly taken later from the spot on the lane where Gleckner first saw her, shows her feet projecting between two cornstalks toward the lane, her legs partially visible behind the tasseled stalks with her pants pulled down and gathered from her shins to her ankles.

"The day I found that body was the sorriest day of my life," Gleckner told us. He complained that the whole thing wouldn't go away, and that it didn't start with the articles I wrote for the *Grit* newspaper in the summer of 1977. He had met with Joe Hubbard a matter of weeks after the trial and had even drawn a little map showing where he found her. His X marked a spot between the seventh and eighth rows of the corn running parallel to Sylvan Dell Road and not further down the lane at the so-called body scene. I still have that drawing with Gleckner's X and signature. However, a mark in a crude drawing of rows of corn is far from clinching evidence of evidentiary manipulation.

Gleckner said he had been hounded by news reporters and skeptics of the outcome of the case over a span of months, even several years, after the jury declared Kim Hubbard guilty of murder.

"It just won't go away," he lamented, his voice rising in pitch for emphasis.

The bespectacled Gleckner stood firmly behind his assertion that he found the body on the 28th as he had testified under oath but conceded that he may have been confused whether she was lying between two parallel rows or across rows between stalks. He suggested that the shock of finding the body "might have messed up my recollection."

"At the time I thought that was the way it was," he said wearily. A machine-planted field of corn, as this was, tends to run in rows 30 to 36 inches apart, with the stalks in each row itself eight to fifteen inches apart. An adult, especially an adult carrying a body, could not walk between stalks across rows without bending, breaking, or stumbling over cornstalks. Coarsely known as the dumpsite because it wasn't conclusive, even probable, that Jennifer died there, the body was carefully lain on her back, according to closeups entered as evidence. That means the murderer, or whoever deposited the body there, would have to physically insert at least the length of her body into the corn to carefully set her into the position described.

Virtually the entire body from the ankles projects farther into the planted corn, but whether it was lying perpendicular to the rows or horizontal between two rows depends on how you interpret the sworn testimony of investigators at the body scene. Several photos admitted into evidence clearly show the body lying across a row—feet between stalks in one row and head between stalks on the other. The only photo of just her head and shoulders depicts her left shoulder atop a bent stalk and the left side of her face touching or almost touching the stalk. In another photo, a close-up of her face, the stalk is pulled away by a hand testified as belonging to Dr. Earl Miller, revealing what appears to be an earring. Only one earring was ever entered into evidence. An earring, at one point, was the target of searchers several days before she was allegedly found, according to CAP records. It raised the question of how they would know that.

Gleckner had walked up that farm lane off Sylvan Dell Road, which was a rough access road to the fenced-in oil ARCO storage tanks on the other side of an earthen wall behind the cornfield. Dr. Miller described it as a "wagon path." The main entrance to the ARCO compound was about a quarter mile further east off Sylvan Dell Road.

Gleckner admitted that he was apart from other CAP searchers between Sylvan Dell Road and the river because "it had been a long day and I was weary of crawling through the brush." He certainly wasn't in any mood to push his way between stalks of corn. He remembered thinking that by the time he walked back to the road, he would likely be summoning members of his unit on the river side of the road, and days of searching would be officially called off. That was the plan.

He testified that he saw the girl's body lying "between the rows" of corn which "ran parallel to Sylvan Dell Road." This would prove to be a contradiction because only the first eight rows of corn, known as sweep rows in planting, ran parallel to the adjoining paved two-lane road. Gleckner testified he saw the body about halfway back, at about 100 feet, where the rows ran perpendicular to Sylvan Dell Road and parallel to the lane.

The base of the stalks of field corn thicken and grow out, narrowing the distance between each in the same row to little more than a foot. The "hills" that form the rows themselves leave a more accommodating 30 to 36 inches between them.

The sneaker-clad feet of the body, as described and shown in evidence photos from the field, do seem to be sticking out between the stalks and not the rows. Other photos of the deceased girl from close up indicate that she is lying across two rows. The problem is how Gleckner, under cross-examination, agrees that she was lying in the same row of corn and that the rows were running parallel to Sylvan Dell Road. The body, according to his testimony, was lying feet first toward the lane between two of the rows running in the same direction as the highway. Gleckner's testimony in itself does not call attention to any discrepancy here if you were unaware how the rows were planted.

Could one mistakenly discern that the distance between stalks was a row when one is more than twice the width of the other? That's possible and this doesn't stand out in the testimony unless you are paying strict attention. This is later complicated by the testimony of Dr. Earl Miller, the county coroner, who describes approaching the body toward the head "through the same row of corn" in which the body was lying. Another discrepancy between Gleckner and Miller's testimony is the distance of the body off the lane. Gleckner says "three or four feet" and Miller estimates "fifteen feet." The latter doesn't match with an evidence photo taken from Miller's "wagon path" with the sneaker-clad feet clearly protruding from the corn.

Coroner Miller testified that he walked out from Sylvan Dell Road into the corn a distance of 20 to 30 feet. He then circled back toward the body, approaching from the head end. The last row between the eight sweep rows measures 26-28 feet up the lane. This would put Miller's and Gleckner's positioning of the body at least 74 feet apart along that lane. At the same time, they seem to agree it was lying between the rows and in the same direction.

Also across the lane at 26-29 feet was an impressionable band of wet clay-like dirt. It had been conveniently deposited there earlier on the same day her body was allegedly placed there, according to testimony, by a contractor cleaning off the tracks of a bulldozer that had been transported up and down that seldom-used lane for earthmoving work on the ARCO levee. It was this three-feet wide strip of dirt that captured tire impressions used to place Kim Hubbard's car in the field, including the only tire with deep treads that wouldn't be put on in the car until October 29—the day after the girl's body was found. Bob Faust, owner of Poole's Service Station in South Williamsport, signed an affidavit along with a copy of the receipt, that a new tire had been installed on the left front wheel of Kim's car the morning after Jennifer Hill's body was found. Faust further noted that all the tires at the time "were either bald or balding." By the time of an evidentiary hearing after Kim's conviction, there were enough tires rolling around in this case to keep two vehicles on the road.

Joe Hubbard had always contended that the body was originally found within forty-eight hours after October 19th in one of the sweep rows at about twenty-six feet down the lane, where she would have been more readily spotted and spirited away with little notice. He believed the body had been removed much sooner than October 28th, preserved by refrigeration, and then returned to the field further down the lane at 100 or 127 feet (both distances from testimony) with minimal notice so it could be officially "discovered."

This also coincides with two individuals signing affidavits that there was a white van down that lane at least twice between the 19th and 26th just off the entrance of that lane. The state police were using white vans at that time for special transport and later as mobile labs specially equipped with investigative equipment. Another man, Donald Decker, attested that there were two vehicles near the entrance of the cornfield lane between 10:30 p.m. and midnight on October 19, 1973—a few hours after the girl went missing and was believed to have been murdered. There was no description of the vehicles because it was dark. It did show that there was activity in proximity to the lane, according to the prosecution's scenario, after the murder victim had allegedly been disposed in the cornfield.

Another odd thing about the questioning of Gleckner comes when District Attorney Ertel is establishing when the body was discovered and asks if Gleckner discovered the body "on or about October 28." Upon repeating the question, he again states it was "on or about the 28th of October, 1973." Using "on or about" in court is generally an attempt at narrowing a time frame or a perceived time, not when establishing a specific date as critical as October 28, 1973, was to this case. Much of the testimony establishing rudimentary place and time seems, in retrospect, to leave room for error.

Suppose, as some of this contradictory evidence from the field indicates, the body was found earlier, removed in hopes, perhaps, of the killer returning to the scene. In the meantime, it is preserved and then returned to the field further down the lane and more distant from public scrutiny. The body is then officially discovered for Gleckner to play his part, either unknowingly or willingly.

And yet there was apparently little here to raise a juror's suspicions. The defense either failed to note these disparities or chose not to notice. As for Joe Hubbard, he didn't pick up on these field discrepancies until after the trial.

There were a couple of new bits of information that stood out. For starters, Gleckner professed that he had not been personally involved in any previous search of that area but believed the Sylvan Dell had been searched before. He stated that he was aware of that area being searched before but "mainly" by vehicles from the highway. That seems strange lack of attention to one of the closest nonresidential areas outside of the borough. One searcher who was a volunteer and not a CAP member, told me that he was part of a search party that went through that field in a line just a few feet apart days earlier than the reported body find. Additionally, state police, in one update reported by the newspaper during the search, mentioned a "ground sweep" of thirty to forty searchers in that area. It seemed a logical maneuver since the body was so close to the South Williamsport Borough line—off the eastern edge where the girl had lived.

The CAP logbook of assigned hour-to-hour searching parties was inaugurated the day after she was missing. There was no confirmation of any searching there prior to the late afternoon of the 28th in logbook entries released months after Gleckner wandered up that lane. However, it made little sense that they would have gone that many days after searching and not targeted that field. Their initial reported searching activity had been in the forested mountainside just south of the borough and a likely dumping place for a car headed in the direction as described by Mrs. Nevel.

The CAP set up its HQ at the Post 617 American Legion Post on South Williamsport's Market Street about three miles away from where the object of their search supposedly lay. Jennifer Hill's father, Jack, spent a lot of time at the Legion Post during the days she was missing, apparently waiting for any word about his daughter. The Hills' house on South Hastings was only six-tenths of mile from there and that much closer to the cornfield in the Dell.

There were no coordinated searches reported (or at least released) in the Mission Coordinator's Report (MCR) from October 20th through October 23rd despite newspaper reports of various searching activities during that time frame. The MCR did report 200 people involved in the search activities starting on October 24th with low-flying aircraft from the nearby airport in Montoursville taking part. On Friday, the 23rd, it was publicly reported they were expecting as many as 400 searchers, including Boy Scouts, students, and other volunteers, to be involved by the end of the weekend.

Had not Gleckner wandered up that lane to essentially kill some time, the body would have had to wait to be found—even if it was by the farmer who would be harvesting that tasseled corn in a matter of days. Some have questioned why airborne searches via helicopter embarked just across the river at the Williamsport-Lycoming Airport wouldn't have spotted that body from above sooner. They would have flown over the Sylvan Dell area dozens of times directly over where the body lay wherever their search destination might have been in or around South Williamsport.

As if in anticipation of why the body was not spotted earlier, the *Sun-Gazette* article on the discovery of the body on October 29th added the following toward the end of a lengthy article: "When asked why air searchers had not seen the body, CAP Major Louis Hunsinger and Captain Warren Peterson agreed that even a low-flying helicopter would not have spotted the girl's body through the thick, unharvested cornstalks." Others have observed since the corn was well tasseled and ready for harvesting that the leaves had shriveled, widening spacing between stalks that should have made it rather easy to see any foreign objects lying in the field.

Gleckner did not describe the body itself in testimony or subsequently in any known interviews, and he made it clear that he had no urge to take a closer look. He saw that it was distinctly a body, offering virtually no description of what he saw. He immediately left the scene to radio Hunsinger, his immediate superior, to confirm the find. His only testimony regarding the physical discovery of the body consisted of: "off to the left of the road (lane) I seen the body." He said he never approached the body closer than five feet.

It was Defense Attorney Patrick Fierro who questioned Gleckner about how the body was positioned in relation to the farm lane and Sylvan Dell Road. At one point he stated that the body lay in the rows "running at right angles to the road," the road being the private lane into the field. And if that was not clear enough:

> Fierro: Her body was parallel and running in the same direction as the rows of corn?
>
> Gleckner: Yes.

Sadly, Duane Gleckner would die in 1985 at the age of 43. He would have virtually no presence on the internet in the years that ensued, except for several things: a partial obituary, a photo of his gravestone in the Find-a-Grave Memorial site and several news articles about his involvement in the search for Jennifer and his testimony at Hubbard's trial about finding the body. That complete testimony in which his description of where and how he found the body—all trial testimony, in fact—can be found at Kim Hubbard's website. Gleckner is pictured in the October 25, 1973 issue of the *Sun-Gazette* planning searching activities for October 24 with his immediate superior, Major Hunsinger, commanding officer of the unit. At the time, according to the photo caption, they were reportedly concentrating on "the mountainous area south of the borough."

The last viewed photo of Gleckner's moss-covered gravestone partially obscures his name. Other information below his name was totally obscured. He would have been pleased to know that, after death at least, he was not the object of public attention.

If he was truthful about it being on the 28th, it should mean that Gleckner was not part of any conspiracy, but he may have taken a unit down there for the purpose of finding the body on that date. The coincidence of the discovery of the body being found just minutes before the searching would have been called off for good and that Gleckner happened to wander up that lane when everybody else was searching near the river have also been questioned.

Gleckner was frustrated about the difference between rows and stalks of corn when we questioned him more than four years after the trial: "Her feet were between two stalks of corn," he stated somewhat petulantly. "I thought it was a row." He then added emphatically: "I don't know which way the rows went. All I know is she was there."

That section along Sylvan Dell Road, including the field lane and other pull-off, was a popular parking place for romancing couples. Kim Hubbard admitted "going to the Dell" himself with his girlfriend, which was used to full advantage by Ertel during the trial. Yet it took them nine days and how many necking couples before searching there—at least for the record.

Gleckner suggested that the shock of finding her body might have "messed up" his recollection. He fulfilled his link in the case's chain of evidence in the case, and it only required a few minutes of observational time. It was Hunsinger who, after reporting to the scene to confirm finding, called in "Code 15," the prearranged signal that the body had been found.

> On October 28, the CAP log reports a team left to search Sylvan Dell at 1525 (3:25 p.m.). At 1630 (4:30) a team was called to assist at Sylvan Dell Road. At 1700 (5:00) "search party located at Sylvan Dell reported a possible find." (The latter was likely the "Code 15" after Hunsinger confirmed Gleckner's earlier find.)

"At the time I thought it was the way it was," he told us, as if the passing years may have played tricks with his mind. He brought up the condition of the body, which wouldn't even become as issue until months after Kim Hubbard's conviction.

"I know of bodies that have been dead a week. You didn't have to find them. The smell was so bad they found you." However, he stated that being suspected of finding the body earlier and then lying about it was "ridiculous," adding that "this thing has ruined my life." He also reiterated "it was something I would just as soon forget." When asked if it was possible someone else found the body, removed it, refrigerated it, and brought it back for someone else to find, he shook his head sadly without comment.

Ironically, in the October 29, 1973, issue of the *Williamsport Sun-Gazette*, a state police investigator stated that "there was partial decomposition of the body"—the only time the condition of the body was mentioned, even by the forensic pathologist at the trial. As it turned out, partial decomposition was an understatement. That might fit any body dead more than a few hours.

It is also noteworthy that in the second paragraph of that same news article—even before probable cause of death and whether it appeared to be a homicide—it was stated: "The body was half nude when discovered but there has been no medical determination yet as to whether the girl was sexually assaulted." Even though the crime was played up as being sexually motivated, trial testimony would reveal that there was no evidence of molestation of the twelve-year-old girl or injuries consistent with any attempt at such.

There was further explanation in the article that the girl's "blue jeans and underpants were down around her ankles when found." It was later seen in photos of the body as allegedly found in the field that a letterman's jacket Jennifer had tied around her waist when last seen was discreetly draped across her body covering all intimate body parts except for one partially exposed breast.

Gleckner said being questioned by reporters like me was part of his frustration, but he was especially offended when Jack Felix, Kim Hubbard's court-appointed lawyer after the trial, burst into his insurance office one day and accused him of "being in cahoots with" state police and Ertel in framing his client.

"I don't know what I can tell you," said Gleckner, who blamed Patrick Fierro, Hubbard's attorney, for getting him involved in questions, and ultimately accusations, about the location and condition of the body. "It's all there in the transcripts of the trial and, other than that, I don't want to go into it."

It started raining shortly after the Code 15 call, and by the time criminal investigators and others arrived to secure the body scene it was coming down steadily, continuing into the preliminary darkness of the evening. Gleckner said in trial testimony that it started to rain about 4:30 p.m.

Peggy Ann Rechel signed a deposition on Oct. 13, 1980, stating she had a conversation with Gleckner in which he imparted the following: "… He was positive there were two (2) sets of photographs showing the location of the body of Jennifer Hill in the cornfield along Sylvan Dell Road and that these two sets of pictures showed the body in two different locations." He also confided to her, in retrospect, that prosecution witnesses, himself included, were being deliberately confused in questioning about the two conflicting sets of photos. She said that he suspected that the prosecution witnesses may have been confused themselves by the time the field evidence was all laid out.

Note: Lou Hunsinger died on December 14, 2020, after an extended illness. He was an Air Force veteran and served in the Civil Air Patrol (CAP) from 1949 to 1980, retiring from the CAP with the rank of Major. Peggy Ann Rechel died seven years after her notarized affidavit. She was only forty-two years of age. Both were respected members of their communities.

CHAPTER 13: THE BODY

"No Way the Body was Dead That Long!"

The pristine condition of the murder victim's body after lying in a cornfield exposed to the elements for at least 216 consecutive hours should not have passed unnoticed in the convicting murder trial of twenty-year-old Kim Hubbard in February 1974. The probable decomposition of a human body subject to specific weather conditions from October 19 until nightfall on October 28, 1973, were spelled out day-by-day, even hour-by-hour, in Chapter Six.

It is what came after—perhaps too long after—that has blurred the shadow of a doubt about this case for several decades. The problem is what to make of it, and how many more straws it should have taken to break the back of this case with evidence that was there all along but not presented to the jury.

Steve McCune was the person who embalmed the body of Jennifer Hill at Noll's Funeral Home in South Williamsport at an unspecified time after her autopsy held between 6:00 and 8:00 p.m. on October 29—more than twenty-four hours after Duane Gleckner allegedly discovered her body. McCune was assisted by James Shaler, funeral home manager at the time, but first they had to pick up the body from the field even as evidence was being collected and casts poured at the body scene. McCune's memories of that night and his shock upon examining the body and prepping for embalming were still vivid when interviewed five years to the month later. He was manager of a Wilkes-Barre, Pennsylvania, funeral home at that time and would move on to become owner and director of his own funeral service in Mountain Top just south of Wilkes-Barre.

McCune chose his words cautiously but admitted he felt less constrained than he might have been had he still lived and worked in

South Williamsport. McCune received a call from the funeral home at around 5:30 p.m. on October 28th. The girl had been found and they had been requested to pick up the body and transport it to the Williamsport Hospital morgue. He remembered it was raining quite hard, having started not long before they arrived at the field in Sylvan Dell shortly after 6:00 p.m. The body still hadn't been moved from its original location, as far as he could tell, and he observed people taking photos and apparently making casts, or trying to, in various locations on the lane and in the vicinity of the body.

Police appeared to be pouring casts, and it seemed to him they were having problems doing so because the ground was so wet. Surface water was pooling on the narrow lane running north to south from Sylvan Dell Road to the Arco Tanks compound behind an earthen wall perimeter at the end of the 250-foot-long narrow lane. And the rain kept coming down. There was a lot of mud around the body itself and he did recall walking along a plank to avoid the mud.

The body was covered with plastic sheeting to protect it from the rain, he noted, but there was no plastic beneath it. At some point, not long after he and Shaler arrived at the scene, they observed the body being moved to take photos of an imprint of something supposedly left under the body. They simply "rolled the body away" toward the south.

The body lay just inches away and adjacent to where they were taking photos of what were said to be prints. McCune couldn't make out any depressions around or under where the body had been. Then again, it was twilight, raining and darkness was descending.

He wasn't sure why they expected prints to be under the body since they haven't moved it until then. He doesn't remember any casts being poured immediate or adjacent to the body, but that may have been done later. He did notice plastic and other evidence of casting on the lane an estimated 45 feet from the body scene toward Sylvan Dell Road.

Did he notice a stick underneath the body when it was rolled away, as pointed out by Dr. Miller in testimony about one of the body photos during the trial as a point of reference? He was certain there was none.

Since he had observed the body closely, notably later during the embalming, he believed it was highly likely that the weight of a decaying body pressed against such a stick for days at a time would leave a significant mark on the skin of the back. He had observed none. The body was remarkably free of any markings that might indicate insect and animal activity. This was verified in the postmortem report of Dr. Robert L. Catherman, the forensic pathologist who conducted the autopsy the next evening. His only description relating to the back was "postmortem changes of the skin" referring to minor or early decomposition. It is significant that Catherman's only reference to overall body condition was "early slight postmortem decomposition."

McCune said the body was then moved again to a temporary location nearby while he and his Shaler waited to remove it from the field. The only thing he remembered about that process, perhaps because of other distractions at the scene, was when it was moved the second time it was lifted slightly to avoid being dragged in the mud.

As for McCune and Shaler, they used a body bag to pick up the body when extricating it from the field. McCune remembers his growing irritation at Allen Ertel's constant cautioning on handling the body.

"He kept telling us not to slide or drag the body in the mud," he said, still peeved at the recollection five years later.

It's funny the things you remember at eventful times in your life.

They transported the body to the Williamsport Hospital and placed it on a morgue table—supposedly undisturbed from the way it was found in the field. It was warm in that room, he recalled, and an air conditioner was brought in to cool it off.

William Nixon, an Emergency Room Technician at Williamsport Hospital at the time, was called to the morgue the night of October 28, 1973, to help move the body of Jennifer Hill from the "autopsy table," where it had been placed by McCune and Shaler earlier that evening, to a litter and then put the body and the litter in the "cooler." It would apparently stay there under refrigeration until Dr. Catherman's autopsy at 5:50 p.m. the next evening. Nixon got to closely observe the body, which was lying on a muddy piece of plastic, and that it was remarkably well preserved with no notable signs of decomposition.

After the autopsy and at the embalming, with McCune as the primary and Shaler assisting, both of them marveled at what they saw. He remembers Shaler saying: "No way that body was dead that long." He agreed. In other observations, he noted that the blood drained out beautifully and the stomach was not noticeably distended. Organs in the stomach area had been removed at the autopsy.

Additionally, he said the vessels were milky pink and the blood bright red. There was a minimum of clotting, a process that begins a matter of hours after death. No staining of tissues, no skin slippage or peeling. As for the embalming itself, McCune said he "cut both sides of the neck and clamped off the head area, pumped in the fluid and then closed with a solution before unclamping."

"If the body had been in the air that long (Oct. 19-28)," McCune said. "The skin would have torn right off if you touched it."

There were maggots but they were "very, very tiny." He would have expected full-grown larvae on a body exposed that long in that setting. He had previously handled bodies that had been outside exposed to the elements for days at a time. It didn't fit.

What about refrigeration? McCune agreed that refrigeration would explain the excellent condition of the body. He became somewhat animated when this topic came up, especially when it was suggested that hospital facilities might have been used. He seemed genuinely surprised that there was a cooler at the hospital which could store multiple bodies. He also admitted that he was not all that familiar with accommodations there since the typical transport of a body from a death scene was to their funeral home.

McCune first noticed the only prominent mark on the neck as an abrasion, but upon a closer examination, said it could be deep enough to be an incision or gash.

Consultation with another long-time funeral director, Homer Graham, not long after the McCune interview, revealed similar conclusions based on what he could determine from scrutinizing photos of the body and Dr. Catherman's findings in his 1973 Postmortem Report. Graham, examining the neck "abrasion," said it looked like an embalmer's incision.

It was another case of things "getting curiouser and curiouser," but this was no work of fiction and certainly no Wonderland. Just when you start to make sense of something in this case, another thing comes along to knock you off balance.

McCune refrained from theorizing about the how's and why's of the body condition, but he was straightforward and consistent. He knew that he was providing sensitive information about a controversial case, but he was candid in what he saw at the cornfield and later during the embalming process. In recent years he has avoided interviews when contacted by others about the case.

> (I was assisting Edward Schumacher, reporter for the Philadelphia Inquirer at the time we interviewed McCune in Wilkes-Barre. The Columbian-born Schumacher went to the New York Times in 1979, later heading its Buenos Aires news office and changing his byline and professional name to Edward Schumacher-Matos. At the Inquirer, Schumacher was part of an investigative team that won a Pulitzer Prize for its coverage of Three Mile Island in the spring of 1979. He ultimately became the Director of the Edward R. Murrow Center for a Digital World at the Fletcher School of Tufts University.)

Now we're getting into the territory of a couple of real heavyweights in forensic medicine. Fortunately, I have a recording and transcript of a January 30, 1980, interview of Dr. Glenn M. Larkin and Dr. Floyd C. Coles conducted by Dwight Schmuck, a freelance journalist, who along with his colleague, Brad English, reported on the Hubbard case in March of that year in three consecutive issues of the *Weekender* newspaper. Schmuck and English expanded on issues raised in previous news coverage with a series of interviews that introduced even more discrepancies and inequities in the investigation and trial. None was more powerful than their Q&A with Coles and Larkin, further edifying and adding to the credibility of assertions that Jennifer May Hill was either not killed when the Commonwealth claimed or her body was refrigerated for days to halt decomposition and placed in the field by someone other than Kim Lee Hubbard.

Floyd C. Coles was Allegheny County Chief Deputy Coroner at the time, and Dr. Glenn M. Larkin, a renowned forensic pathologist who worked with Cyril H. Wecht & Associates, was recognized as a leading expert in determining time of death. Larkin dedicated the last two decades of his working life as an expert pathology consultant in more than 100 criminal trials for both the defense and prosecution as well as 30 civil cases. He also did pro bono work in assisting in cases of people who may have been wrongly convicted. Aside from his role as chief deputy coroner, Coles was a funeral director and embalmer. Coles was chief deputy to Coroner and renowned forensic pathologist, Dr. Cyril Wecht, and chief autopsy technician for fourteen years.

Coles died in 2010 and Larkin in 2013 at the ages of eighty-four and seventy-eight, respectively.

Both forensics experts closely analyzed Dr. Catherman's autopsy findings, as well as photos taken there and at the body scene. They also took into consideration comments made by the embalmer, McCune. Finally, significant attention was paid to hourly localized meteorological data for all nine days the girl was said to be lying in that field near the Susquehanna River.

The key question was, based on their expert opinions, whether the body depicted in postmortem report could have been dead for nine days.

"Only if it was refrigerated," Coles responded.

"The belly wall is flat, and this is very inconsistent with a person being dead for even a two-day period because the gas formation would have happened there," he said, explaining that the food identified in the stomach would have caused the gas formation, resulting a green color due to the putrefaction process. "This is completely inconsistent with anything other than a fresh body." He took note of the fact that McCune's description of the embalming indicated "a fresh body"

Larkin agreed and was especially attentive to where the body was located.

"It is unlikely that this body could have been at the spot without being attacked by various animals in the field and without having more ravages of post-mortem feeding," Larkin explained.

By using blowflies and other insects feeding on a dead human body, forensic entomologists can come pretty close to calculating an estimated time of death. This is known as insect derived time, providing a tight time frame known as the minimum post-mortem interval.

"Stomach contents here were easily identifiable and they're described (by Catherman) with a great deal to detail," Larkin stated. "In a body dead for nine days most of the material would be one of an amorphous (lacking structure or shape) junky mass...."

He went on to point out that under magnification there was virtually a complete lack of fly larvae. Just a very few around the eyes, which again indicates twenty-four or fewer hours.

"The flies would have really attacked this body along with the ground larvae and other insects," Coles added.

Catherman's findings indicate that he examined sections of the brain, said Coles who added that it was "very improbable" slides could be taken after nine days in the conditions indicated.

"It would be almost liquid. It would just run out when you open the head," Coles speculated with Larkin adding that this would also be true with the adrenals, which Catherman had examined.

Bodies are supposed to be examined in autopsy, initially at least, as near to its condition and appearance as possible when photographed at the body scene. Coles expressed concern "that there was tampering of the body" between discovery and when autopsied by Catherman. He said the body in the field was photographed with the bra partially off and a breast partially exposed but in place when examined in the morgue the next evening.

"Because of this, any statement relative to the condition of the clothing is suspect," Coles concluded in an addendum to the interview.

The defining exchange in the interview was to the point:

Schmuck: "Would it be dead for nine days?"

Coles: "Only if it was under refrigeration."

There was little mention of body decomposition and the implausibility of the murdered girl lying in the field for nine days nine full days until after Kim Hubbard had been convicted and sentenced to ten to twenty years for second-degree murder. However, the one person who should have noticed that there seemed to be insufficient decomposition for a body dead that long would have been Dr. Catherman, Deputy Medical Examiner for the City of Philadelphia, who conducted the autopsy on the evening of October 29, 1973. His-time-of-death estimate was that Jennifer Hill was murdered ten days before. He testified that, based on stomach contents and other factors, "that the death occurred on the day of disappearance and that the death occurred between when she was last seen alive (4:30 based on Nevel's testimony) and 6:00, perhaps 8:00 p.m.... more likely to be between roughly when she was last seen alive and up until 6 (p.m.)"

He was asked no questions by the prosecution or defense that would require him to comment on the condition of the body, but in his postmortem report (not entered into evidence) he referred to postmortem decomposition being "early slight;" soft tissues as "well preserved;" the condition of the brain as "consistent with early decomposition;" the spleen showing early changes of decomposition," and adjectives such as "unremarkable" and "not significant" in reference to virtually all bodily systems and organs.

"There is nothing inconsistent with the decedent's death occurring on or about October 19, 1973," was Catherman's formal proclamation of when her death occurred in his postmortem report.

The words "nothing inconsistent" and "on or about" certainly aren't a clarion call of certainty. Indeed, it seems that uncertainty is consistent in the Commonwealth's case. Ertel also falls back on "on or about" in his direct examination of Dr. Catherman when he asks, "Did you have the occasion to examine the body of Jennifer Hill on or about October 29,

1973?" Ertel used "on or about" in other interrogatives to his own witnesses as was the case with Duane Gleckner, the body-finder.

Was the body found on October 28th? Or was it within a day or two or three or four? Was the autopsy conducted on October 29th as indicated on the postmortem report itself? The term "on or about" widens the parameters of the facts. The Black Law Dictionary defines it as "a phrase used in reciting the date of an occurrence or conveyance, to escape the necessity of being bound by the statement of an exact date." It essentially protects the witness or the questioner from being challenged as inaccurate and would be up to the defense, in this case, to challenge the ambiguity or implied uncertainty of the question or response as a protection from perjury.

Even though no sign of advanced decomposition was assessed in Catherman's testimony or in his written postmortem report, Ertel takes him into interesting territory that might set the stage for the possibility that the girl was murdered days later and perhaps kept alive by her captor for more than five days. Catherman concedes that he could take the time of death up to 8:00 p.m. on Oct. 24th if, as Ertel phrases it," you were told that girl was still alive on the 24th and ate substantially the same food."

This was dropped and never really brought up again, but it could have served as a reprieve in their case if evidence suddenly arose that she may have been seen later or to cover the possibility of artificial preservation. Either scenario might have been a tough base to cover, because that would mean their appointed killer would have had to hold the girl captive for up to five-plus days and feed her the same food her playmates reported her eating on October 19th within a few hours before she died.

My reporting in the July 31, 1977, issue of *Grit* brought up the issue of decomposition, or more accurately, the lack of it, and drew a letter from Catherman dated three days later (August 3) which described my effort as "commendable," but with a terse criticism: "Your failure to review with me the references in the articles dealing with my part in the case before going to press is regrettable, perhaps, inexcusable."

In the article, I reported that Joe Hubbard had visited Catherman in his Philadelphia office and that the forensic pathologist had told him the body was "refrigerated long before the 28th."

I had deemed his formal testimony and six-page postmortem report as plentiful opportunity for him to state his opinion, as he did multiple times with references to decomposition as "early slight" or "not remarkable" or "not present" or "well preserved." He did invite me to call him to discuss "this interesting case." It turned out to be a pleasant enough discussion, and when the issue that the lack of decomposition could be the result of artificial refrigeration, he readily conceded that refrigeration could be a factor. However, he made the following statement for the record:

"I have no personal knowledge as to whether the body was artificially refrigerated or not. It was refrigerated, in my opinion, by the cold air it was exposed to in its resting spot in the field."

He suggested that cooling breezes in that field could have had that impact but offered no reason why there was literally no damage to the body from animals and insects. Of course, Coles and Larkin would loudly disagree based on temperatures and weather conditions during those nine October days of Indian summer.

Catherman preferred not to say what consistent minimum temperatures would be required to halt decomposition at the "early slight" level. He said that it would depend on other factors like dampness and breezes. There had been no precipitation during the nine days in the field, nor any immediately preceding that span, and the National Weather Service readings had wind speeds as "negligible." Even dew formation was described as minimal and the general environment classified as dry, which accelerates decomposition.

Catherman, in his defense, would have to rely on supplementary data provided to him, most likely from Coroner Dr. Earl Miller who pronounced Jennifer Hill dead on October 28, 1973. Ertel, prior to questioning Catherman in the trial, did read to the jury the maximum and minimum temperatures during those nine days, which averaged 51 degrees, surpassing 60 degrees on seven of the nine days and approaching 70 degrees (67, 69, 69) on three of them—the same temperatures upon which Coles and Larkin based their opinions. This was not addressed in questioning of the forensic pathologist.

Interestingly enough, when Catherman was asked if he could state the body was not, or most likely not, refrigerated by artificial means, he reiterated that he could only say the body was refrigerated, "possibly by natural means."

While appealing the case several years later on Kim Hubbard's behalf, Attorney Peter Campana received a letter of response from Dr. Catherman which stated that the body had been "consistently exposed to low temperatures at all times."

He also explained that there is a difference between high and average high temperatures, which might make a difference. He mistakenly remembered that the highest highs were between 50 and 60 degrees during those nine days, when they were actually ten degrees higher than that. He also did not take into account that temperatures and other conditions were recorded hourly.

Time of death is often established by stomach contents, its state of digestion and the day and general time when the food was eaten. Under cross-examination Catherman stated that after an average meal the stomach empties via a bowel movement after two to four hours, if not longer. The stomach content that Catherman described in the October 29th autopsy was readily identifiable but after nine days it should have been "an amorphous junky mass," as per Dr. Larkin's description.

Catherman, in his postmortem report, described the stomach contents as "moderately well digested," which would have preceded a bowel movement, and then went on to identify "fragments of bread, French fries, tomato, lettuce, onion, (and) one whole brown-green grape skin." He recognized the "central portion of a grape with seeds" and "pink-brown material consistent with meat." He also pointed out a watery substance with particulates "with an odor suggestive of slightly oily vegetable matter." This matched a hoagie with dressing Jennifer ate at the

Humdinger for lunch on the day of her disappearance, later eating some of the ammunition of an afternoon "grape fight" in which she was involved with her friends about two hours before her fateful walk home.

On October 22, six days before Jennifer's body was allegedly found, South Williamsport Mayor R. David Frey, came to the Hubbard house asking about Jennifer's activities on the 19th and was especially interested in what she had for lunch. That seemed an odd question at the time for Dorisann Hubbard. On the 23rd, Police Chief Charles Smith showed up at the Hubbard home asking questions supposedly to shed light on where Jennifer might have gone. He asked Ruthie, who had been with Jennifer all that day, what she had for lunch and then wondered if her friend had a "B.M." Ruthie didn't know what that meant so he rephrased it to "if Jennifer pooped before she left." That seemed even odder, bordering on weird, but it was Joe who realized after the murder trial that it was probably information used to establish time of death on behalf of the state police.

The state police frightened and intimidated Dorisann, but Frey and Smith, who were both known and liked by the Hubbards, might have felt they were being helpful. Whether they were well-meaning or complicit, it seems someone had targeted their prime suspect for a murder case early in the investigation.

Had the body already been found? If not, was this information they needed to know were they to find Jennifer dead instead of merely missing?

CHAPTER 14: KIM IN JAIL

"They Like to Play with Your Mind"

For Kim Hubbard, doing jail time for almost a decade—a third of his life at the time—was an educational, if unwanted, experience. He was learning a lot about human behavior in the initial years of his sentence, and, considering the environment, that was seldom heartening. One lesson was that he had trust issues when it came to getting close to other people. He became what you might call an active loner. What alienates you from society works remarkably well in prison unless you are there for a training course on committing crimes.

On one hand, you needed to have an alliance with a group where you can watch each other's backs, but an alliance didn't mean investing yourself in making friends or hanging out all the time with your own kind. What he lacked in trust when it came to other inmates, he compensated for with his family and the impenetrable belief right from the beginning that he was going to—at the very least—get a new trial. There were the news stories casting doubt on his guilt and the fairness of his trial. Plus, there always seemed to be a court decision pending on another appeal.

There was no mystery about the guards and other caretakers behind bars, whether it was a county jail or state prison: "They like to play with your mind. It's like any place else. Some you can get along with. Some are assholes."

He does have many memories, mostly unpleasant, about his time in the Lycoming County lockup and in two state prisons: Rockview near Bellefonte and the Chase Correctional outside of Dallas, Pennsylvania.

When Kim was in the county jail, the only property he owned was his 1967 Oldsmobile Cutlass, which wasn't worth more than $500. Other than that, he had $10 to his name, which was being held by the warden. He was in the county jail for, what, almost four months? It was something of a training camp, prepping for prison, you might say, and ultimately an introduction to for-real killers and sadists.

Kim had been taught to respect his elders and say sir or ma'am. His time in the Army was also a factor. Mostly because of his mother, he wasn't all that big on cursing. Maybe some with peers he hung with but not in general. His language became more colorful while in prison, and after he did his time, his vocabulary picked up a handful of words he wouldn't have dreamed of saying before in polite conversation. Then again, he wasn't much more than a kid when he was arrested and a prime-time adult when he got out. The people with whom he associated when doing his time weren't great examples of moral behavior or toeing the line, as the guards liked to say. Still, he was careful and polite in mixed company, especially with women and older people who might be offended or intimidated by profanity. The biggest adjustment would be to the language of women, with whom he hadn't had much exposure in prison. He and Colleen had parted ways not far into his incarceration but not with any ill will, at least on Kim's part. He suspected she might have served something of a prison sentence of her own, what with her being the highly publicized girlfriend of a designated killer and having been accused of being a liar in court by her own father. She got caught up in this nightmare, and she had probably been under a lot of pressure to turn against him, but she told the truth all the way through. He gave her credit for that.

His first stop after county jail was State Correctional Institution (SCI) Rockview. There was a guard there who terrorized him, seeing as he was young and polite. He probably thought it was an act, but he was just being respectful as he had always been. This guard kicked open his cell door and knocked his radio over. He apparently preyed on other inmates too. You had to pretty much take it without cowering or being a wiseass, which only made them come after you harder.

"The one (guard), when I first got to Rockview, he knew the Hill family. He talked a little nasty and I was scared to death at that time....

He's the one that took me in that... well, it was very, very scary. Because here I come in still a boy, worrying about getting raped, getting in fights, getting stabbed. This 'n' that. They took me in and they cuffed me. The took me into the BA Unit, you know, behavioral adjustment. They put me in for the first... I forget how long I was in there. A couple of weeks anyhow. It was scary. They didn't say nothing to me. Just holding out until they found a cell in the orientation unit...."

Another confrontation with a Rockview prison guard may have made life a lot easier for Kim then and later when transferred to Chase Correctional not far from Wilkes-Barre. "Baby rapers," as killers and molesters of children were known in prison are among the lowest regarded by fellow inmates. Kim was watching television on B Block when a guard eyed him for several seconds and then sat next to him.

"How could you have raped that little girl like that?" he abruptly asked.

Kim wasn't sure how to respond, except to blurt out, "I didn't rape anybody, and I can prove it." He then told the guard to come back Friday, knowing that was visiting day. He then got word to his parents to bring a copy of the postmortem report from Jennifer's autopsy. Sure enough, the guard showed up right on time, sat down next to him as he had before, and Kim handed him a copy of the report, which stated clearly that there was no evidence of sexual molestation or injuries confirming intent to do so. The guard read it carefully, stood up, looked at Kim and said, "I'll be damned," as he handed the documents back.

"He handed me the paper back, walked out of the block and I never saw him again," Kim recalled. No guard or inmate, for that matter, ever brought up the subject again.

It was prudent to find a group to hang with in prison—a group of like-minded guys who have your back. He chose the jocks. He was a natural athlete, so sports made sense. He wasn't very big, but he was wiry, muscular, and coordinated. "I got into sports heavy. From day one, the day I hit the yard." He played on the prison baseball team at Chase, and his main prison job was in the gymnasium, passing out and taking care of equipment. He was basically quiet and, though sociable, he avoided getting tight with other inmates. You get involved in their troubles and you've got problems. "I never really developed a friendship in jail. I knew a lot of people, especially in sports, but I didn't really have friends."

"When I was playing sports, I tried to get the recreational director to transfer me to Camp Hill. It was a prestige thing. Prisons against prisons. They got good treatment down there... You got special privileges and travel around outside the jail to other jails. You got the outside look."

He never got so he was "bitten," prison jargon that generally means you've pretty much accepted your lot, maybe like biting the bullet or bitten by the reality of your fate. His parents faithfully visited the prison every week, and there always seemed to be another appeal, more evidence uncovered that might get him another trial or another journalist looking into his case. He made up his mind to avoid getting in trouble at all costs.

Joe Hubbard counted 423 weekly visits—most of them after Kim was assigned to Chase Correctional, which was about a three-hour round trip every week for them. The tally of letters sent reached 1,112, an average of at least two a week.

"I had a piece of freedom every week, plus they always had good news. I always stayed on a high key, you know? I always had that hope. Other prisoners don't have that hope... I always stayed up. Every day I figured I might be getting out this day. I never got depressed."

However, he had put his fate in his father's hands for so many years that he knew little about the murder case itself or the evidence used against him. His dad would tell him stuff about appeals and whatever he had in the oven, but it washed over him, with him catching a chunk here and there. It was like this had all happened to somebody else, and he wasn't any position to uncover anything. He couldn't even remember most of the stuff that happened in the trial. He didn't know where to start. It was years after he got out, after his father died in 1989, upon taking possession of the transcripts, evidentiary photos and documents, affidavits, and other case-related material, that he really got into the evidence.

"I just blocked things out," he said of his decade in the state correctional system. "I was always thinking Dad would show up and say, 'Pack your clothes and let's go home.'"

He spent a lot of time in the gym and in the yard working out. His job was on the gym crew for "yard time" in the morning and afternoon. One of his jobs was to go in early to get the equipment out for distribution, ranging from baseball bats to weights. Cigarettes were still the jail currency at the time, and he'd get paid by this cancerous currency for saving somebody basketball court time or some other favor in the gym or yard.

He was what was considered an "upper class prisoner" because he got involved in the system and stayed out of trouble. Upper class prisoners took jobs, be it in the library or laundry, instead of sitting in their cells. Some inmates probably thought of him as a suck-ass, but it was better than having your head up your ass. For one thing, you could use your job to make money for snacks, cigarettes, and essentials in the commissary. He did all right on that end, because his mother would make sure there was money there for him there too. It was money, as he learned later, that his family couldn't afford.

The whole process of doing time consisted of "shit that doesn't matter." Even conversation was mere fodder to blunt the boredom. People are always in control, taking care of you. "You can't do much in there but preserve yourself."

After doing nine years of hard time in state prisons, Kim would get his first taste of freedom at a halfway house in Johnstown where he discovered, as the song says, "freedom's just another word for nothin' left to lose." It was a year of transition before he returned to society as a paroled felon.

"Hey, everybody thinks it's easy or something, but I was used to having people doing everything for me… I don't know what it was; a coping factor having to do all this for myself again after ten years, you know, of not doing it. It was weird. I had problems too, mentally. I mean just being there," his voice trails off and his eyes take on a far-away stare and you can tell he's feeling what he was feeling back just a few months before. "It was the first time I was by myself, so to speak."

This conversation took place after he was paroled—out of prison and away from the halfway house—and back in the town where he had been arrested for and convicted of murdering a child. She was just a kid, and that was the sad part for both of them. Being known as a murderer is bad enough. Doing time for the murder of a little girl was total bad news. And yet he never got targeted as a baby raper by fellow inmates, and he believes it was because of the various news articles over the years casting doubt on his guilt. Then again, hard-core inmates knew a perv when they saw one and he liked to think they could tell he wasn't one of them. That news coverage also played a big part in his acceptance by the community after he returned to South Side a decade later.

He had spent a lot of time in a cell by himself, but there were schedules to follow and time out in the yard, wherever, with fellow inmates. You did what they told you and there was a routine you got accustomed to. You didn't decide what you were going to do or where you were going to do it, except in the context of your immediate surroundings. It could be the yard, in the gym, the cafeteria. Now he was in a halfway house in a strange town, Johnstown, whose biggest claim to fame was being flooded big time—twice. The town was already a two-time loser.

"It was actually too much freedom. I didn't know what to do with it. I'd get out there and walk around. I didn't know what to do. I didn't have a game plan is what it was. If I had got out of jail, went right to Johnstown, and got an eight-hour-a-day job, it would have been so much easier. There would have been something to take up all that time.

"All I did was walk around. There were people at the center, counselors, but they didn't really tell you anything except to get a job and stay out of trouble. I started having problems. It all started caving in on me. I guess the best way to explain it is like you see a dog. It's tied up all day. As soon as you let that dog go, take its leash off, it runs. Doesn't know where it's going or why. It's just running. That's just what my mind was doing. My mind would never get tired, but my body was dead tired… I wasn't eating. I wasn't sleeping. But I was still going a hundred and ten."

He was this close to going home and getting back to life, but, at first at least, prison almost seemed better than the halfway house, which its inhabitants called the center. Corrections people called them transition centers, which seems innocuous enough, but when Kim Hubbard, a convicted murderer, went there in the early 1980s, they were starting to "transition" an increasing number of men who had done hard time for serious crimes of violence. It could be argued that nobody needed a transition more than these people. Yet the counselors seemed out of their depth with these supposedly rehabilitated criminals. The recently unpenned inmates, conversely, looked at their keepers as clowns.

"I tried to explain the problem I was having to the counselors, and it was like they were playing too deep in left field somewhere. They didn't know what I was talking about. These guys were supposed to be trained professionals and know everything about inmates. I think we were the first ones to ever go to that center who did time like that. They don't know how to talk to you either, you know. It was like we were aliens."

They didn't even offer advice on how to get a job in that desolate place—except go to the employment office and get yourself on the list.

"They had a lot of escapes while I was there. We were starting to get some hard timers in there and they didn't know how to talk to them… I can't tell you how many people were shipped back. Didn't know how to relate to their counselors and stuff.

"It's not like the typical employer is just waiting to scoop up someone who had just served hard time for God knows what. So, you tried to figure it all out. You know, where to go and who might hire you. If people in that town only knew there were for-real killers running around with nobody paying attention to them, they wouldn't have come out of their houses.

"I was actually free. I would just go over to the park and sit down and sort of smile to myself. There were people runnin' around and stuff. No guards. I kept thinkin' that, hell, I'd just done nine years, four months and some odd days and I'm finally on the way out… I'd just go over there and sit. I had no game plan.

"In prison, you never knew when you were getting out. Because they played mental games with you. They played with me for months with that. Learning to cope with everything again was my biggest problem. I pretty much got over that, but it took me almost a year after I got out.

"I was scared down there actually too. Here I am. I did all this time. I'm used to being in a cage at night. Secure. No one could get at me there… I didn't look at it as not being able to get out. I looked at it as people couldn't get in. It made me feel secure that way… I was out on my own, or so it seemed. I thought for a while I was going to be permanently mentally damaged, feeling the way I did in Johnstown, because I couldn't talk to none of those guys."

A counselor even suggested he go to the mental health unit… "I just needed to talk to somebody to explain how I was feeling… I was fortunate, because it dawned on me that I had too much spare time… You see, I had to work it out for myself, because they didn't have any idea what I was going through and stuff like that. And then Hoss came."

He eventually found a job, working for a tire distributor by traveling around and selling tires to garages in the Johnstown area. It paid below minimum wage, considering the ten to twelve hours expended each day, but that, in itself, was a benefit. "It took up my time. It gave me something to do."

Another resident of the center, Hoss, who had also been sentenced ten to twenty years, had bigger problems than Kim, and he resolved them, or tried, by getting drunk a lot and doing some drugs.

"He got hung up on what he did, which was pretty violent… When he was going through his coping factor, he was going to kill one of those guys, and that guy (counselor) just didn't know… Hoss was telling how he was going to cut him up in a thousand pieces and flush him down the toilet, and that guy didn't know he was serious… We couldn't get that guy to understand he was in danger."

Kim didn't think about the crime for which he had been convicted like Hoss did, because he hadn't taken a life and he really had only a fuzzy memory of the girl, Jennifer, who was just another kid hanging around with his little sister. He tried not to think about what they did to him. He just thought they had played all of them for fools. They had been expendable, and everybody was happy except the Hubbards and a handful of people who knew he hadn't killed anybody.

Kim made the transition from prison to life unfettered, through the Pennsylvania Department of Corrections and its transition-back-to-the-community phase known as the halfway house. He looks back on it as something of a farce, because the whole point was to get a job—any job. There wasn't a lot of help in doing so. He was in Johnstown, and the first thing you did was go to the unemployment office where you got an emergency check and food stamps for starters.

"They're nothing. They just said there's your room, there's your unemployment office and welfare office. When you get a chance, get a job. We want you to have a job. That was it."

Hoss, as it turned out, mellowed a bit after he became romantically involved with a woman who soon became his girlfriend. It might have been a happy ending for him—or at least for the halfway house program—had he not joined the ranks of escapees: "One day he just woke up and said, 'Look, Hub, you got a few bucks?' And I said, 'Sure, here,' and he was gone. To my knowledge, to this day, they still haven't caught him." Hoss was Hoss. He didn't need to know any more than that, so he had no way of knowing his fate.

There were no jobs in Johnstown 1983-84, which had one of the highest unemployment rates in the state (as high as 15 percent), and he didn't know anybody there. So, it had been a struggle. He counted being turned down for jobs 109 times. He got so he was just going through the motions, figuring he wasn't going to get hired, anyway. Then he got the job selling tires.

Getting back to Williamsport was different. There was work there and his ambition and work ethic got him off to a fast start. He was soon a supervisor on a commercial cleaning crew. He would eventually take over his father's business as a contractor specializing in slate roofs and chimney repair and cleaning.

The first year or so after he got out, he would visit some old friends, but he never got close to anybody. Old friends were approachable, but he felt strange trying to reestablish old ties.

"I don't associate with anybody I associated with back then. I don't feel compelled to call anyone," he said back in 1984 during his first few months of freedom in Williamsport. "I just don't want to be around a lot of them."

It seemed to him the ones who went out of their way to be friendly were not all that sincere and stuff would come back they'd say about him. They were getting off on being around a killer and being able to tell people stuff about him, true or not. It had happened in the trial too, because the cops were looking for kids who saw a helmet in his car. Stuff like that, and everybody, probably their parents, were getting off on helping them get a crazy pervert off the streets.

Meanwhile, Kim Hubbard went on to marry Susan in 1990, achieve business success and father a daughter, Kyrstin, a pharmacist who works in a clinical setting at the same hospital, now part of the UPMC Health System, where Jennifer Hill's body was autopsied in 1973.

Susan and Kim met at the Country Ski Shop in Montoursville. Suzie, as he calls her, is a private person like the mother-in-law she came to admire and love, but she remembers their meeting with fondness:

"I worked there for a summer before returning to college a second time. Kim would come into the store and shop. It was December. I know we were both attracted to each other. With me it was how he carried himself, his chest out and shoulders back, and for him he overheard me talking and that was what struck him about me. I decided that next time he came into the store I'd ask him to go skiing with me.

"It was a few days, and he didn't come in. Then he did and his father had just passed away. So, after the funeral, we finally went skiing. I remember going to his house and he was a gentleman. We'd talk. I met his mom fairly soon after a couple dates."

It all seemed so natural, even with him being fourteen years older than her at the time. He was thirty-six. Susan had to tell her parents who she was dating, because she knew it was going to get serious. It had reached that point already, and they reacted angrily when they learned more about him. They were worried and concerned, as any parent would be under the circumstances.

"They forbid me from seeing him again. Kim asked me to move in with him only after about one month after meeting. I did. My parents disowned me for a short time because I was living with Kim. They finally called and knew I was serious, so they came around, you might say. They started to give Kim a chance and read the *Weekender* papers and started to believe Kim's story."

By 1990, she and Kim were living together, and she admits that he is not a romantic guy. He was kind and generous, but you could say he was very practical when it came to love and marriage. A few months into the relationship, Kim was not one to get down on one knee and ask for her hand in marriage. His proposal went this way: "If we're still happy in May you can buy a ring." When the time came, they concurred that they belonged together.

"He gave me the money and I went alone to pick out the ring I wanted," she recalled. "We were married and almost to the day, nine months later, Kyrstin came along, May 15, 1991." They celebrated their 30th wedding anniversary on August 15, 2020.

As Susan and Kim embarked on their relationship about five years after Kim's return to society, Joe Hubbard, critically ill and still obsessed with exonerating his son, died in his home on December 7, 1989. Kim was able to tell him he loved him—something he had never done before—while his father was still conscious enough to hear him.

Not long after that, Kim took possession of his father's records about the case. These records sat, boxed, and ignored, for years. One day after work, Kim came home and found Susan with the case records, evidence photos and documents spread out on the dining room table.

Kim asked, "What are you doing?"

Susan replied, "I'm thinking I'd like to try to write a book." Kim, his head bowed to the floor as if the muscles in his neck deserted him, looked at her and said, "There's no way; it's too complicated." The truth is that he only knew as much about the case as he could handle.

It was then that Susan, who was just learning the facts of the case herself and realized there was so much more she hadn't known, reacted angrily.

"Do you know what these people said about you?" his usually soft-spoken and thoughtful wife asked defiantly.

This sparked Kim's interest, motivating him to closely examine what his father, investigators, journalists, and forensics experts had discovered over the years after his conviction that had never been brought to public attention. Both scoured through boxes of files about the case, comparing evidence photos and analyzing trial testimony.

There were trial transcripts, interviews, research findings, depositions, and compendious notes on virtually every aspect of evidence used to convict him of the murder.

In a sense, the father had literally reached out to the son from the grave to do something he had not been able to accomplish while alive. Kim Hubbard became a student of his own case and picked up his father's pursuit of exoneration, experiencing similar frustrations to those suffered by Joe Hubbard over fifteen years of unflagging determination. This is when Kim and Susan decided to make all this information public via the internet where they could let people see for themselves at a website about the case.

Much of what appears on the website, *Kim Hubbard: The Real Story,* developed in 2013, reflects Joe Hubbard's zeal to exonerate his son—even as many of those people so instrumental in this saga of crime and punishment moved on in their lives or are no longer with us. The latter include, Allen Ertel, the prosecutor; Patrick Fierro, the defense attorney; Charles H. Greevy, the judge; Norma Hill, mother of the murder victim; Steven Hynick, Edward Peterson, Ronald Barto and Joseph Keppick, state police criminal investigators; Duane Gleckner and Louis Hunsinger, finders of the body; Floyd Coles and Glen Larkin, forensic pathologists; Francis X. Ross, town cop, and many of the witnesses, both for the prosecution and defense, who testified at his trial.

CHAPTER 15: DORISANN

"Don't You Ever Make a Deal with God!"

Dorisann Hubbard might be considered a tragic figure if one's life is judged solely on suffering and loss. She certainly had her share of both. Yet, even after her son was formally pronounced the murderer of a young child she had treated as her own, she quietly rose above it, absorbed yet another tragedy and moved on in expectation of "everything turning out all right," as she often predicted. She was clearly a better person than those who conspired to despoil her character.

Here was a very private person who found herself frightened and alone on a very public podium—the witness box during her son's murder trial. She faced the jury as the only witness who, if believed, could end a nightmare that had enveloped her family for almost five months. For a successful prosecution to be engineered, it was essential that this significant source of reasonable doubt be erased. And that meant continually pounding away at the credibility of this sincere but disillusioned woman, who had always valued her privacy, and, despite her unease, believed that being a teller of truth would outweigh maternal obligation.

Truth is biblical because it is always the right thing to do, no matter what the immediate consequences. Fidelity is loyalty to family, community or country that may not always demand truth, because this is the very trait exploited by purveyors of injustice who count on disregard of truth if it advances fidelity to the state and its prosecutors and enforcers of the law. Cops and prosecutors are human. They are influenced by ambition and ego. Some may be able to rationalize cutting a corner here or there to get a murderer off the streets. If you have your mind focused on one suspect, you are more likely to ignore contrary evidence. And once you get in deep enough you have to stay the course to achieve the common goal. If it means crippling the credibility of someone who may threaten those ends, you do it.

Dorisann testified, admittedly terrified because she had never been one to seek attention, but, as a religious person, who knew she had truth on her side, believed that the jurors, most parents like herself, would see that she was telling the truth. However, just as Allen Ertel accused her son of being a liar, he dismissed her as a mother lying to protect her son. How was she to know that nobody would believe her when she testified? Everyone shrugged it off. Any mother would lie to save her son, right? That's what Ertel would tell the jury. It seemed they agreed, and that bothered her more than anything else, other than her son being found guilty.

In a letter to Judge Charles Greevy, the presiding judge, shortly after the trial, she stated: "Sir, I am not prejudiced, and I am not a liar. If my son, Kim Hubbard, were guilty of this terrible crime, then I, his mother, would be the first to say he had to be punished." It was important for her to tell this to someone who was supposedly an objective arbitrator of fact and, by extension, truth.

"It would be different if Kim was guilty," she told me the first afternoon I met her and her husband, Joe. I, armed with the required skepticism of a journalist, needed to be convinced. "I would move out of town to a new home, and we'd all start over again."

There was something about her that seemed the essence of sincerity as she faced me across her kitchen table that day. I believed her as I would come to believe Joe who buried me in an avalanche of trial transcripts, evidence photos and compelling affidavits. She, of all the parties involved in this complex web of lies, distortions and half-truths, was the purest of heart and knew her son could not have committed this crime. Not just because she knew him as her son, but because she alone knew he was not capable of doing it as spelled out in the Commonwealth's carefully nurtured scenario. In her mind, they had convicted her son because she had been branded a liar. Then there was the betrayal of cops pretending to be friends and protectors when she was facing them alone, without Joe, and then failing to step forward with the truth of their deception. In their eyes, these were the things they had to do to throw onto the growing heap of so-called evidence. She was morally outraged, not with the sparks-flying indignation of her husband, but with the sense of unfairness of being subjected to an injury that wouldn't heal. Everyone who testified contrary to the Commonwealth's evidence against Kim was branded a liar or simply as a friend or relative of the Hubbards.

There are some losses from which you can eventually recover like seeing your son escorted away in handcuffs for at least a decade of imprisonment. To suffer the double indignity of being declared the mother of a murderer and someone who would lie after taking an oath on a Bible was something that she found very difficult to process. To her lying after swearing the truth on a Bible was the most unforgivable thing she could do as a child of God. She did not react with anger like Joe but continued to believe until the end that the truth would set her family free. It did not free Kim, but he served his time, nevertheless, and she enjoyed having her entire her family back together for the final 25 years of her life. She lost Joe too soon and in a horrible way, but Kim was back, married and a father, presenting her with another grandchild to treasure and love.

The truth did set her free, in a way, which is also biblical. So is, as stated in Ephesians that "each of you speak the truth with his neighbor, for we are members one of another." It was the lack of the truth from former friends and associates throughout the investigation and trial of her son that led to the injustice. It was others, as she saw it, not her, who violated the Bible's commandment that "you shall not bear false witness against your neighbor."

Where Joe saw what happened as evil and villainous, to her it was human frailty that should be forgiven if confessed. That forgiveness, she conceded one of the last times I talked to her a decade or so after Kim was released from prison, had been very difficult for her and she was still struggling with it at that time.

"I guess we're all just human," she said resignedly as she refreshed my cup from her bottomless pot of coffee. That was Dorisann, and it just confirmed that "truth and grace" were essential in her mind to being a loving Christian.

The persistence of Joe, with her at his side, did serve to partially heal her wounded spirit and sustain her belief that good will inevitably prevail over evil. It did, at least, for those who really mattered in her life. She had been abandoned by the church—even before the mid-winter trial had started. Being forsaken and disrespected, to which even Christ had been subjected, had come before from those closer to her than a fickle congregation of churchgoers. Some, she liked to believe, may have changed their minds as they learned more about the discrepancies in the evidence against Kim. She came to believe that mysteriously delivered gifts of funds and food that showed up during the toughest of times after Kim's conviction may have come from a member or members of that congregation. That helped sustain her belief in both humanity and organized religion.

She prayed for all of them and moved on with the years she had remaining, although she faced the last two decades without Joe. He had suffered enough, and she knew he was at peace now and waiting for her. They would have so much to catch up on.

"Dad was the brains. Mom was the strength," was the way Ruthie described their partnership.

As a mother, she had mourned the death of a six-year-old son in an unimaginable after-school accident in February 1962. She endured the survivor's guilt that came when doctors had to take the life of a fully developed baby trapped in the birth canal to save her own as she lay near death herself in the operating room. Only a mother who has gone through the soaring expectation of the impending birth of her third child and first daughter, followed by the horror of the taking of that life inside her own body, would understand. Ruth Elizabeth, as her name would have been, had no chance of a normal life—if she would have lived outside the womb at all—with an oversized head and fluid flooded brain. It was condition known as hydrocephalus whose best prognosis was severe brain injury for the child.

"They took an X-ray, and her head was in the birthing canal. She was a water head," according to daughter, Ruthie, who knows all the chapters and pages of her mother's life. "Mom was dying, so they actually went in with a chisel and broke the baby's head so it would pass through the canal."

Dorisann was feeling spiritually alone and searching for sustenance during the years between the death of son, Donald, by accident, and the taking of Ruth Elizabeth at birth. Despite her deep religious convictions, she was struggling for peace of mind after the disappointing New Tribes missionary experience. She even considered joining the Catholic Church, and, after Kim's conviction, settled instead on nourishing her personal faith as a congregation of one. She would continue to believe in the possibilities of happiness, and, unlike Joe, who could not get past his guilt and failure to exonerate his son, she was always expecting some kind of redemption for them all.

This was Dorisann Hubbard then, but she was also other things. She was an abused daughter who was shunned by her adoptive brother as being beneath him. She was a fervent believer in truth and honesty, but she was portrayed as something she despised the most, a liar, in her only real public portrayal in an otherwise unobtrusive life.

She was critical to establishing Kim's alibi, but how was she to know that nobody would believe her when she testified? Any mother would lie to save her son, right? That's what Ertel would tell the jury. It was not enough to use motherhood against her, but he essentially heaped scorn on everything she said happened the day Jennifer was said to have walked to her death. It seemed the panel of her peers agreed with Ertel's denigration of the one witness who must not be believed.

Joe had turned his back on religion, as had Kim and Ruthie, but Dorisann, the one with most reason to do so, stuck with it even as the tragedies mounted. Ruthie, contrarily, would continue to believe in God but found congregational worship as hypocritical.

"She made a deal with God when Donald fell over the bank," recalled Ruthie, named Ruth after Dorisann's mother as was Ruth Elizabeth who never emerged to take a breath as a living human being. Donald's fall occurred not long before that and was an accident that might normally have claimed his life. He landed on a sharp protuberance jutting from the ground that sliced into his neck. It struck the jugular vein, the most vulnerable in the human body, and there was tremendous loss of blood, swiftly draining the life from the little boy. He should have died and seemed on the threshold of doing so when Dorisann made a prayerful deal with God.

"Mom said take what I have now and spare my Donald," said Ruthie, her mother's closest confidant. Donald lived, because the jugular was not directly penetrated. The big vein had been moved slightly aside and, according to the doctors, that is what saved his life. So, it seemed God had kept his part of the bargain, but what "I have now" was in her womb. "Well, she lost the baby, and because of that she would say, 'Don't you ever make a deal with God!' That was a big thing."

Although she had been advised not to have any more children, Dorisann had put her trust in the Lord and made a bargain she would come to regret.

Sadly, Donald only survived to the age of six. Another slip-and-fall under the back tandem wheel of a school bus just outside the school in February 1962, killed him brutally, but instantaneously. A teacher at the school lay a coat over Donald's body that day, a gesture etched in her memory. She called Dorisann years later, still unable to shake the memory of the little boy dead in the blood-soaked snow.

Dorisann's deal with God had spared a life, if only for a matter of months. Two children lost in such a short span of time, and though the circumstances were different, the causes of death were eerily similar.

That left Ruthie, who was barely eight months old when Donald died, and Kim who was eight years old. Ruth Marie was born on June 13, 1961, and about six months later her maternal grandfather, Donald Forsburg, was struck down suddenly by a brain aneurism. He was only 51. His grandson, inexplicably named after him by an abused daughter, perhaps as a last desperate attempt to gain his affection, would carry on his name. But not for long.

Ruthie's closeness to her mother revealed some things about Dorisann Hubbard that she may have taken to the grave otherwise. Dorisann and her sister, Janet, received little affection from their father. There was clearly emotional abuse, but the physical abuse of the sisters must have turned their childhoods into a horror story at times. Janet, the younger of the two, was not abused as her older sister was. Ruthie believes her Grandfather Forsburg was bipolar based on her mother's descriptions of his behavior. He once threw a brick at Dorisann, just missing her and striking and severely injuring a dog. There were tales of him coming home drunk and sharpening his axe to commence chopping up the furniture. "He was really mentally out there," as Ruthie put it.

There were severe beatings at the hands of her father, and it is likely she was targeted due to a suspicion that Donald Forsburg was not her real father. Dorisann confided in Ruthie that she believed she was the child of her uncle (her father's brother). "I think he knew and that's why he took it out on her," Ruthie theorized. Dorisann's father had broken up with "Grandma Ruth" for a period early in their marriage and she had been seeing the brother. This relationship apparently coincided with Dorisann's time of birth.

It is not clear whether Donald Forsburg, as her father of record, expressed this to her when he was abusing her or if she figured this out for herself. Of course, Dorisann would have been embarrassed for this family secret to become common knowledge, but Ruthie sees this as just another example of her mother's courage and protectiveness of her grandmother, a sickly and timid woman who was apparently abused herself and more vulnerable than Dorisann. Janet and Dorisann would live next door to each other on West Central Avenue for several decades. Janet and her son, Mike, would both testify at Kim's murder trial, placing Kim's car in front of his home around the time he was accused of picking up Jennifer Hill.

"Mom had the worst life. Her whole life has been nothing but bad luck," Ruthie said. "She had one horrible thing after another that would have sent some people to the mental ward."

Donald Forsburg, the elder, was born June 5, 1910 and died in December 1961. He had a sixth-grade education but was a successful contractor whose specialty was steeplejack work, climbing high above the landscape to repair towering smokestacks and church steeples. He started in that kind of work at the age of fourteen with his own father. He was apparently an intimidating man with a big personality and an explosive temper. His wife, Ruth, was demure and quiet, opposite from her husband.

Children in descending age were Richard, three years older than Dorisann, and Janet who was two years younger than her sister. Joe met Dorisann when he worked for the man who would become his father-in-law. Dorisann's brother, Richard, though adopted, was their father's favorite and went on to a college education and become a teacher. He paid little attention to either of his siblings, and his chief connection with them as adults were weekly visits to his mother, who lived with Janet in the home where they all grew up. It was the property adjoining the Hubbards, and Richard, who also testified at the trial about seeing Kim's car, helped support his mother financially.

Kim, who was only eight when his grandfather died, called him "Pop Pop" and, though his treatment of his daughters was known to have been unkind, even cruel, he was always good natured and generous to his grandson. He seemed to be wealthy, as Kim recalled, and generous in buying him expensive toys. He had Cadillacs, eighteen-wheel trucks for his business, and loved the grandkids. He had a merry-go-round and gravity-fed roller coaster in his yard on West Central Avenue. Kim's grandmother always had dogs. All kinds of dogs. Don Forsburg traveled around the region with his crew as a steeplejack, attracting attention wherever he went and occasional newspaper coverage. His photo in the April 23, 1958, issue of the *Syracuse Herald Journal*, high on a church steeple, stated in the caption that he "fascinates old and young from his lofty perch."

"I admired both Joe and Dorisann. They continued to be decent, caring people despite getting the short end of the stick too often," said Kim's wife, Susan, whose parents first resisted her marrying Kim but were eventually won over. "I came to love and respect Dorisann greatly. I learned a lot from her and was amazed by her courage and compassion."

Susan has heard all the family stories and has learned a lot about the pasts of both Joe and Dorisann. She says the fourteen-year age difference between Kim and her is negligible because "it's like he lost those years he was in prison and got to live them over again after he got out." She wasn't around then, but she was always impressed by how Dorisann stepped up when cops were accusing Kim in the early days of November 1973 after Joe's breakdown, possibly exacerbated by meds and alcohol, and hospitalization in the Way Unit at Williamsport Hospital.

"That sort of left Dorisann and Kim on their own when they were setting up Kim, and I don't think Joe ever forgave himself for not being there," Susan said. "They took advantage of him and his family and he literally fought to his death to set the record straight."

Although prospective jurors were asked if they would regard the testimony of friends and loved ones of the accused with equal credibility to police witnesses, the testimony of Dorisann Hubbard, Kim's chief alibi witness on the afternoon of Jennifer Hill's disappearance, was apparently disregarded. Why? What good and caring mother would not lie for her son to save him from being convicted of murder and possibly a death sentence?

It was October 31st around noon when she received a visit from Lt. Stephen Hynick and Sgt. Edward Peterson of the Pennsylvania State Police. "They asked if they could talk to me about Jennifer Hill, that maybe I could help them find the murderer." Joe was there and, by the way, would it be a problem if the District Attorney came over? Again, they regarded their friendly demeanors as a sign that Kim may not be the target they had feared he was. Ertel just happened to be a few blocks away at the borough hall, so he was there is a matter of minutes. She remembers that Ertel arrived and that she, Joe, Ertel, and the two cops were talking over coffee when Ertel casually asked if we might be able to call the school and see if Kim would come home. It still didn't seem threatening to her, though she could see that Joe was looking somewhat concerned. He had been leery of Hynick from the beginning and wasn't getting a real positive impression from Ertel, despite a continued pleasant demeanor.

After Kim arrived, Ertel wanted to talk to them privately for a few minutes without Kim. Dorisann sent him next door to her mother's home. She remembers Peterson asking if he could go to the bathroom, which happened to be upstairs where the bedrooms were. So, Joe went up and quickly closed any open doors and Peterson ascended to supposedly do his business.

"Joe and I were asked to call Kim in, and we were to stay in the kitchen with Sgt. Peterson while Mr. Ertel and Lt. Hynick questioned Kim in the dining room. Most of the time the door was shut. Sgt. Peterson again went to the bathroom (upstairs). Mr. Ertel then requested Kim's shoes and then for Kim and Joe to go to the borough hall with him." This, by the way, was where Kim's vehicle would be taken—not the elusive red sports car into whose trunk Bob Shoalts had claimed to see him throw a body. Ertel also asked permission to talk to Ruthie in school, and then Dorisann was alone as they all apparently went to the borough hall.

In what seemed like a matter of minutes, Joe was standing on the porch with two different detectives, and now she was getting scared. "Joe told me not to be afraid and that we had nothing to hide. They wanted to search the house." Dorisann wasn't sure what they would want in their house. She suddenly felt alone and frightened. "Joe did not come in and then he was gone or taken away. The two detectives wanted to see Kim's room first.

"The one man started going through Kim's dresser. The other set his brown case on Kim's windowsill, pulled out a clear plastic packet and said, 'Mrs. Hubbard, do you recognize this shirt?' I grabbed the packet and, turning it over, a label said: *Evidence Blood-Stained Shirt*." There would never be any blood-stained shirt in the case, and even then, she suspected this was some kind of scare tactic. At the time, she was nonplussed. Two cops were searching the house, and now she could see that Kim was clearly a suspect. Ertel, in his summation to the jury, would use this recollection to attack Dorisann's credibility by pointing out to the jury that it was paint on that shirt, not blood, and this was somehow "a cover up" on her part to influence the jury:

Mrs. Hubbard brought up this shirt. The police never made a deal of it. It was a mistake. They thought maybe it was possible blood stains. They had to be careful... Why would she bring this up on the stand to say it was not Kim's...? Was she afraid they were blood stains from the killing, and was she saying it was planted there by the police?

If anything, by admitting this incident and confirming that there were suspected blood stains, he was attacking her credibility in a round-the-barn attempt to show she realized Kim must have killed the girl. Think about it. Cops come into her house and search Kim's room with her permission and then, while going through his clothing, pull out a shirt labeled evidence and identified as a "blood-stained shirt." Neither of those two men believed to be detectives were ever seen by Dorisann again, either during the investigation or at the trial.

Meanwhile, Joe has been hospitalized and it is just Dorisann and Kim, who are still trying to cooperate with police. Dorisann was probably seen as the vulnerable one, because she was a prim and proper, soft-spoken woman. In retrospect, they were seeing her as a way to get information about Kim that they could use against him. That is what criminal investigators do, and that itself is procedure when they have a suspect. Then there was South Williamsport Chief Charles Smith, who had apparently been assigned to cull incriminating information from her. She knew him and he was playing the role of concerned friend, but was it to gather evidence or create it?

"Chief Smith over and over stressed he was my friend and that I could trust him. He said, 'Doris you're just upset and you can't remember. Tell me you made Kim take Jennifer home.' I'd say, 'No, Kim wasn't home then.' Then he said, 'Doris you made Kim take Jennifer's coat after her. You know, she left it lay on the counter.'" Then Smith said he had to make a call to the DA, and when he came back his mood was not as friendly. "Doris, you might as well tell the truth," he said sharply. "I have two witnesses that saw Kim go to the Dell Friday the 19th!"

By the way, people who are her real friends, do not call her Doris. Dorisann wanted to know who those witnesses were. Smith said it was the "Mauro boy" who lived on the way to Sylvan Dell Road and that Kim had waved at him. How many murderers wave when they dump a body? This so-called witness never testified to put Kim at the Dell that day but his family business, the Mauro Music Store, was mentioned by Chief Smith in his testimony as the first Commonwealth witness as if he were someone who was expected to testify but never did.

Now she was confused and said she wanted to tell Kim. He was being accused, that was for sure, and they were only going to believe what they wanted to hear. "He asked me not to tell Kim about what he had said." It was then that she asked Smith if she should get a lawyer. He said no. They wouldn't need one. Joe was in the hospital by this time and Kim was sleeping upstairs. Smith said that with Joe's medical bills a lawyer would only put them in debt. *(Note: It turned out that their lawyer, Patrick Fierro, retained after Kim was arrested, did put them in debt and, with a lien on the house, they were hamstrung for legal help after the trial and for an appeal. Jack Felix, the public defender, would take over from there.)*

Dorisann, after Chief Smith testified, said she asked him directly outside the courtroom at the trial why he lied (about the Mauros), "He said, 'We can't talk here." She persisted: "Charles, you must look in my face and tell me why you lied. He said, 'Later.'" She said she walked away from him and "later" never came.

"On October 31, 1973, Sgt. Peterson asked me if I sewed and if I had a sewing machine. I told him that I neither sew or own a sewing machine." She didn't understand the reason for this question until after she saw and examined the clothing at the state police barracks in Montoursville at a later date. While looking over Jennifer Hill's clothing there and the ripped seam of the crotch, which was partially sewn, she came to realize that someone attempted to sew up that area of the elusive dark blue jeans with the red hearts at the knees.

They were the pants she was wearing when she left the Hubbard home. The pants were identified by several witnesses, including a neighbor on the next block, Mary Mundrick, as being dark blue and with bell bottoms. These were the jeans with brightly colored material at the bottoms of the jeans that were apparently sewn as an extension to keep up with the growth of a maturing girl. There were also red hearts sewn at the knees, apparently as decorative patches, but at the body scene, these pants were enclosed in the nearby Glick bag she had been carrying on her walk home.

"My son does not carry a sewing machine in his car, nor would he know how to use one," Dorisann argued referring to the irregular white thread from the partially sewn crotch. That meant that Jennifer had to go somewhere with a sewing machine, perhaps during that unaccounted for half hour, with light blue pants put on her before she was found.

Did Jennifer go home during that time, try to sew up her jeans and then opt to put on the other pants before running off to rendezvous with her killer? In that event, why would she take the bag with her with the partially sewn pants inside? Her family was supposedly waiting for her, but they all testified that Jennifer never made it home. Why would they be so desperately searching for her within an hour? It certainly wasn't typical behavior on their part.

The problem with all this conflicting testimony seems to challenge the credibility of either the Hills or Mrs. Nevel. And, finally, there was the question of time. Jack Hill called the Hubbard house to ask when his daughter had departed from there and it was Kim who answered. Norma Hill said she looked at the clock when Jack made the call and it was between 4:45 and 4:50 p.m. Jack, who was in the courtroom when his wife testified three trial days earlier, said he made the call at "around 5:00," which gave the Commonwealth another ten to fifteen minutes of time for their anointed killer to, among other things: pick up the girl on Hastings Street, try unsuccessfully to sexually assault her, kill her, dump the body and, during or after all of this, driving to the cornfield about two and a half miles away and back to his own home almost three miles from the body scene.

Now we have Dorisann Hubbard, who was dismissed as a liar to eliminate her son's alibi. Her recount of the time of Jack Hill's call, actually agreed with the time given by Norma Hill. She remembered taking the phone from Kim and Jack asking, "Dorisann, did Jennifer leave there yet?" Her response? "I said, 'Yes, Jack.' I looked at the clock, 4:45. 'She left one hour ago.'" It was an odd question because at 4:00 p.m. Ruth answered the phone and Jackie, Jennifer's older sister, wanted to know if Jennifer had left yet. "I said tell her Jenny should be walking in any minute now and that she left here about fifteen minutes of four." When Jack testified, he said he was sitting there drinking coffee when Jackie called with the same query. He obviously knew the answer to his question.

So, the woman who Allen Ertel dismissed numerous times in his summation as a liar was never shown to a liar by his own witnesses. But it was important for her to be a liar, because she said Kim was home buffing the floor when he was supposed to be in a car in front of the Nevel House. The only other person there, aside from Kim, was Ruthie Hubbard, but you know how kids are when it comes to keeping track of time.

CHAPTER 16: DEATH THREAT

Joe Hubbard: Still "Out There Making Waves"

Joe Hubbard's barber made a house call to his South Williamsport home on Saturday, October 16, 1982. Hubbard wanted to look good just in case they came for him. He saw no need to disturb the state police conspicuously parked nearby.

"They" were supposedly coming to get him. Although hair had not yet overlapped the tops of his ears, he wanted to look his best when and if they arrested him. It hadn't taken him long to spot the guys in suits who had him staked out, monitoring him and his home. If he departed to go somewhere, a car followed while another remained just up the street. They were making no secret that they were watching him, tailing him wherever he drove.

Joe Hubbard knew the person behind this was the man he had come to regard as his nemesis. They hadn't met face to face in almost nine years, and during that time frame he had challenged this powerful political figure in various appeals, generating some unwelcome negative publicity for a man seeking the highest office in the Commonwealth of Pennsylvania.

It was Allen Ertel again.

The three-term Congressman was on the ballot for Governor in November, advancing as the choice of Pennsylvania Democrats in the spring primary. Courthouse rumors had spilled out into the community that Joe Hubbard was soon to be arrested for making death threats against Ertel. It was true that he hadn't had much good to say about the prosecutor who orchestrated his son's conviction. Making death threats wasn't one of them. If anything, he preferred Ertel to stay around to see Kim exonerated and the case against him unveiled for the fraud it was.

There was an unmarked car sitting just a few yards from the front of his West Central Avenue house, making no attempt at concealment. He soon learned they were plain clothes state police assigned out of Harrisburg. In fact, they told him who they were. They worked in shifts and followed him wherever he went.

Joe decided he should have the barber come to him rather than imposition law enforcement and waste taxpayer dollars in gas money. That was Joe. Had they been any of the state police from the Montoursville barracks who he saw as complicit in his son's murder investigation he probably wouldn't have given a damn about their convenience. What had been convenient for law enforcement in 1973 had ruined their lives. Joe truly believed that the state police, their investigation orchestrated by Ertel, a hands-on prosecutor, knew they had channeled their investigative powers to arrest and prosecute an innocent—and exceedingly vulnerable—man.

This was different. These guys knew nothing about Kim's case. They were just doing their job, he reminded Dorisann, and they were actually his alibi if something did happen to Ertel. As it turned out, there never was any death threat revealed. Just playing it safe, you know. Joe Hubbard was out there, pledging to expose false prosecution and making waves. His language in news coverage after his son's conviction had never been threatening—just strident in blaming the former DA, Congressman (at the time) and gubernatorial candidate for perpetrating an injustice.

These cops on watch in front of his house were not the enemy. Joe had made a point of letting his designated stalkers know whenever and where he was going. He had even become quite cordial to the occupants in the car—usually in pairs working in shifts—as they had to him.

The "death threat" stories had appeared in Saturday and Sunday editions of newspapers across the state, as well as TV and radio stations. Joe Hubbard was not mentioned by name, but United Press International (UPI) reported that a press release revealed the suspect being watched resided in South Williamsport. An anonymous source further revealed that the threat was made by a man whose son had been convicted of murdering a young girl while Ertel was the DA there.

That pretty much narrowed the field, and the stakeout confirmed it. Almost three weeks prior to the press release, the Hubbards had been driving to the Chase Correctional Institute in Dallas, Pennsylvania, where Kim was imprisoned, when Joe realized they were being followed. Again, there was no subterfuge, and as they were leaving the prison, Hubbard would subsequently recall, "they read me my rights" and questioned him. However, there were no charges asserted, no arrest and no forewarning of such.

"The only threat I've ever made against Ertel is that we aren't going to give up until we beat him in the courtroom," he quipped.

Other than their generic press release, the Pennsylvania State Police in Harrisburg would not comment on the matter.

Ertel himself said nothing publicly about a specific death threat, but he had come under fire in one newspaper editorial for his lack of political manners as election day approached. He may have been going for the sympathy vote, as well as using it as a reminder that he once put bad guys in jail.

Nevertheless, UPI reported in newspapers across the state, as well as the Williamsport *Sun-Gazette* locally, that there had been an alleged threat on the life of Ertel, who was campaigning to unseat Dick Thornburgh, the Republican Incumbent, as governor. Readers in Williamsport and well beyond didn't need any more clues to guess who must have made the alleged threat.

Who would benefit from such a tip? If the word spread, it would be a reminder that Ertel had successfully convicted the murderer of a young girl. It would serve a double purpose of marking this passionate man who continued to plague the Congressman as dangerous and therefore disreputable. Ertel had sued the *Harrisburg Patriot-News* and Harrisburg Attorney William Costopoulos for defamation by publishing a Costopoulos case analysis of the Commonwealth of Pennsylvania v. Kim Lee Hubbard. The analysis, reported in that newspaper, concluded that "a strong pattern of prosecutorial manipulation and/or tampering of evidence in this case has highly significant merit."

It went all the way to the Pennsylvania Supreme Court where it was dismissed, reinstated in appeal and killed in 1996. The high court said they found no evidence of "falsity" or "actual malice" in the part of the newspaper or Costopoulos.

In response to learning about the death threat accusation, Dorisann Hubbard, who had been dismissed as a liar by Ertel in Kim's trial, expressed her opinion: "Kim has been in prison almost nine years. Why would we conveniently wait until a few weeks before the election to give Allen Ertel front-page publicity?"

The state police were officially mum about the origin of the alleged threat. Ertel was clearly not averse to using any tactic to grab the attention of voters, as reported in the Williamsport area news media. There was Ertel's campaign appearance at the most famous place in South Williamsport and in all of Lycoming County, for that matter, the headquarters of Little League International. He had brought reporters with him to issue a challenge to Thornburgh, there on an official visit, to a public debate. It was there that Ertel wondered aloud to the news media in attendance, according to a newspaper report, whether Gov. Thornburgh should be held responsible for a Wilkes-Barre killing spree weeks before by George Banks.

Why? Banks had been hired as a state prison guard at Camp Hill during Thornburgh's administration. Once again Ertel was showing his mastery of circumstantial evidence and how to stretch it for maximum effect.

A murder conviction of Kim Hubbard and branding his family as low-lifes and liars apparently weren't enough of a godsend for Allen Ertel's career. He was able to reap another round of publicity in the two-and-a-half weeks leading up to the election off the mysterious Joe Hubbard death threat. After a brief flurry of coverage, the death threat story fizzled. In the end, it never made much of an impact. The bottom line was taxpayers paid the bill for relay teams of state cops following Hubbard over a two-week span.

Ertel had been elected to Congress in 1977 after Kim Hubbard's conviction in March 1974. He subsequently went on to become the Democrats' choice for Pennsylvania Governor in 1982, losing by only 2.65 percentage points of the 3.65 million votes cast in the November election.

It was an impressive loss for Ertel, considering Thornburgh's popularity and his high profile in Pennsylvania politics at the time. However, each subsequent defeat in quests for higher office transformed the former up-and-comer into a political down-and-outer. He subsequently vied for, and lost, a bid for Pennsylvania Attorney General and, finally in 1988, he failed in pursuit of a seat on the Pennsylvania Supreme Court, an endorsement from the governor at the time, Bob Casey, notwithstanding.

If the Congressman had hoped the death threat scenario would prove politically expedient and gather momentum in the days leading up to the election, it seemed to fall short of generating any significant subsequent news coverage after the initial reports.

Ertel's unsuccessful bid for Attorney General, the state's chief prosecutor, was in 1984—the same year Kim Hubbard returned to society. In his failed campaign for the Pennsylvania Supreme Court, Ertel touted his "experience in public office," his integrity and his exposure to statewide political campaigns, as well as his "rare and valuable insight into the people and the legal system of the Commonwealth."

Ertel returned to his Williamsport law practice, still in his early fifties. After almost 25 years in private practice, he died suddenly on November 19, 2015, twelve days after his 78th birthday. He collapsed on West Fourth Street a short walk from his office.

Ertel and his law practice outlived both Dorisann and Joe Hubbard. Kim Hubbard had been out of prison for several years but had no direct encounters with Ertel. After being elected to Congress in 1977, he was able to wash his hands of the Hubbard case in subsequent appeals, leaving that up to his successors in the Office of the Lycoming County District Attorney.

Anyone who watches true crime shows on television knows that prosecutors seldom admit they convict the wrong person—even when new exonerating evidence surfaces.

That is contrary to the Pennsylvania Supreme Court standards for "Ethical Duties of Lawyers in Criminal Cases:"

> *The District Attorney… represents the Commonwealth, and the Commonwealth demands no victims. It seeks justice only — equal and impartial justice — and it is as much the duty of the District Attorney to see that no innocent man suffers as it is to see that no guilty man escapes. Hence, he should act impartially.*

It can be argued that few prosecutors "act impartially" once they sink their teeth into a case—especially when convincing evidence emerges that they may have engineered the conviction of an innocent man.

Ertel was forceful, even hostile, in prosecuting the case, depicting Kim Hubbard at various times as a sexual pervert who picked up young girls or made inappropriate comments to them. He also portrayed the defendant as a druggie with a proclivity toward violence. In truth, Hubbard did "smoke some weed," as they termed it back then, but Kim has never disputed that, other than to clarify that it was for recreational and occasional use only.

His friends and many of those with whom he associated at the time tended to have long hair and what you might call casual attire. There was still an anti-Hippie attitude in small-town America in 1973–74, and these were the witnesses attesting to Kim's character, whereabouts, and his general behavior. The trial itself resembled a rally with people literally hissing and booing the young defense witnesses. Presiding Judge Charles F. Greevy himself said the courtroom "resembled a theater without the popcorn."

Joe Hubbard was identified in newspaper coverage of the trial as a "chimney sweep," which was not his chief source of income. It was something he did for publicity during the Christmas season, and a feature article about him performing that task appeared in the local Sunday weekly, *Grit*. He was a roofer, specializing in slate roofs, and chimney repair. He was also an avid community volunteer, serving with the volunteer ambulance as an EMT, and later working in the Emergency Room at Williamsport Hospital.

Allen Ertel never had to fear violence from Joe Hubbard. However, the publicity about the murder case since Hubbard's conviction hadn't portrayed Ertel favorably and may have cost him some critical votes in central Pennsylvania. That may have been the real concern.

It was in the midst of the death threat drama and state police tail that Joe and Dorisann Hubbard took a long Saturday drive to my home some sixty-five miles away. My wife and I gave them a tour of some local sights and sites in our part of Pennsylvania, including French Azilum, a state historical site between Wyalusing and Towanda that was a planned settlement built in 1793 for the French Queen Marie Antoinette to escape the French Revolution. She famously never made her getaway, losing her head in the process, and the site achieved prominence for something it never became, the asylum for despised French royalty. It did bring in French families, royal or just loyal supporters of the queen, with subsequent generations continuing to inhabit the area to this day.

The lowlands flanking the Susquehanna River were fertile fields of Native American history, and Joe Hubbard had been an ardent hunter of arrowheads and Indian relics. It was a pleasant afternoon with little discussion about "the case," but we were being followed wherever we went. We even witnessed a shift change returning from French Azilum, as a car with a tandem of plain-clothes cops, waiting at a convergence of back roads, took the place of the one that had been tailing us.

Returning to my home in our small town, we settled in for a visit and noticed that our tailing tandem was sitting in plain sight in a dark-colored sedan on our street about 100 yards away. At some point, we decided we needed coffee and snacks. Joe jumped in my car with me. I backed out of my driveway and proceeded to the grocery store just a few blocks away. Dorisann, looking out our front window, noticed that the shadowing police suddenly realized their assignment had left the scene and lurched ahead, driving down the street in pursuit. Dorisann ran out of the house, hailing them to a squealing stop.

"They just went to the store," she assured them, as I learned upon our return. "They'll be right back."

The two reportedly looked at each other, looked back at her and nodded obediently. With that, they turned around and slowly returned to their stakeout. And, yes, we were back in a matter of minutes. About an hour later, we escorted the Hubbards to their car and wished them a safe trip home. A few seconds after they pulled away, their friendly stalkers followed, and we were pleasantly surprised to see a wave from one of them as they passed us standing at the foot of our driveway.

I think I saw Joe Hubbard only two or three times after that. After he died at the end of 1989, we did keep in touch with Dorisann now and again, and she seemed content with both her son and daughter nearby and granddaughters to fuss over. Then we lost track for a few years and were saddened to hear that she had died in 2012 after months in nursing care due to failing health.

By election day, November 2, 1982, Joe Hubbard was no longer of any interest to the Pennsylvania State Police or apparently to Allen Ertel for that matter. There seemed to be even less interest in Kim Hubbard upon his return to society in 1984. Despite his fears he would be hassled every time there was an unsolved murder or sexual assault in the region, he has been left alone by state and local police.

CHAPTER 17: DETECTIVE INVECTIVE

Solved at Last or Framed Again?

Publisher's Disclaimer: *"Any opinions, statements of fact or fiction, descriptions, dialogues, and citations found in this book were provided by the author and are solely those of the author. The publisher makes no claims as to their veracity or accuracy and assumes no liability for the content."* – Wild Blue Press, Denver, Colorado, inside title page of *Unsolved No More* by Kenneth L. Mains

If the arrest and conviction of innocent people too often occurs when police are pressured to solve a case too quickly, it follows that painstaking and principled detective work is a must in prosecuting and convicting the real guilty party. There should be no shortcuts to justice. This too often leads to concentrating on one suspect who seems to have the motive, opportunity, lack of a convincing alibi and maybe even a criminal or personal history that convinces even seasoned investigators to proceed without a more thorough investigation.

"When you rush, mistakes happen," declares Kenneth L. Mains, a cold case investigator, in the prologue of his book, "Unsolved No More," which includes a chapter on the investigation and conviction of Kim Hubbard for the 1973 murder of Jennifer Hill. "That is why cold-case investigations are easier, I feel. You are not ever rushed. You can be meticulous, thorough, and perfect."

Mains will conclude his investigation by agreeing with the jury's guilty verdict and applauding the police and prosecutor, even though the investigation and trial fit the classic example of innocent people being convicted of crimes they didn't commit, as Mains himself wrote:

How can we arrest and convict an innocent person? Easily, because not enough time is given during the initial investigation. You are pressured to solve the case quickly and when you do that, shortcuts happen.

On the 19th day after Jennifer Hill's body was alleged to be discovered, Kim Hubbard was arrested. Fifteen weeks to the day after he was arrested and incarcerated in the county jail, a jury delivered a guilty verdict after seven days of testimony capped by the requisite summations by the Commonwealth and the Defense.

People are prone to believe that law enforcement doesn't arrest people without good reason, especially for violent felonies, and that neutralizes the "reasonable doubt" hurdle each juror must clear before rendering a guilty verdict. The best hope for a defendant at trial is damaging the credibility of the police or prosecutor by showing the jury they may have acted hastily without considering more viable suspects; behaved unprofessionally or, worst of all, may have sought a conviction while ignoring, even failing to share, exculpatory evidence or witnesses.

In his book, Mains, who depicts himself as a protector of the innocent and brilliant investigator of cold cases, allows his prejudices against Kim Hubbard to cloud his examination of the Hill murder case. The book is comprised of a mélange of essays ranging from his background and credentials; his philosophy of solving cold cases; his calling as guardian of the innocent while going to bat for murder victims and their families; criminal profiling as a tool for solving cases, and an overview of several cases that he has investigated and solved—at least in his own mind. Among his most memorable cases portrayed in the book, published in 2017, are missing persons who he concluded, with mixed results, to be murder victims.

He takes great pride in his accomplishments, which will be mentioned later, handing out the following advice: "Don't be afraid of greatness; seek it out and embrace it." He subsequently reminds those who choose to pursue the greatness he believes he has attained to "remain humble." As an example of that humility, he declares himself a "True Crime Legend" on his self-congratulatory website.

The centerpiece of the book, in location at least, is a seventy-page chapter on the murder of Jennifer Hill and how he has solved the case via the latest in DNA technology, declaring Kim Hubbard guilty of that crime. Hubbard's conviction, of course, does not qualify as a cold case, or, technically at least, an unsolved case. Kim is stating his case for exoneration, featuring a website that presents evidence, circumstantial and physical, contradicting key aspects of the case against him. Mains is clearly offended that Hubbard's website (*"Kim Hubbard: The Real Story"*) contains photos of the body of Jennifer at the scene where her body was found and on the autopsy table. All were submitted as evidence and there are multiple parental warnings regarding not just the photos but some of the testimony. Potentially offensive body parts, notably genitalia, are artificially blocked or covered by clothing. It is not an example of sensationalism. Body condition and testimony corresponding with body scene photos are critical in showing exclusionary evidence.

Mains sees these photos as offensive and seems to imply this as further proof of perversion or a fondness for provocative photos of young girls. The fact that a law enforcement veteran would see body photos in a murder case as provocative is disturbing itself. It is another apparent attempt to undermine Kim's character, ignoring something you might expect in a murder case with questions about body condition and handling.

Elsewhere in his book, Mains is most passionate in a chapter on Dawn Marie Miller, a young Williamsport woman who suddenly went missing in 1992 after she traveled to Bellefonte in Pennsylvania's Centre County to visit her boyfriend. Mains failed in persuading the Centre County District Attorney to bring anyone to trial for the murder of the twenty-one-year-old woman despite "the strongest circumstantial evidence I've ever seen" against two suspects, but it was admittedly a life-changer, or at least a career-changer, for him: "Dawn gave me the ability, the hope, and the passion to never let another victim to be forgotten...."

His credentials are impressive in the field of cold case investigations. Even more so when you consider his rough start as something of a high school "ruffian," by his own admission, who got kicked out of school repeatedly, even tossed out of his home, fathering a child in the process, and ultimately earning a high school degree while washing dishes on the side. After that he enlisted in the US Marines.

It seems he and Kim Hubbard had a lot in common, although Hubbard took a detour with a ten-year murder sentence, and Mains earned a college degree in criminal justice on the heels of his military service. After finding his niche in law enforcement and, from there, in cold case investigations, he founded the nonprofit American Investigative Society of Cold Cases (AISCC), achieving a high profile in the field. Where his photo and name were once prevalent on the AISCC website, an updated site does not mention Kenneth Mains except as a 2019 annual conference attendee and as one of the contacts for a sponsored DNA Lab.

The murder of Jennifer Hill and the conviction of Kim Hubbard for that crime occurred before Mains was born. He presents a lot of his so-called facts without attribution, which seems to have come from pro-police sources, perhaps local scuttlebutt, or from his own imagination.

Mains shows his dislike of Hubbard from the beginning, betraying his lack of objectivity in this investigation. His first depiction of Hubbard in his overview of the case is as "a young derelict." A derelict is a vagrant, who is often jobless and homeless. Hubbard, in actuality, was serving in the US Army's 82nd Airborne Division when he was honorably released on a hardship discharge to provide for his family when his father was hospitalized with serious head and facial injuries. Hubbard was back to school in pursuit of a delayed high school degree. At the same time, he was working full-time while receiving a monthly check from Uncle Sam under the provisions of Active Duty Enlisted Administrative Separations. He was essentially the main provider for his family until his father was back on his feet.

Mains either needs to consult a dictionary when defining people he chooses to portray negatively or learn more about the people he investigates.

Again, when Mains first introduces "the accused," he describes him as "prone to violence" and that troopers during surveillance... "saw him punching his sister and pulling her hair" (and)... "slapping his girlfriend and choking her." There is no attribution here. Most of those involved in the investigation are dead and gone, so this was hearsay at best. Proving Kim Hubbard had violent tendencies, especially connecting him to strangulation (choking), would have been invaluable for the prosecution to prove through testimony. Seeing someone doing something, even while hidden in surveillance, is not the same as unlawfully tapping someone's phone (electronic surveillance) for incriminating statements. If the cops had this "evidence," they would have assuredly used it. Mains is already taking those same shortcuts he abhors that get people wrongfully convicted.

I think of my interview with Lt. Steven Hynick, overseer of evidence and personnel during the investigation, and I can assure you he would be the one to know, at that time in the investigation (up to Kim's arrest and imprisonment on November 16, 1973), of such things. At that time, the type of surveillance used would be fixed or stationary surveillance from a distance with at least two people. This is the so-called a "stakeout," which may have been used when investigating their suspect but never brought out as far as I know. The idea that Kim Hubbard was witnessed by law enforcement personnel violently choking a female without it being offered for the record at the trial seems ludicrous.

Stories make their rounds as murder cases drift further into the past, but a trained investigator should know better than to offer scuttlebutt as fact.

The litany of statements without attribution is almost embarrassing for the esteemed cold case detective. For instance, who was the source when Mains stated that deception was indicated when Kim volunteered to take a lie-detector test at the state police barracks two weeks before he was arrested in November 1973?

"People were very mad that I was looking into this case again. Very mad," Mains writes. "I met resentment from every side. I got grief from the old cops who investigated the murder, the victims' family who just wanted it to go away and, of course, the accused and his minions."

It appears that Mains was looking into the case as early as November 2013 when he interviewed Hubbard for the first time. It was at that meeting while Hubbard was telling Mains he was set up that Mains wrote that he "began to see through Hubbard's charade."

But Mains, despite this foregone conclusion, said he nevertheless intended "to do a thorough and accurate review of the case."

Thorough, that is, except for anything he chose to dismiss as "ridiculous" and not worth looking into or even considering doing so. That included any of the body-scene evidence and body condition.

Allen Ertel, who died suddenly in November 2015, was still alive and still involved in his private law practice at the time. It seems someone working as an investigator for Lycoming County DA Eric Linhardt, one of Ertel's successors and later a county judge, would learn what he could from Ertel about the case. Ertel, in the meantime, had been plagued by the Hubbard case for decades and may have blamed his loss in a close 1982 governor's race to negative publicity emanating from news coverage. However, Mains does not mention ever consulting with Ertel. It was his evidence and prosecutorial conduct that was being challenged, but it is hard to imagine that he would ignore him as a source. At the same time, Mains's negative characterizations of Kim seem eerily similar to those offered by Ertel forty years before.

Mains does some serious psychoanalysis of Hubbard, someone with whom he may have spent a grand total of forty-five minutes to an hour. He describes the accused as "an in-your-face kind of guy" who "wants to dominate and be in control." He may have discerned this from his short time with Hubbard, who can become quite intense when talking about the case.

He describes him as a Type-A personality whose "paranoia is not brought on by being wrongly convicted. It is from knowing he is guilty, and he understands that there are people who unequivocally know this, which scares him."

> *(There is no question that Kim Hubbard believes he is innocent. Take it from someone who has analyzed his life, character, and personality from all sides. And why would he be scared? He has*

already been convicted and paid the penalty. The one thing he
did fear for years as a convicted murderer was that they might
come after him again to "solve" another murder case.)

The problem is that Mains does not know when to stop when talking about Kim as a person and some of his perceived motives. He states something point-blank that is clearly prejudicial and unfounded, apparently not knowing or refusing to admit that Kim was reluctant for 25 years to take a proactive stance on his case after returning to his hometown. He kept a low profile for a long time, preferring to get on with his life while still young, but Mains wants his readers to believe that he was chomping at the bit to present himself as an innocent man wronged upon release from prison.

"He moved back to the same area out of spite, continuing the charade of innocence," Mains writes. "He likes the notoriety."

He also states that despite adopting a low profile when he was released from prison, he chose to ride on his infamy because "he wanted to be the center of attention." Obviously, Kim opted to become the "center of attention" some thirty years after he returned home to resume his life. Mains didn't even take the time to thoroughly investigate the guy he was supposedly investigating.

These observations are all made so he can depict Kim as the bad guy as he embarks on his meticulous investigation.

As for Allen Ertel, who he apparently never took the time to interview, or prefers not to mention it if he did, he has nothing but praise for him:

> *The former district attorney Allen Ertel should be*
> *congratulated for properly and successfully trying the*
> *murderer of Jennifer Hill. If I could, I would personally shake*
> *all their hands for the diligent and through investigation*
> *culminating in the arrest of Kim Hubbard.*

I'm getting ahead of myself here, because I'm not out to promote his book, but I do feel it is important to provide a few examples of how "meticulous, thorough and perfect" he wasn't, despite his claims. Not that he didn't raise some legitimate issues on how such a conspiracy could be pulled off, other than dumb luck, and I have wrestled with that myself. At the very least, for Kim Hubbard it is a mystery worth sharing and sheds some light on small-town justice and human nature.

There are some truths you can never uncover. The truths, in my opinion, lie in the character and consciences of the people involved, and it is from exploring them that we learn more about ourselves.

I think Dr. Norman Wengert, one of the early proclaimers of Kim's wrongful conviction, may have captured who Kim was at the time:

> Kim was no goody-goody. He had been around: girls, to some
> extent, drugs (marijuana), etc. A typical youth of our times,
> not atypical, fitting with the majority, not the minority of
> either end. He always treated me with respect, with a "Yes, sir,"
> for instance, which many youths do not do.

Wengert, a chiropractor, who closely followed the case before, during and after the trial, knew there were many things wrong with evidence used against Kim. One of his patients worked for South Williamsport Borough and confided that he personally witnessed that there were tire casts poured in the borough garage, as did two other men who signed affidavits attesting to the same. But even with this knowledge, Wengert wasn't convinced there had to be a conspiracy per se:

> I can understand how it could happen. I can also understand
> how some feel a large conspiracy was involved when, in truth,
> it may have been simply a complex web of one unfortunate
> event after another.

Mains allows his imagination free rein instead of following the evidence by suggesting that Jennifer, described by those who knew her as a "tomboy" not yet interested in boys, may have been part of the following scenario:

> Perhaps she removed her ripped pants and underwear to prepare
> for intercourse and Jenny changed her mind or stopped Hubbard

because it was going too far. However, I do not believe
intercourse was the plan.

Whose plan—the victim, defendant or mutually? And why bring it up if you don't think it was part of "the plan?" He also smears this pubescent victim by seeming to make her complicit, not only in agreeing to a rendezvous, but willing to participate in a consensual act. Prior to making this remarkable statement, Mains introduces another morsel of conjecture, the stuff of juicy fiction, without the support of legitimate evidence:

I think it was Hubbard's plan to watch her change her pants,
have Jennifer perform oral sex on him or both.

This is leeringly suggestive stuff for someone offended by body photos on a website. The superhero detective, protector of the innocent and defender of victims, can't help himself in revealing his prejudices.

After all this descriptive language to establish that Hubbard may have convinced her to pull down her pants, he later states that forensic testing in 2014 (forty-one years after the murder) proves the jeans were "above the pubic area" when she died "because they were urine soaked." That proves in this investigator's mind that the urine was released when he strangled her, and, what, the pants had to be up when he strangled her? It is true that this release often occurs at death, but it has nothing to do with Kim Hubbard except in imagined dramatized scenarios.

Furthermore, it is extremely doubtful that the jeans entered as evidence were soaked in urine without forensic examination at the crime lab revealing this. The strong odor of generous amounts of urine on clothing, even after days in dry weather, would have been noticeable by everyone who had been in proximity to the body from the forensic pathologist on down. The body and clothes were reportedly tested for any sign of human discharge, particularly for evidence of semen, but heavy concentrations of urine wouldn't have gone without notice. We again find that Mains conveniently mentions nonspecific testing as the basis for claiming his discovery that urine was released from the bladder more than four decades before.

The word "urine" is only mentioned once in 1,200 pages of trial testimony and that was by Dr. Robert Catherman, the forensic pathologist, when stating that he collected the required blood and urine samples at the autopsy. There was no mention of urine, or elements indicating such, on her clothes or on her person, let alone being "soaked." It is quite natural for the bladder to release urine, saliva from the mouth and even stool from the rectum as muscles relax after death. After a few hours, the body muscles stiffen into rigor mortis (rigidity of skeletal muscles after death) and the muscles will usually become flaccid again between twenty-four and thirty-six hours after death.

Perhaps we are to believe in yet another anomaly about this murder case: the murderer not only attempted to sew up her torn pants after changing them but washed them to remove the urine.

The evidence based on forensic analysis, as credited initially to a police chief (Charles Smith) as an "I'm sorry kind of murder," was confirmed by a renowned forensic pathologist (Dr. Glen Larkin) and a state policeman (Lt. Steven Hynick) intimately involved in the investigation almost four years after Hubbard's trial. It seemed more of a sudden striking out than an attack, which often signifies someone who strikes in anger without contemplating its impact, later to regret it. Manual strangulation of a young, healthy victim requires tremendous, violent pressure constricting the breathing tube. The victim may pass out in fewer than twenty seconds, but it typically takes several minutes for death to occur.

Look at the evidence—even some of the convicting evidence—instead of the vivid imagination of a trained investigator who prides himself on being "meticulous and thorough."

As noted in a previous chapter, nails on two of Jennifer's fingers were described by Dr. Catherman as "irregular and ragged" but not indicative of being torn off resisting an attack. James L. Miller, a chemist at the Harrisburg Crime Lab, compared the partial fingernail from the car to one of Jennifer's: "I could draw no conclusions as to the source of the identity of the fingernail," he testified. He added that he saw no points of comparison that identified the partial nail in evidence as belonging to Jennifer. Kim Hubbard chauffeured a lot of people in his car in those days.

And yet Mains stated erroneously in his book: "During the struggle (with her attacker), Hill broke a fingernail that was found in his vehicle." He defended his blunt assessment by stating DNA technology would have proven that. So would a close analysis of both the nail and the dead girl's finger even during those pre-DNA years.

Mains added something else without attribution: "Most people who claim Kim Hubbard is innocent, do not know that Joe Hubbard (his father) told police on Nov. 3 that his son had been acting unusual ever since Jennie went missing and even more so after she was found in the cornfield..." He quoted Joe Hubbard as vowing, "I will speak out in court about this. My son, Kim, is not right."

Where is the attribution or documentation here? If he made such a statement to police, why wouldn't they have put him on the stand along with corroborative testimony from whatever investigator, if any, elicited this from him?

Any of the criminal investigators who interviewed Joe Hubbard, even a heavily medicated Joe Hubbard when hospitalized with a mental breakdown, would have been able to testify to this without fear of objection. In fact, this is exactly the kind of witness evidence they needed to bolster their case instead of having young girls testify that Kim had given them rides in his car and that he allegedly made suggestive comments, as they called them in the seventies—much of which Judge Greevy ruled as inadmissible. The judge knew that this was the kind of testimony that, if allowed to stand, could result in a new trial. This was also ruled in the preliminary hearing concerning a young woman who would have provided similar testimony.

The photo of Mains on the cover of his book immediately troubled me. It more than exemplifies his high opinion of himself rendered like a drumbeat in chapter after chapter. He stands as if posing for a movie poster depicting some heroic figure, his chest thrust forward and peering out at some distant horizon in semi-profile. The stubble of a developing beard on his face is reminiscent of a movie action hero.

"It wasn't easy to get to where I am. I have traveled an incredible journey, at least so I'm told," he writes in the prologue of "Unsolved No More," which is subtitled, "A Cold Case Detective's Fight for Justice." He continues: "I have fought, laughed, loved, and cried. I have won wars and I have lost a few battles along the way. I try to make a difference because this life is too short not to try."

His chief concern appears to be self-promotion, and his investigation of this case shows that he decided to take the easy way out and go along with the Commonwealth's chartered course so many years before by claiming that he was able to retrieve Hubbard's DNA, presumably off an envelope containing a letter in his handwriting that he miraculously discovered in a box of evidence believed to have been destroyed in the spring of 1996. Kim, who met with Mains twice, remembers the investigator showing him a photo on his smartphone of old case evidence he said he had found. Curiosity got the better of him, and before Mains took the device back Kim recognized a photo of Jennifer's pants with the torn seam low in the seat of the pants approaching the crotch. He had seen similar photos taken by his father when examining these pieces of evidence more than 40 years ago. I have those photos in my possession.

Mains would include two photos of the "torn crotch" of the dark blue jeans at the end of that chapter in his book, because he felt it disproved something that Joe Hubbard first brought up years ago. It was a finding that further complicated the prosecution's version of how and when the crime occurred and the tight time frame Kim would have had to do the following: (1) pick up Jennifer at 4:30, (2) have some kind of confrontation, (3) kill her, (4) drive a couple of miles, mostly through town, (4) drive up the farm lane, (5) remove the body from the car and deposit in the cornfield. Then (6) drive back home through Friday after-work traffic and then (7) answer the phone within a half an hour at most. (If you believe Norma Hill's testimony that time frame was only fifteen to twenty minutes.) My clocking of the drive itself alone back in 1977 was fourteen minutes. State police Cpl. Ronald Barto testified that it took him an average of between twelve and fourteen minutes.

The torn dark blue jeans with a red heart on each knee that Jennifer was wearing when she left the Hubbard house was confirmed by Mary Mundrick, a neighbor a block away, who saw her walking toward home at approximately 3:45 p.m. This verified the time Dorisann Hubbard said she left her home. When twelve-year-old's body was discovered nine days later that pair of dark blue jeans would be in a plastic (Glick) store bag she had been carrying with other clothes she had brought with her to stay the previous night with Ruthie Hubbard. The pants she was wearing in that field, however, were light blue trousers she had apparently wore to school the previous day before spending the night and much of the next day with Ruthie. Obviously, the pants had been switched before she was placed in that field, curious in itself because it indicated she or her murderer had changed them. Mains might have you believe she may have taken them off herself in a willing—and very brief—tryst.

During the trial, the Hubbards realized the pants had been switched, but it was after the trial while examining evidence at the state police barracks in Montoursville that Dorisann Hubbard noticed the tear in the crotch had been partially machine sewn in a haphazard, jagged manner with distinct white thread. When Jennifer tore the pants while playing earlier on the day of her disappearance, she had improvised by using a safety pin to pull the split fabric together. It was the partial stitching that raised the probability that she had been somewhere with a sewing machine—after leaving the Hubbard house. It is quite safe to say Kim Hubbard would not have been carrying one around with him in his car in anticipation of performing an emergency repair. As for Dorisann Hubbard, she did not have a sewing machine. Nor could she sew with one.

This added another element to where Jennifer Hill had been for at least a half hour during which she hadn't been seen until her alleged sighting by Betty Jane Nevel at 4:30. Had she made it home? She was so close to her destination when seen at that street corner at 4:00 p.m. by Joe Mendez.

The threads and the safety pin were on the ruptured seam of the pants when Joe Hubbard saw them in the state police evidence room. He took a photo there where it was in state police custody and the pin and the thread are clearly visible. The safety pin is mentioned by Ertel himself when he cross-examines Ruthie at the trial.

"Well, that pin there," Ertel asks when showing her a photo of the jeans. "Do you know who put the pin there?"

Ruthie remembered the pin but not where Jennifer got it from that day.

Mains, however, believes he has trumped Joe Hubbard's claim of the stitching on the jeans by introducing two photos of the split crotch he said he found in the long-missing Hubbard evidence. The photos are published in his book. A caption beneath one of them states: "The rip in pants. You can clearly see the white stitching is part of the fabric and not from an attempt to repair." The strands of thicker white thread that had been photographed in the evidence room are indeed not there. You can see what seems to be the rusted section of a safety pin, which validates that these are jeans she wore when she left the Hubbard home that were supposed to have been "disposed of" all those years before. It also validates that the extraneous and hastily sewn thread could have easily been pulled by someone, anyone over a span of two decades away from the chain of custody. You can even see, when the Mains photo is magnified, the holes through which a larger thread would have been woven compared to the remnants of smaller thread in the original stitching.

The photo Joe Hubbard took of the jeans while under evidential custody years before shows both the thread and pin. It appears that somewhere along the way the thread was pulled out if the photo Mains uses in his book is legitimate. The bottom line on the thread is that this, as with other evidence, does nothing to disprove that the pants were changed at some point before she was deposited in the cornfield. It is also a reminder that a thread would be vulnerable for removal over the span of four decades.

Again, a more thorough investigation or reading of the trial transcript would have added to the credibility of his findings in what appears to be a hastily investigated crime. The claim of being meticulous and thorough loses credibility when Mains refuses to even consider evidence pertaining to body condition, the probability of refrigeration and that the body may have been found earlier and removed, perhaps hoping the killer would return to the scene, and then replaced to the same cornfield. His attitude is that just saying that evidence may have been planted is proof of a suspect's guilt, regardless of what the evidence tells you.

"Frankly it is a waste of my time even to entertain this notion, as it is completely false and ridiculous," reasons Mains, who opts to take the shortcut he supposedly deplores by citing "overwhelming evidence" of Hubbard's guilt with a handful of subjective bullet points. Most importantly, he takes the position that if he decides someone is guilty, you can believe it 100 percent "because my integrity is beyond reproach."

How Mains found the long-lost Hubbard evidence box and was able solve the case through DNA is a chapter all to itself. It also necessitates a serious look at DNA evidence and how it has become something of a magic bullet when it comes to solving cold-case homicides.

CHAPTER 18: DNA

Crime Solving's Magic Bullet?

Whether Kenneth Mains did or did not have Kim's DNA or had somehow discovered the case evidence with which to compare that DNA, as he alleges, doesn't matter. Two essential conditions clearly mar, even destroy, the integrity of this conclusion: (a) broken chain-of-custody of evidence missing without oversight for almost two decades; and (b) probable contamination of that evidence after the trial and wherever it had been for the years it was missing.

There is a saying that continues to gain credence among crime solving professionals: DNA technology is only as good as the weakest link in the chain of gathering and preserving evidence.

We know all this evidence was handled by various parties, including Joe and Dorisann Hubbard, Charles King and at least two of Kim's attorneys, starting a mere weeks after the trial when the case was being appealed through a 1975 evidentiary hearing and beyond that to Pennsylvania Supreme Court through 1979. The handling of evidence and photos taken of clothes, tires and casts took place in the evidence room of the Pennsylvania State Police (Troop F) in Montoursville, Pennsylvania. The chain-of-custody was still in effect, but the contamination was ongoing.

Mains himself even complains in his book about Joe Hubbard being allowed to handle the physical evidence at the state police barracks where it was stored and that the elder Hubbard dropped a foot cast and damaged it. Instead, it was the Hubbards' attorney at the time, Public Defender John "Jack" Felix, who accidentally dropped the cast as he subsequently stated in an attested affidavit. That is not the point, other than to show the detective's lack of meticulousness.

"It is unknown why they were allowed to handle physical evidence from this case," Mains complains in his analysis of the Commonwealth v Kim Lee Hubbard. "I can say that practice would not be acceptable today. *The parents of a convicted murderer handled and destroyed physical evidence in this case.*"

They did indeed handle it, but a chipped foot cast is a long way from destruction. The Hubbards and others handled all the evidence, and there are photos of the jersey and pairs of pants taken out of their plastic bags and photographed. Not only was much of this evidence unavoidably contaminated, but DNA of the defendant's closest relatives would have been on the evidence itself. They apparently had no restrictions such as wearing gloves while handling case evidence in those years before the emergence of DNA testing.

Contamination is the introduction of something to a crime scene or evidence derived from it that was not previously there. Most contamination at the crime scene itself comes from the humans who examine or transport it.

Mains is right about this being unacceptable today, and it would be regarded as lax back in those days too, mostly because of potential damage to, or distortion of, evidence still viable while the case remained under appeal.

As for the chain-of-custody, it was broken nineteen years before it was brought to the attention of Mains in a story line that seems to indicate the cold-case investigator was directed to it by a heavenly or ghostly being. Documentation is essential in protecting the integrity of the chain-of-custody, which is vital for any type of crime-scene evidence. If laboratory analysis determines that DNA evidence was contaminated, anyone who handled that evidence must be identified for the record. Television crime shows bring us actual cases where case-breaking DNA is found squirreled away for years, unopened and forgotten, in the far recesses of some storage facility. Chain-of-custody has been maintained and contamination minimized, but even that's not a given.

The shorter this chain and the fewer people handling the evidence, the less probability of contamination. If you lose track of where the evidence has been and who may have handled it, the integrity of DNA testing may be destroyed and therefore disputed.

This brings us to March 5, 1996, when Kim Hubbard received a Rule to Show Cause from the Lycoming County Court of Common Pleas signed by President Judge Clinton Wilcox Smith. He was a successor to Judge Charles Greevy, the trial judge in the Hubbard case, who stepped down from the bench in 1981. It was a motion requested by the Office of the District Attorney for Disposition/Destruction of Property of the remainder of evidence still in custody in the Commonwealth V. Kim Lee Hubbard. Kim had until March 28, 1996, to show cause if he chose to contest the motion. He chose not to.

"I just wanted to get along with my life. Dad had been gone for, what, seven or eight years, and I guess I wasn't expecting to go through all that stuff." Kim recalled. "Plus, we had photos or copies of every piece of evidence. I guess I just didn't want to go through all of that again."

In another dozen years or so, he found himself perusing all that evidence his father had accumulated and came to regret not contesting disposition/destruction of the physical evidence that had convicted him.

Most of the property admitted as evidence at the February 1974 trial was in a list of fifty-six numbered exhibits, including: thirty photos, tires and casts, all the clothing Jennifer Hill was wearing or had in her possession, as well as soil samples, scrapings from the victim, road schematics, a climatology log, and the most intriguing item, "bloody corn." It was the only thing bloody involved in the case. Curiously, there was no helmet listed or any letters or envelopes.

After the disposition process, third-party evidence, if not crucial for future adjudication, may be returned to the original owners and the rest supposedly discarded or destroyed. However, this should not have been done until the motion to show cause was granted at the end of March 1996.

That leads us to the miraculous rediscovery of the evidence which Mains said gave him the opportunity to "solve" the case after which he says he discovered touch DNA identified as Kim's on the inside of the waistband of one of the pairs of pants Jennifer allegedly wore.

So, approaching two decades after the disposal motion was granted—conveniently, shortly after Mains was assigned to look into the case—he writes that he was sitting at his assigned desk as an investigator for the DA's office. He recalls that he was contemplating how to proceed and in the process of reviewing the evidence, when he heard "some people in the waiting room" conversing about ghosts. At first, he paid little attention to the chatter as he was typing up a report: "Then I overheard a statement that took this case in a whole new direction for me."

They were talking about a large box in the basement of the Lycoming County 911 Center where one of them mentioned "seeing orbs or ghost activity in the basement of their office." They had supposedly seen these otherworldly objects floating around this box. Finally, one of them remarked: "Yeah, it was the Hubbard box."

Not only was this a miraculous break, but there were apparently ghost-like figures, perhaps guiding angels, pointing him toward finding the truth: "This evidence was supposed to be destroyed, but here it was. Fate," he observed. Fate is essentially destiny; something often interpreted as inevitable, predetermined by something beyond mortal control.

Mains sprang into action and grabbed one of those unnamed conversationalists to take him to that basement where he encountered a large wooden box. Upon removing the top, he found "the mother lode" of evidence, among them tires, various samples, clothing, including "a famous blue '33' jersey," shoes, "letters from Hubbard" and even a white hard hat. All of these items were listed in the March 1996 Motion for Disposition/Destruction of Property that were supposed to be destroyed. All, that is, except two of them. Mains said he found two items in the box that were not among the items and exhibits listed in evidence in March 1996: letters from Kim Hubbard and a white helmet.

It was an envelope containing one of those letters from which Mains said he was able to obtain a sampling of Kim's DNA that allegedly proved he had touched or handled a piece of Jennifer's clothing in that box.

Much of his incriminating revelations about Hubbard, prior to the fortuitous DNA opportunity, is based on unattributed information, his personal observations about Hubbard and dime store psychoanalysis. DNA apparently wins the day and signals the undoing of Kim Hubbard's hopes for exoneration. In his previous meeting with Hubbard, Mains described him as having a bullying, tough guy persona, but he apparently knew the jig was up when Mains told him he had Jennifer's clothing from which he could collect DNA.

"He began to shake and spill his coffee," Mains says, as if he had suddenly cowed the bully. Kim Hubbard has morphed into a defeated weak-kneed worrier with the mention of three letters—DNA.

Kim says this dramatic description may have come from when Mains showed him a photo on a smartphone, surprising him by announcing he had found the long-lost cache of evidence. He admits he was interested and surprised, briefly holding the digital device to look at the photo of pants with the torn crotch on the tiny screen. He remembers holding the device up and stretching the image for a closer look. The pants appeared to be black, not blue, but he only had a few seconds to examine it. It did, however, give Mains a surface from which to extract Kim's DNA.

It seemed to him that Mains was no longer interested in what he had to say, and, for whatever reason, he had already decided that he now had something that would discredit Hubbard's hopes for exoneration.

Here's how Mains saw Hubbard's decision not to have any further dealings with him: "Initially, Hubbard was happy that I was looking into his case. However, once I told him I wasn't doing it to exonerate him (which is what he thought) and I was doing it for the truth, his demeanor shifted, and he became standoffish."

"I certainly didn't need his assistance at the time, and I didn't ask for it. He approached me," Hubbard states, conceding that he was initially excited that someone with Mains's apparent qualifications was interested. "I already had a reputable exoneration program looking into the case. He just popped up on the internet like hundreds of other people. I did take his advice about emailing someone in the courthouse. I emailed all five judges, but it wasn't to ask them for help. I just wanted them to look at my website and know that this happened in their own criminal justice system."

In a way, Mains manipulated the sending of letters that would lead to him being assigned to nose into the case. Might as well get paid to find the truth, which was apparently already established in his mind.

Mains indicates in his book that he was requested by the Chief County Detective and District Attorney to follow up on an email Hubbard had sent to the county judges. Hubbard, on the other hand, says he was contacted by Mains, who in their initial communication advised him to email the county judges calling their attention to the website. The judges, he reasoned, might direct the matter to the attention of the office of Chief County Detective William Weber.

The exoneration program involved at the time was Duquesne University's Pennsylvania Innocence Project, which relies on the efforts of law students with faculty advisors and externs, including attorneys and technicians in a volunteer capacity, to assist in cases as needed. Kim was later informed that the law professor in charge of a student team looking into the Hubbard case called it off after learning from Mains that he had proven his DNA was on the clothing of the girl in evidence.

Hubbard said he soon became suspicious of Mains and his motives, though he was initially impressed by his association with the American Investigative Society of Cold Cases, its website and the heavyweights involved in the cause. He regarded him as an independent investigator when first contacted and was unaware of his association with the district attorney at that time. But he came to regard him as lazy and biased as a detective, especially after Mains stated he had no interest in going through trial transcripts about field testimony or examining corresponding photos admitted as evidence.

We've got two seemingly different stories of how and why Mains got involved in the case in the first place and who initiated their subsequent encounter. They seem to agree that Kim emailed the five judges in the Lycoming County Court of Common Pleas about his website, and this was passed along to DA Eric Linhardt who in 2017 was elected to one of those judge slots himself.

I remember hearing from Kim a few years back that there was a detective with impressive credentials interested in his case, but he expressed some reservations about the guy's attitude; "He's got that cop mentality," he said, "and it took me back to the state cops, Hynick and Peterson. You know, like he was doing me a big favor even talking to me?"

Mains lays out his investigation over seventy pages in a paperback and, with a boost from state-of-the-art DNA software technology, ultimately declares Kim Hubbard the killer of Jennifer Hill. The story of the cold-case detective's findings was reported in the Williamsport *Sun-Gazette*, the paper of record covering the 1973 murder and 1974 trial. The paper, by the way, never once delved into the case and the questions raised about it over those years. Maybe they were just waiting around for a renowned detective to close the case?

"Despite Mains' book," concluded *Sun-Gazette* reporter Seth Nolan, "Hubbard continues to assert his innocence."

Kim's reaction?

"All this man has to do is step up and say, 'Hey, I found some DNA on Jennifer's clothes.' Case closed. None of all that sleight-of-hand evidence, now so obvious in trial transcripts, evidentiary photos, and autopsy findings, means anything at all."

The newspaper, to its credit, did at least seek a response from Kim, which included the preceding comment. The young reporter may or may not have been familiar with the discrepancies in the case that drew impressive attention and coverage from various news outlets in the late seventies and into the eighties. It apparently came down to this. You've got a convicted murderer's credibility weighed against an acclaimed investigator with impressive credentials as a defender of the innocent. I do understand from personal experience how a reporter might lean toward someone seemingly loaded with credibility versus someone adjudged guilty by a jury of his peers.

Let's look at how Mains locked up the case with DNA despite all the flaws in the sanctity of the evidence from which he was able to conclude that Kim Hubbard left his unique hereditary material in a "DNA mixture" on the inner waistband of the jeans Jennifer was wearing on the day she is believed to have died.

The process known as TrueAllele® Casework is a product developed by Cybergenetics.

The go-to person at Cybergenetics and developer of that product is Dr. Mark Perlin, who described it thusly:

"So basically, it takes low-level or mixed DNA results and enhances those to produce probabilities with correlating statistics."

Dr. Perlin, whose tagline for Cybergenetics is "Justice Through Science," has testified in state, federal, military, and foreign courts about objective computer DNA. Perlin confirmed on his company website that these samples were forwarded to his lab from the Pennsylvania State Police in reference to the Hubbard case. He added that DNA "as inferred from the envelope," was found on the waistband or the murder victim's pants. This was as stated by Mains in his book, noting that they couldn't get a reading from the first envelope sent but connected with a second.

In other words, the required reference sample from the envelope matched with a mixture (more than one person's DNA) to ascertain that Kim had touched that waistband. According to Mains, the envelope and pants were contained together in the same large box. We do know that while they were in evidence, most everything was segregated, and each item of the clothing was separately packaged. It might be assumed that this was the case when Mains opened that box, but he doesn't get into that much detail aside from naming some of the items inside.

TrueAllele® is a computer program that "rapidly infers genetic profiles from all types of DNA evidence samples." So far, so good. As of this writing, Cybergenetics has maintained secrecy of its source code, reasoning that it is a trade secret. The problem in a court of law is that opposing attorneys, whether arguing for the prosecution or defense, have no way of questioning computer instructions used to determine results.

"TrueAllele is being used on the most dangerous, least information-rich samples you encounter, and typically in the most important cases," Dan E. Krane, a defense expert witness and biology professor at Wright State University, as quoted in a November 18, 2015, article of the *Wall Street Journal*. "And I don't know how it arrives at its answers."

That begs the question of how much Cybergenetics knows about the reliability of the samples it receives. Dr. Perlin's email address was on the website so I thought it might be interesting to see if he would respond to the background of a real case scenario that I didn't identify as the Hubbard case. It was disingenuous, I suppose, but I wanted to know how he would regard the sanctity of his findings if he knew more of the story behind the sample. Otherwise, it might deter him from saying anything about it on the record with recent controversy over his process as well.

I still have the notes about the description of an unnamed case "I was looking into as a crime writer" that I presented to him about two years ago.

It contained the following points:

> —*physical evidence in the case was collected and submitted as evidence in the trial almost 45 years ago—during the appeals process, which included an evidentiary hearing in front of the trial judge well before the DNA era, various individuals handled this evidence multiple times, including both of the defendant's parents. This evidence included the murder victim's clothing from which a sample of low-grade, mixed DNA would be taken years later...*

> —*the individual convicted had been notified by the Prothonotary, the custodian of records for the county court, that all evidence from more than 25 years before was to be destroyed unless he filed objection, which he didn't...*

> — *a box with the name of the defendant on it is found in the basement of a county office building about eighteen years later (twenty years as of this date) with no record of how it was transported there or who may have handled or examined it in the interim...*

> —*This included the envelope containing a letter written by the defendant mentioned in the trial, though never identified in the trial transcripts as being submitted as Commonwealth's evidence. Nor was it listed among the exhibits as listed ...*

My question is how reliable would this DNA evidence be in linking this defendant to a single piece of clothing due to loss of chain-of-custody and probable contamination from handling by close relatives?

I received no response from Dr. Perlin, which is not meant to disparage him, but his reaction might have been instructive. An attempt for some kind of response from Mains through contact phone number and email at his Jersey Shore, Pennsylvania, office at the time was similarly unproductive. It wasn't really an imperative. He had laid out his whole shaky case against Hubbard for public record. I could analyze by buying his book. Another investigative crime writer looking into the case, Angela Laskodi, posed some of the questions I've brought up here and was subsequently blocked by Mains from communicating with him online.

"Mains just throws trash out there hoping no one will do any fact checking," Laskodi said in a critique of his book. "If he fabricated the Jennifer Hill murder to the extent he took it, I can't believe anything he writes or, God-forbid, investigates."

And yet Mains is quick to respond when it comes to self-marketing one of his books, the cold case organization he founded or even his association with the History Channel's discontinued series, "The Hunt for the Zodiac Killer," which was dropped after its first season amid complaints that the fifth and final episode was especially disappointing for viewers expecting a dramatic lead-in to a second season that was not to be.

In most all cases, a touch DNA sample is a mixture of more than one person. There is a lot of science behind pulling out a definitive match based on a reference sample, and now with increasingly popular software programs like TrueAllele® in the game, it often depends on coding or the so-called instructions inherent in the software.

Touch DNA is material transferred to a surface by touching or handling. It is much touchier, so to speak, than blood or semen samples. With the ever-present possibility of a mix with touch DNA, the analysis becomes a challenge, which is why TrueAllele® is such an attractive commodity in showing a statistical likelihood based on complex mathematical formulas to separate the genotypes of individuals from each other.

This in known as probabilistic genotyping. Probability may lead you in the right direction of what is probable, but probable is just something that is likely to occur or be. Then consider that this approach is almost impossible to explain to members of juries who know little about how it works, other than it solves crimes and frees people convicted of crimes they didn't commit.

You can cross-examine a DNA analyst on how he or she connected a certain person to a surface, from metal to skin, but you can't put a computer on the witness stand. Not yet anyway. The truth in a software program is derived from whatever is programmed into it.

"Still, probabilistic genotyping remains on the outer edge of scientific acceptance," *ProPublica* reported in an investigation of "algorithmic injustice" published on Nov. 4, 2016. Perhaps this will change by the time you read this. Thus are the advances of science.

Utilizing software computing to identify someone's DNA means that properly collecting and handling of evidence to avoid being tainted by contamination is more important than ever. The promise of powerful software in identifying killers, rapists, and other perpetrators of violence from the surfaces they touch is balanced by skepticism within the legal community.

"Many trials involve highly technical testimony about the chemistry and biology of evidence and the physics of how it was analyzed," it was reported in a newsletter published in January 2014 by the Missouri Division of the International Association for Identification. "But all that science can easily be thrown out when the method of actually collecting the evidence is in question." The International Association for Identification is proclaimed to be the "largest forensic association in the world" with a specialty in the scientific examination of physical evidence.

This is clearly a concern even among organizations and college curriculums supportive of DNA technology while, at the same time, raising cautionary flags.

The skepticism has been advanced with even greater urgency by investigation journalism, with *Atlantic* magazine reporting on "The False Promise of DNA Testing" in its June 2016 issue. In this report highlighting the propensity for error in DNA labs, William Thompson, a DNA expert and criminology professor at the University of California at Irvine, is quoted as stating on the heels of botched test results that sent an innocent sixteen-year-old Josiah Sutton to prison for rape: "It was no longer a question of whether errors are possible. It was a question of how many, and what exactly we're going to do about it."

Sutton was exonerated due to faulty testing but not until he served four years for the crime. This was not through TrueAllele®, which would have been much harder to challenge and show human error, other than through how the material was handled. This is the Achilles heel for Mains's claim of solving the case.

And just as DNA exonerates and brings about justice through science, as professed by Cybergenetics and other true believers in the field, it is also subject to human error and difficult to challenge in a criminal trial. Human error becomes even more of a threat to evidence tested more than forty years after it was collected when contamination, a shattered chain-of-custody and human prejudice combine as factors.

In matters of conscious or innate human prejudice, I am not about to psychoanalyze Kenneth Mains as he did Kim Hubbard, but this case alone provides proof that he was far from meticulous in this investigation and more interested in following a path taken almost four-and-a-half decades before by people for whom he has expressed great admiration on behalf of the agency that prosecuted Hubbard. I am not even interested in getting into his personal life and the nitty-gritty of his early career in law enforcement, other than what he says about himself, because my interest in him is behavior and views that reflect how he dealt with the Kim Hubbard case.

You see, Ken Mains was at the threshold of something even more impressive than his connection with a respected organization that he founded in 2013 and subsequently served as president. Now I'm probably giving Mains more attention than I should, extending into an additional chapter, and he certainly has a right to his opinion. However, he went on record with a published overview of his investigation that was consummated by declaring Kim Hubbard the killer based on a preponderance of his so-called evidence. It went beyond opinion, and he conveniently pulled it off by crediting disputed DNA technology and easily contaminated evidence.

It was more malicious than that with salacious characterizations of what may have happened between his anointed killer and a pre-teen girl who was victimized again in an additional indignity. This is the same person who was offended that Hubbard included body photos on his website to establish valid points about body condition and crime scene evidence. Throughout his analysis of the case were characterizations of Hubbard as a derelict, a bully, a liar, and a man of violence seen physically assaulting his sister and his girlfriend in unspecified and seemingly nonexistent police surveillance.

Mains was a producer of the History Channel Mini-Series, "The Hunt for the Zodiac Killer." One who did review it was Steve Hodel in the *New York Times* who said, "the one good thing the series did was to try (accent try) solving it by, for apparently the first time, getting access to the killer's alleged or probable DNA."

Now Mains was a producer and costar in a reality TV version of a buddy movie, although the History Channel labeled it a "nonfiction limited series" that turned out to be more limited than originally intended. Mains buddied with Sal LaBarbera, a retired LAPD homicide detective, as an on-screen tandem of investigators. As Mains promoted the show, he boasted that he was a consultant/advisor and did some of the key detective work. Zodiac Killer premiered the same year (2017) as his book, "Unsolved No More," and he was riding high.

The series was "quietly discontinued" after five episodes, abandoning plans for a second season. Hodel, a former homicide detective himself and an award-winning true crime author, saw problems from the first episode:

> It becomes apparent that neither of the two-man team of
> detectives "working the case" has any serious background

knowledge of the real facts. They have not done their homework, and that mistake will undermine and play a major negative role throughout the entire series.

...Regardless, they quickly focus on two old Zodiac suspects and rather than following where the evidence leads them (Basic Homicide 101) they decide to see if they can make the evidence fit their preconceived "prime suspects." Unfortunately, they stick with this plan throughout the entire series. (The series is subsequently dropped for a second season with no comment by anyone from the History Channel.)

Sound familiar? Mains used this same approach to make the evidence fit his preconceived suspect, Kim Hubbard, trying to "make the evidence fit" his prime suspect. What seemed to be a promising approach, exposing a serial killer in the reality television version of real time, was just another contrived effort, promising much but delivering the same old stuff with DNA coming to the rescue.

There was an element of lifting touch DNA from "two bloody handprints" Mains found at the bottom of the pants of murder victim, Cheri Jo Bates, who was never officially linked by detectives to the Zodiac Killer but as "a possible Zodiac Killer victim." She was killed more than two years before the rest of the "official" serial killings, starting in December 1968 and numbering as high as thirty-seven.

It may seem unfair to blame Mains for the content of this serial, but he, true to his style, got his publicity out of it in interviews by making sure everyone knew he was behind it and assuring that DNA would ultimately unmask the killer. In an interview with FOX News, he depicts himself as being literally hands-on in gathering so-called evidence used in the series.

"It's probably the greatest American unsolved serial killing case," he claimed. "I'm very confident it can be solved."

As it turns out, the case of the Zodiac Killer remains open after another disputed attempt in 2020 to resolve it via DNA technology. As for Mains, maybe he'll get it right next time.

CHAPTER 19: HYNICK

"I'm Through Fighting the System!"

The most unwelcome visitor to the Hubbard home within a matter of hours after the alleged finding of the body of Jennifer Hill, was Lt. Steven Hynick. Dorisann Hubbard remembered him as an ominous figure from the moment they met, with a steely, penetrating gaze that had assessed hundreds of criminal suspects over thirty-seven years with the Pennsylvania State Police at that time. He was the man in charge as he and his partner, Sgt Edward Peterson, drilled them with questions about that day when Jennifer left their house. Questions were systematically repeated, often irritatingly so, with the apparent strategy of tripping them up and exposing intimations of guilt.

"Even his smile made me shudder, and I'd find myself wanting to make him like me, because I thought if he went away, we could go on with our lives," Dorisann would say repeatedly in different ways whenever his name came up as if they were somehow at fault for not winning him over.

After fleeting interest in Joe and his truck, the cops turned their attention to Kim. It was when they requested that they call Kim home from school and brought Allen Ertel into the conversation that she came to realize it was an interrogation. Yet it was Hynick they sought to please. Ertel would look them over as they answered questions, occasionally offering one of his own. She doesn't remember him having much of a personality. He seemed uncomfortable in their humble but always meticulously clean home.

It would be Hynick who took Kim into custody at the local fast-food hangout on November 16, 1973, for what would be the first day of some ten-and-a-half years of continuous imprisonment in three different institutions and a halfway house. By the time of the murder trial three months after Kim's arrest, Hynick had been reduced to just a minor figure in the trial and was apparently deskbound as the guy who basically oversaw personnel assignments and the aggregate evidence as "administrative head" of the operation as it proceeded into trial.

Hynick and Peterson were the most prominent state police in the investigation right up until the arrest. Despite being the cop who took Kim into custody and sent him off to be processed for incarceration in the county jail, Hynick was supplanted by Cpl. Ronald Barto as the designated arresting officer who formally filed the arrest warrant and moved to the front of the line.

"My role in this investigation was administrator to see that the proper persons were doing their job," Hynick would explain in his trial testimony. He added that he was not in charge of the investigation itself and was more involved in duties like inventorying evidence. Those in charge of the investigation, he explained, were Corporal Barto and Trooper Keppick, respectively.

In a matter of months after the jury found Kim guilty, Hynick himself was being forced out of the state police, threatened with imprisonment by Ertel for allegedly tampering with a witness. "The allegations against me are totally untrue, malicious and politically motivated by Lycoming County District Attorney Allen E. Ertel," he was quoted as saying in the January 20, 1975, issue of the Williamsport *Sun-Gazette*.

Hynick's first public exposure in the 1973 Hill murder investigation is in a front-page photo in the October 29th *Sun-Gazette* as one of the figures gathered around "where the body of Jennifer Hill was found" illuminated in the darkness under a tarp held over them to protect them from the rain earlier in the evening. Others in the macabre photo op included Ertel, Dr. Earl Miller, Barto, Keppick and South Williamsport Police Chief Charles Smith.

Hynick seems to be the spokesman for the state police in the October 31 *Sun-Gazette* when he reports the crime as "sex-related," that they were looking for known sex offenders and that they "believe the Hill girl was strangled by a man, not a woman or young boy..." By that date Kim had been questioned at least twice, and Hynick would concede in the trial that the defendant was a suspect on that date.

Fierro: "Because at that time (Oct. 31) Kim Hubbard was a suspect, wasn't he?"

Hynick: "Yes, sir."

It was on October 31st when the car was impounded and boots taken as evidence. The state police seemed to have limited their suspects to one by that date—if they ever had others, that is. It seems that the point of that public statement might be to get the following information out to the public: there was sex or attempted sex and only a man could have been the killer.

But the alliance between Hynick and Ertel would soon be fractured, and there are strong indications that this may have started in the latter stages of the Hubbard case over another investigation involving the high-profile prosecution of Williamsport Mayor John R. Coder.

In an Associated Press article on March 1, 1975, the case against Fred R. Sechler is resolved with the plea of guilty to criminal solicitation for using a woman to trap Ertel in a sexually compromising position to learn information about another criminal case. In the meantime, Hynick would be accused of keeping Sechler apprised of the case Ertel was building against him. Ertel had successfully escaped losing Kim Hubbard's appeal in oral arguments for a new trial ten days before the Sechler resolution. Hynick, who had been suspended with pay in January 1975, had hearings postponed twice—the first time because he was hospitalized with high blood pressure and blood sugar issues, and again when his wife was hospitalized.

Hynick had previously vowed that "I will not resign for anyone" and that he would fight Ertel's prosecution "to the end."

Hynick was challenging charges that he kept Sechler informed of the ongoing investigation conducted against him. He was accused of tampering with a witness and warning Sechler of his pending arrest. Hynick wasn't backing down—at first, that is—publicly calling for an independent investigation by the state Attorney General. Within a year after the Hubbard trial, Lt. Hynick was stating this about Allen E. Ertel for the record:

*If I, as a veteran criminal investigator with 37 years with the
state police, can be harassed and shabbily treated by superiors
and a politically motivated district attorney, what effect will
this have on the enforcement of officers in the performance of
their duties in the future?*

He would additionally, most likely to Ertel's discomfort, put it out
there that the district attorney was willing to break the law to enforce and
prosecute the law.

"Is it fair to arrest and prosecute for the illegal use of wiretapping
(successfully against Mayor Coder in 1974) and… on the other hand, use
the same methods in attempts to obtain evidence on police officers and
other people?" was his rhetorical challenge.

Despite his vows to fight to the end, the former head of the Criminal
Investigation Division at Troop F headquarters in nearby Montoursville
made a deal and exited into retirement with his pension intact. He was
just a year shy of his sixtieth birthday.

On August 13, 1975, about seventeen months after Kim Hubbard
started serving his sentence, Hynick was placed on one year's probation
in connection with the alleged tampering with a witness. According to a
report from United Press International some eight months after charges
were filed against him:

*Visiting Judge Earl Handler of Indiana, PA, accepted the
agreement for Hynick to take part in the state's Accelerated
Rehabilitation Development program, under which a first
offender can complete conditions of a probation sentence and
charges are dismissed. Hynick, a thirty-eight-year veteran of
the force, under conditions set by Judge Handler must retire
effective August 20, 1975 (and) must not engage in any police
or investigative work of any kind.*

The guy who might provide insight into the maneuverings of the
Jennifer Hill murder investigation got to keep his pension which is

something he wouldn't want to endanger by suggesting tampering or worse in a murder case. Nevertheless, I, along with Ed Schumacher, then a *Philadelphia Inquirer* reporter, were able to track down Hynick somewhere along the looping Dutch Mountain Road in Sullivan County—one of the two least populated and most scenic counties in Pennsylvania—about three years into his forced retirement.

Not surprisingly, he was hesitant about commenting on the investigation of Kim Hubbard beyond stating that "Ertel would bend any rule for a conviction at that time." He did confirm that he was the chief criminal investigator up until Hubbard's arrest on November 16, 1973, when he was subsequently reduced, if not officially demoted, to administrative duties. Cpl. Ronald Barto, who did not have a high visibility during the investigatory phase, was the arresting officer and signee of the arrest warrant. It was Hynick who took Kim into custody on the day of his arrest, pointing a gun at him and snarling, "Run if you want."

Kim remembers those words vividly. Hynick not so much almost seven years later, but he said that sounded about right: "If the suspect thinks you want him to resist, he is going to be more accommodating. It's simple reverse psychology."

Did he really expect Kim Hubbard to resist arrest? Hynick shrugged that question off with a mirthless smile.

He insisted that his superiors and unnamed Lycoming County officials constantly harassed him to get him to resign from the force, which he resisted until August 1975. He said the one thing he learned from his career-ending prosecution was that guilt or innocence did not matter "if Ertel comes at you."

Asked if that also applied in the Hubbard investigation and trial, he turned cautious again: "All I can say is I'm through fighting the system, and I'm not in the position to help you."

He implied that if he did know something that might be helpful to us, it wouldn't improve his situation. I remember him nodding when we said there were suspicions that Mrs. Nevel was taken to the car in impoundment, where there was a white helmet on the back window ledge and was subsequently hypnotized. Was what she described on the witness stand the impounded car? However, he would not verbalize agreement or would just shake his head and say, "I'm not in the position to say."

In truth, he was in the position to say, because he was the guy in charge of the evidence, including the impounded car. He was just as careful when confronted about that subject by Fierro during his cross examination at the trial.

Fierro: "Did anybody point out this car to any prospective witnesses in your presence?"

Hynick: "No, sir."

We know Mrs. Nevel was taken to see the impounded car for identification, but the question would get a follow-up from an irritated Fierro that would raise an objection from Ertel and turn it into a clash between them in which Fierro threatened to put Ertel on the stand to answer the same question.

Fierro to Hynick: "Were you present when somebody from the police showed this car to Mrs. Nevel and pointed out this white helmet on the ledge?"

OBJECTION!

Then Fierro announces: "Yes, I say it was done and I intend to prove it." The judge calms things down, bringing that line of questioning to a sputtering end.

Hynick's role at the trial was reduced to providing one link in the chain of evidence—taking Kim's 1967 Oldsmobile sedan into custody and establishing that a white construction helmet was on the back window ledge. He would subsequently, under a withering cross by Fierro, state that he and Peterson, a veteran of more than twenty years in the state police at the time, did take a pair of the defendant's combat boots into custody. They disagreed in their testimony as to whether Kim was a suspect at the time, with Hynick stating that he was, as well as being given a Miranda warning. Peterson, in his testimony, stated he wasn't and that they didn't Mirandize him.

I did get to ask Hynick if he agreed with Chief Charles Smith's assessment of Jennifer's death as an "I'm sorry kind of murder." What he saw of her, he said, you couldn't see any signs of obvious violence. "I didn't get to look at her closely, but she looked like she could have fallen asleep there."

I asked him why he told the local daily newspaper that the girl must have been strangled by a man. He professed not to remember saying that but noted that any updates released to the news media were carefully orchestrated from "on high" and that he was merely passing them on.

We would interview a reluctant Joseph Keppick at his residence near Montoursville about six years after the trial. He was very close-mouthed about his role in the Hubbard investigation and characterized the idea that the girl's body was returned to another location in that field as ridiculous. Unlike Gleckner, who may have inadvertently become a pawn in such a scenario, Keppick would have had to know what was going on. He was the chief cast maker, according to the testimony of Dr. Miller, and would certainly be knowledgeable of any irregularities and evidence tampering at the body scene. If so, he didn't want to talk about it, either to admit or deny.

Keppick was one of the four state policemen who went after Jack Felix for defamatory remarks in a September 1974 press conference and damaging their professional reputations. He died at the age of eighty-seven on February 18, 2020, in a nursing home in Laporte, the modest Sullivan County Seat.

Sgt. Edward B. Peterson, another of the four to sue Felix, died on February 12, 2018, at the age of eighty-five. He would have been about forty-five during the Hill murder investigation. Peterson outlived Barto, who died in 2013 at the age of sixty-nine.

As for Hynick, he was eighty-three when he died in 1998 and was buried on Dutch Mountain not far from the tiny village of Colley in Sullivan County where he retreated after retiring from the state police. He got to keep his pension, despite charges filed against him in December of 1974, fewer than ten months after Kim Hubbard was convicted. He apparently lived out his twenty-three years of retirement in relative comfort and seclusion.

CHAPTER 20: FELIX

"They're Going to Say, 'Are You Crazy?'"

If I was a cartoonist for a newspaper, I'd draw a picture of a public defender with two guns pointed at him from either side of their head: On one side, the (Office of Chief Disciplinary Counsel) and the Supreme Court saying, "I dare you to take that case and I'm going to take your law license." On the other side is the local court who says, "I dare you to not take the case. And I'll hold you in contempt." That's our world right now. – **Malia Brink, Assistant Counsel for the American Bar Association's Standing Committee on Legal Aid and Indigent Defendants**

A 1975 evidentiary hearing—oral arguments based on inconsistencies, falsehoods and evidence not introduced at the trial—was held on February 19. It was a year from the week of Kim Hubbard's murder trial. Lycoming County President Judge Charles Greevy, who had presided over the 1974 trial, and Judge Thomas Raup, who at age thirty-six was one of the youngest Court of Common Pleas Judges in Pennsylvania at the time, would decide if a new trial was warranted based on evidence presented. Hopes were high for Joe Hubbard and court-appointed attorney, Public Defender John A. "Jack" Felix, despite one potential barrier. Judge Greevy would have to decide if a new trial was warranted based on faulty, missing, or contrived evidence that would have taken place under his watch. The pros and cons of the same judge presiding over an evidentiary hearing challenging the findings of a trial over which he had also presided were, on the one hand, that he was familiar with the case and, on the other, that it might bring into question his own role leading to the conviction.

An evidentiary hearing is part of the appeals process devoted to newly discovered evidence that had not been in transcript or presented to the jury at the convicting trial. The oral arguments were supported in briefs filed by Felix that would have to be countered by District Attorney Allen Ertel. Such a hearing may be petitioned under Pennsylvania's Post Conviction Relief Act (PCRA) after the defendant is convicted at trial and, if granted, remanded back to the trial court in which the defendant was convicted. Thus, the same judge who presided over the trial gets a second opportunity to uphold the conviction or call for a retrial.

The motion for a new trial would be denied by Judge Greevy with Judge Raup, who did voice some concerns about illegal search and seizure regarding Sgt. Peterson taking possession of the boots, concurring.

If the trial was a setback, the evidentiary hearing must have seemed a fatal blow to Kim Hubbard's hopes. It was devastating for Felix, a firm believer in the innocence of his client, because it irrevocably shattered his faith in the justice system. In retrospect, it was the beginning of the end of his law career. The state police would soon be coming after him, and it would be their turn to take their case beyond the Lycoming County Court of Common Pleas.

Mostly it was about the tires, but that was only part of what appeared to be tampering with evidence used in convicting Kim Hubbard barely a year before. Worse than tampering. Some seemed to have been manufactured out of whole cloth. Make that synthetic rubber and plaster, as in tires and casts.

It all fell apart at the evidentiary hearing—a day that started with wary optimism for Felix, who had devoted, by his reckoning, at least 200 hours reviewing the trial evidence, preparing and arguing post-trial motions, and noting alleged discrepancies with respect to some of the physical evidence. Joe Hubbard had proven to be an invaluable resource as they spent many hours analyzing, evaluating, and handling the physical evidence in a supposedly secure property room of the Pennsylvania State Police at the Troop F Barracks in Montoursville. The hearing culminated disastrously with Felix literally fleeing the courtroom to shut himself away in his courthouse office. He was admittedly distressed, even fearful, as he struggled to understand what he'd just seen in the courtroom as Joe Hubbard pounded on his door in anger and frustration.

"You were worse than Fierro!" the distraught father of the convicted murderer howled.

He soon regretted directing his anger at Felix, but the young attorney could never come to terms with what he had seen in what he considered hallowed ground, the courtroom, and his helplessness and inability to rise to the occasion.

As they awaited the hearing to be called to order, it seemed to them that the picture was finally clear as to what they must have done in making the tire and foot casts. That confidence started to dissipate as state cops started rolling in tires and carrying in casts, photos, clothing in clear plastic packaging and other exhibits. That clear picture—everything the public defender and his clients thought they had learned—was shattered like shards of jagged glass almost impossible to piece back together. Felix, shaken, stood and approached the judges, wondering where to start.

"I had to call Mr. Felix back from the judges and tell him to sit down," Joe recalled several years later, his eyes momentarily ablaze with the vividness of the memory. "There were Kim's two recapped tires covered with mud. The same tires the police said were so clean during the trial that they had to go clear up into the wheel well to get mud samples. That's when they were trying to say Kim must have cleaned his car real good to get rid of any evidence showing he had been in that field."

I remember asking Felix a few years after that why he didn't point out the changes to the judges then and there.

"You can't go up and say, 'Judge, well I saw something at the police barracks two weeks ago and they've done this and this to it...'" he said his voice fading into a few seconds of silence. "It was really frustrating because we had planned to explain the tire situation." Another long pause as it came flooding back to him. "I started looking and so forth and I tried to explain what could have happened and what I saw didn't match the evidence... Our diagram didn't line up with the evidence then."

Except there was one judge who had seen the trial evidence a year before, although it would have undoubtedly required scrutiny on his part to pick up on any modification of the physical evidence.

Felix stepped down as Hubbard's attorney and resigned as Public Defender within a span of three months after the catastrophic evidentiary hearing. Felix did file an appeal to the Pennsylvania Supreme Court as Public Defender effective April 9 "on behalf of Kim Lee Hubbard from the Jury Verdict of 1 March 1974 and from the Court's denial of the Defendant's motion for a New Trial in its Order dated 19 February 1975." Felix would not to be the one to handle that appeal, however. He stepped down as Public Defender on April 1, and he formally notified Joe Hubbard via letter on May 1 that "Judge Greevy has informed me that as my duties as Public Defender officially concluded on April 1, 1975, it would be inappropriate for me to personally represent Kim on appeal."

It is not clear why a judge would consider it inappropriate for a former public defender to continue to represent a client in the appeal process as a private attorney. Perhaps it was because the transition from public servant to privately contracted attorney could have created issues as the case continued via appeals to a higher court. If that was a conflict of interest, how about a judge presiding over both the trial and the evidentiary hearing that raised questions about it?

Nevertheless, Felix recommended to the Hubbards that they should notify President Judge Greevy "of your desire to have the Public Defender Office represent your son on the appeal now pending." The new Chief Public Defender at that time was Peter Campana who would subsequently take over the reins of the case.

Whether or not it was inappropriate or typical judicial involvement, Greevy certainly diverted potential Pennsylvania Department of Justice interest in looking into allegations of evidence tampering. An appeal by Army Chaplain George Rathmell, a fervid advocate for Kim Hubbard, to investigate charges of evidence tampering brought a response from Pennsylvania Deputy Attorney General Peter Foster nine months after the evidentiary hearing indicating that the judge had put the kibosh on such an investigation before it got off the ground.

Foster, in a letter informing Capt. Rathmell that "state police found no evidence to support these charges," indicated that Greevy had told them he had seen no indication of evidence tampering. Foster then included the following comment: "Judge Greevy pointed out that Hubbard's father broke a cast of a tire print when permitted to examine the evidence. Therefore, we are not opening an investigation into this case."

The judge should have known at this time that Felix had, in fact, attested to have been responsible for inadvertently chipping a small foot cast (of a partial footprint) while examining the evidence prior to the oral argument. Charles King, who was present at the time, described as what happened thusly: "Mr. Felix was handling the foot casts when another foot cast fell a couple of inches to the floor and a small piece broke off of it." Obviously, the implication was that Joe Hubbard was somehow manipulating evidence that was in state police custody. Only the state police would have the control and opportunity to do that.

The evidentiary hearing before Judges Greevy and Raup set in motion several more years of frustration in the appeals process. It also appears that it may have done more harm than good, stymying a Department of Justice investigation into evidence tampering. The judge, with some misinformation about "Hubbard's father," seems to have sealed the deal for a closer look at the evidence while the people who might have tampered with the evidence, if such was the case, were final arbiters of whether such an investigation was warranted.

Tires, casts, and other physical evidence were viewed at the state police barracks. Photos and documents were filed at the Lycoming County Courthouse at this time in the office of the Prothonotary, the keeper of court records, and were viewed in the public defender's office by the same foursome who did so with the physical evidence in the state police barracks: Felix, Joe and Dorisann Hubbard and Charles King, who, became a human repository of case evidence.

"All the tires I saw (at the barracks) were standard Kelly Springfield tires," King maintained. "None of them were recaps.... All of them were spotlessly clean and the best one had four shallow treads. Like the man who changed the tire on Kim's car after the body was found said. They were all bald or balding."

Felix's Brief in Support of the Defendant's Motion for a New Trial revealed his game plan for what he would be arguing before the two Court of County Pleas judges. It also gave the opposition a heads-up in countering what was in store for them if they were going to waylay this challenge to a conviction. Furthermore, it disarms Fierro's later contention before the Pennsylvania Supreme Court that calling for a mistrial would have negated "the best chance... of ever getting whatever favorable verdict a jury might give us" and that "a second go-around would have been a disaster." The new evidence, often inexplicable, even trivial, should have at least had a jury questioning the origins of the evidence being used. For Felix, he has been as tormented by the whys more than the hows of that evidentiary hearing. Was it overkill? Why did it matter that the jersey, when they took it out of the plastic bag at the police barracks, had a sour smell and then, at the hearing, it was damp as if it had been washed? If you're going to tamper with evidence. Why that? Again, this was years before the consideration of DNA and the possibility of any that might be present on the clothing.

"They're going to say, 'Are you crazy? We didn't wash the jersey,'" Felix was still trying to figure it all out years later. "You wonder why would something had been changed that would appear to be somewhat insignificant."

Also alleged in the brief:

√ The verdict rendered was against the weight of the evidence, which was circumstantial.

√ The court erred in allowing a hypnotized witness to testify without informing the jury or allowing defendant or his counsel to be present.

√ The court erred in not granting a mistrial due to the Kenneth Whitenight outburst.

√ The court erred in admitting evidence obtained as a result of illegal search and seizure.

√ The court erred by condoning prejudicial and inflammatory remarks by the DA in his summation.

√ The court failed to completely instruct jury on alibis and effects of alibi testimony on the burden of proof.

Note: Most of this information has already been detailed in previous chapters and the discrepancies and inconsistencies have become voluminous. Explaining what tire went where, should be as simple as one, two, three, four, but it is excruciatingly maddening, especially after the evidentiary hearing, that it can seem incomprehensible and even inexplicable. A Philadelphia Inquirer reporter in 1979 ended up lying on the floor, his hands over his ears as Joe Hubbard tried to explain the various tires, casts, prints and photos from the trial through the evidentiary hearing. If you want to seriously analyze the evidence, especially prints, photos, tires, and casts, you should go to Kim Hubbard: The Real Story.

The response from the court denying the motion for a new trial dated February 19, 1975, the day of the hearing, could not have conceivably been written with the few hours remaining after the hearing that day with almost eighteen pages of opinion, citing legal sources, quoting sections of transcripts, and repeating key points made by the prosecution as fact that have since been discredited. It was certainly written by the sixty-year-old President Judge who had been on the bench almost twenty-four years at that time. Judge Raup, still in his rookie year as the county's second judge, seemingly concurred with the opinion because it is written in the "we" perspective as required. That is not unusual when a junior and senior judge hear an oral argument, especially when the latter presided over the original trial and is much more knowledgeable of the facts of the case.

Felix had previously called a press conference based on allegations in his briefs for the evidentiary hearing, which included alleged tampering with evidence by the state police. This would years later become part of a milestone Supreme Court decision on whether a Public Defender should benefit from judicial immunity granted to judges and district attorneys. It was ultimately decided that because Felix made his statements at a press conference and not as part of a judicial proceeding, he was not protected by that immunity. The catch was that the comments at that press event came directly from the brief entered prior to the oral arguments, which the Superior Court of Pennsylvania considered part of a judicial procedure and that Felix, as Public Defender, would therefore have that immunity as a "high public official." In a legal drama that played out over several decades, ending with Felix's disbarment in 2014, it added another layer to the impact of the 1974 murder trial. More on that later.

Judge Greevy had a distinguished thirty-year career on the bench and served in leadership roles in his community, his church, the Masons, and other organizations. He was active in the evolvement of the Pennsylvania Juvenile Court and, according to his bio in the Lycoming Law Association, "devoted much effort to improve the community's understanding of the needs of children who are neglected and emotionally disturbed." He was an acclaimed protector of youth and had no tolerance for those who harmed and abused children.

He was clearly convinced—"without the slightest doubt to prove murder in the second degree"—that Kim Hubbard was guilty and was therefore fairly tried and any errors, namely failure to move for a mistrial on two separate occasions, were the burden of the defense attorney.

In a way, Fierro became something of a fall guy in this opinion, but the Pennsylvania Supreme Court, by a narrow majority, would later decide not to grant a new trial due to ineffectiveness of counsel because of Fierro's contention that circumventing a mistrial was part of his trial strategy.

The brief off which Greevy and Raup rendered their decision included much more than newly discovered evidence: tires, casts, differences in clothing, body condition indicating it was found earlier then transferred to a location in the field, and "false or unreliable testimony" from a key Commonwealth witness (testimony relying on hypnosis during the investigation). The evidentiary findings addressed most in depth in their opinion was the impact of hypnosis and how it was used. The judges' opinion reveals that hypnosis was of no consequence in the case, but it also mistakenly characterized the defendant as implying that the witness in question was in a hypnotized state while testifying.

The court deemed it had not erred in allowing a witness who had been hypnotized to refresh her memory without notice to the jury, especially in her identification of a car with a helmet in the back window she saw when impounded.

"Hypnotism was used only as a recall stimulus prior to the defendant's arrest," it concluded on that matter.

The point is there was no authentication of how, why, when or where it was implemented. Was she taken to where the car was impounded and then hypnotized? Did she see a car generally resembling Kim's, adding the helmet because it stood out in her memory later? It is minimalized as "just one of the factors in the arrest" even though she was represented as the only eyewitness linking the defendant to the victim that day—a point emphasized in newspaper coverage before the "eyewitness" was identified.

"The tape of the hypnosis was offered to the defense prior to the trial," the opinion notes. Not according to what was in Fierro's file from Ertel, which said nothing about a tape being available. Was Fierro made aware of this via conversation? Why were the Hubbards kept in the dark about this until weeks after the trial?

The opinion makes another interesting observation: "The hypnotist (who we now know was Dr. Larue Pepperman) was present at trial in the event the defense sought to examine him prior to admission of the hypnosis-elicited testimony."

It seems that, if this is true, the defense attorney again chose to withhold this from Kim and his family. At least it confirms that Judge Greevy was fully aware of the hypnosis, if only after the act. He's blaming the defense for not taking advantage of this potential flaw in eyewitness testimony. He also suggests that the Felix brief implied Mrs. Nevel was under hypnosis during her testimony. That was never an allegation in the brief, even if suspected. Felix merely stated that because the use of hypnosis would confuse what the witness saw and where, resulting in inconsistencies, "that she was not competent to testify."

The opinion points out twice for emphasis that Kim had not been arrested at the time Mrs. Nevel was hypnotized, that her contribution to the evidence apparently became instrumental in his eventual arrest. But she was identifying the car, not the killer, and the car was impounded more than two weeks before the arrest. They had their prime suspect. They had his car, and they took the witness to see it at least twice, according to testimony. The judge seems to be intimately aware of what the police and prosecution did throughout the trial and investigation while the defendant and his family were totally oblivious of much of it until taking possession of Fierro's case file.

As far as not making a mistrial call over Kenneth Whitenight's outburst, the ruling minimizes it at first as "a spectator's outburst" and then denies it is an error by the court "when there is no such motion on behalf of the defendant." Again, it becomes the defense attorney's obligation and that it must have been Fierro's strategy to allow the outburst to pass. Greevy credits the court (himself) with having Whitenight "immediately removed from the room and the trial continued without further mention..." Are we to think that courtroom drama wouldn't have been discussed among jury members during deliberation if not before? Is it logical to suspect that the lack of action, whether via defense motion or by the court itself, might have influenced the jury into thinking the court sympathized with the father even as he was escorted out while apologizing to the judge?

"Not every unwise or irrelevant remark made during the course of a trial compels the granting of a new trial," the judges' opinion explains. The father and daughter give differing accounts of what is alibi testimony. Who will the jury—most of them parents—believe: the distraught father or the eighteen-year-old daughter who has just truthfully admitted in a public forum that she had been sexually intimate with the twenty-year-old defendant?

Continuing to address the issue of a mistrial, a case is cited (Commonwealth v. Goosby) where the brother of the decedent stood up and yelled at the defense attorney: "He murdered him. You are a bum!" No mistrial there in that case—and that was during the defense's summation to the jury. The judges seem to regard it as exclusionary for a mistrial by pointing out that "it was already a matter of record that the father strongly disapproved of the romance and of the defendant." It was certainly an opportunity to finally put an end to that relationship with the unwelcome lover behind bars.

Finally, the opinion states that not giving "a cautionary instruction" to the jury in such a case may benefit the defendant by not "refreshing the jury's recollection of this brief incident." Brief? Maybe. But they were probably the most memorable words spoken in the trial. It was reported in the headlines and leads of all the news coverage of the trial the following day.

Reading the judges' decision, it could have been written by Ertel himself, especially an overview of the case presumably authored by Judge Greevy in the following narrative.

"Tire prints were found approximately 100 feet from where the body lay, as well as footprints around and under the body. Certain of the tire prints were identified as having been made by tire from defendant's car. The boot print under the body was identified as having been made by a boot obtained from defendant."

Nobody brought up the sanctity of the convicting evidence during the trial, except when Fierro expressed concern about how it was taken and processed in cursory remarks to the jury in his summation. It is true that the judges' opinion reiterates the prosecution's scenario as expounded in the trial, but this is not to say the judge knowingly declared disputed evidence as fact.

"In closing, we note that in a criminal case a defendant is entitled to a fair trial, not a perfect one," the opinion concluded, echoing a familiar refrain in Pennsylvania Supreme Court denials for new trials and was, in fact, used in rejecting one of the Hubbard appeals to the high court. "The defendant, Kim Lee Hubbard, received a fair trial and the verdict of the jury was merited under the evidence and the law."

On February 21, 1975, Jack Felix submitted a sworn deposition outlining what he'd seen when he inspected physical evidence at the state police barracks compared to what he saw later in the courtroom during the evidentiary hearing.

- √ The blue jersey inspected at the state police barracks "smelled both musty and sour" when removed from the clear plastic bag in which it was encased. At the hearing, there was no such smell and the jersey was damp as if recently washed.
- √ Tires marked Commonwealth's Exhibits 87 and 88 at the barracks were on rims with barely discernible treads and worn "to the outside." Tires identified as 87 and 88 in the courtroom at the oral arguments "appeared to be recaps with mud visible on the rims." One of them had "six fairly good treads."
- √ Guidelines in photo exhibit of tires and casts (#110) that were drawn in red ink at the barracks and during the trial were blue at the evidentiary hearing.
- √ The dark blue jeans that had been mysteriously changed from when last seen before her disappearance had been partially sewn in the crotch with white or red string that did not match the thread in the pants, and
- √ The bra of the deceased has a pin in the back holding sections of the strap together, not previously seen at the state police barracks, in evidence photos or described in testimony.

Evidence in custody during the appeals process, no matter how significant or seemingly inconsequential to the prosecution or defense, is not to be disturbed, manipulated, or tampered with. This devalues the importance and relevance of all the physical evidence.

Jack Felix firmly believed that Kim Hubbard did not receive a fair trial and was committed to his client, but circumstances forced him to turn his representation over to a successor in the Office of Public Defender, Pete Campana. Within two years, four state police criminal investigators who played integral roles in investigating the death of Jennifer Hill would sue Felix stating that they "suffered grievous harm to their reputations and interference with the proper performance of their occupations." In their initial challenge to Pennsylvania Superior Court, they requested several thousand dollars for each of them in restitution for damages incurred when Felix had held a press conference stating allegations of evidence tampering in the investigation, prosecution and prior to oral arguments on February 19, 1975. The appellants were Ronald K. Barto, Donald J. Houser, Edward Peterson, and Joseph D. Keppick.

The overview of the case before the Superior Court of Pennsylvania was presented thusly:

> Statements made to the press by appellee concerning the case form the basis for the present defamation action. All appellants were state police officers who were involved in the investigation of the murder. The complaint alleges that appellee's statements were defamatory in that they were made maliciously and accused appellants of improprieties during the course of the investigation. Shortly before the statements, appellee had filed a brief with the lower court in support of his client's post-conviction petition. The lower court has found in its opinion, and it is not disputed by appellants, that the statements "[were] no more than a reiteration of the contents of that Brief."

The Superior Court found that Felix was a "high public official" entitled to absolute immunity for defamatory utterances made in his official capacity. The court also ruled that the remarks in this case were "closely related to appellee's official duties and therefore were entitled to protection." It was further determined that Felix "was absolutely privileged" to repeat information from a recently filed brief for a new trial that was later argued in in an evidentiary hearing in the Lycoming Court of Common Pleas.

The opposing view was that he was more like a "privately retained defense attorney" than a public prosecutor who enjoys judicial immunity and may make comments about a trial or hearing outside of the judicial process as the attorney for the Commonwealth, a.k.a. the citizens of Pennsylvania. Even though it was noted that a public defender may have that immunity inside a courtroom, in this case "remarks made by him at the press conference" were made "outside the judicial sphere."

This was an argument over whether Felix, as Public Defender, enjoyed the same judicial immunity as judges, prosecutors and others representing or speaking on behalf of the Commonwealth as witnesses or investigators. The Superior Court would take a different view of Felix's role and standing as a public official with a reversal on October 6, 1977. The argument that turned the tide against the claim of immunity for Felix (the appellee) was curiously based on the contention by the four state policemen (appellants) that Felix made his public statements about evidence tampering knowing they were not true:

> In the appellants' complaint, it is alleged that appellee's statements at the press conference were known by him to be false or were made in reckless disregard of the truth. If that allegation can be proved, appellee's qualified privilege will not protect him. Therefore, appellants' complaint stated **a cause of action** and should not have been dismissed. The order of the lower court is reversed, and the case is remanded for proceedings consistent with this opinion.

Felix's fate was probably sealed by the quick disclaimers from Judges Greevy and Raup in their February 1975 opinion stating they strongly supported all the evidence the Commonwealth had wielded to gain a conviction. The Superior Court would then turn around and add credence to the allegations of the state police foursome that Felix knew his statements to be false and that he engaged in "reckless disregard of the truth." This has never been supported by evidence, whether it showed "a cause of action" or not. The cause of action is defined as "the facts or circumstances that entitle a person to seek judicial relief." Felix, by the way, has never stated he made accusations knowing they were false. Quite the opposite.

Jack Felix was still working in the legal profession as he approached his eighties. At last report, he was still active in the Williamsport Community Theatre League as a founding member.

> *NOTICE OF DISBARMENT NOTICE IS HEREBY GIVEN that by Order of the Supreme Court of Pennsylvania issued July 17, 2014, John A. Felix is Disbarred on Consent from the Bar of the Commonwealth of Pennsylvania to be effective August 16, 2014. Elaine M. Bixler Secretary of the Board. The Disciplinary Board of the Supreme Court of Pennsylvania.*

CHAPTER 21:
UNANSWERED QUESTIONS

It Keeps Getting "Curiouser and Curiouser"

A popular long-standing column in *Grit* was called "Odd, Strange and Curious" which might be compared to "Ripley's Believe It or Not." I am reminded of that column when I think about all the strange oddities and curiosities replete in the prosecution of Kim Hubbard that raise more questions than answers.

Some are head-scratchers and you can't help but wonder why.

For example, the exemplary condition of the body was persuasive proof beyond mere curiosity for people who handled the body on the evening it was "discovered." Perhaps more impressively, two nationally respected forensics experts swore on their exemplary credentials that the only explanation for this anomaly was that the body had been refrigerated. Since the body couldn't have been refrigerated even by the lowest transient overnight temperatures in that cornfield, refrigeration that literally halted decomposition must have taken place elsewhere. Yet it may seem ridiculous, even laughable, as one doubting detective disdained, that the body was removed from the field within forty-eight hours after death, placed under refrigeration and then returned to the field in a location further from the purview of any passerby.

Doesn't happen in real life, right?

It was regarded as even more preposterous that the refrigeration may have taken place just across the river in a hospital morgue that could accommodate multiple bodies in its cooler under presumably tight security with the county coroner a senior member of the medical staff. It's a possibility, not an accusation, and would have been the more convenient location were the prosecution and/or police investigators behind such a body exchange.

Arguably the most important Commonwealth witness in the trial was Dr. Earl R. Miller, the county coroner doubling as chief crime scene investigator. Aside from his access as county coroner, Miller was a respected member of the medical staff of what was then Williamsport Hospital and fittingly had access to and oversight of morgue accommodations. Several integral figures contributing to a successful murder conviction had ties to the hospital and unique access. They included the physician hypnotist of the prosecutor's acclaimed chief eyewitness, a department head (Carl Pfirman) who accused the eventual defendant of killing the girl several days before her body was found, and Dr. Miller himself.

Therefore, as outlandish as it might seem, it was possible, if not probable, in a conventional criminal investigation. Few aspects of this case might be described as conventional.

Why would misrepresenting the day the body was really found be a strategy in finding the killer? It comes to mind that the prospect of the killer returning to a crime scene under surveillance might be a motivation to set such a trap. As previously noted, there was a forested area that included a tree with outreaching thick branches supporting a makeshift platform directly across the road from the "wagon-type path" as Dr. Miller described the lane intersecting the cornfield in his testimony. It was still roosted there, in the latter stages of deterioration, when I went to the field three and a half years after the trial and four after Duane Gleckner discovered the body. Such structures are not unfamiliar in deer hunting country, but a cornfield on one side and trees, marshy ground and underbrush bordering the river on the other aren't exactly prime deer hunting terrain.

Suppose the plan was to keep the search going, fooling the perpetrator into thinking the body was still there? That's the stuff of TV crime shows of the time. The murderer walks into a trap to what, move the body, as an act of penance or to relive the crime? The police would then let the public know they had run a bluff on the killer who fell for the ruse. They might even be celebrated as clever and imaginative. However, if the ruse fizzles, do you come clean and admit you've had the body all along? It would give a defense lawyer plenty of ammunition to attack the credibility of the investigation during the trial.

Odd, strange and curious, for sure, but so is going to all the trouble of replacing a body in a cornfield. Either option would require the knowledge of several reliable conspirators—if not the prosecutor's approval. Again, one must consider that a body couldn't emerge from a field in pristine condition after all that time under the stated weather conditions with no evidence of significant deterioration or animal and insect damage.

Another recourse is the killer himself refrigerates the body up until a matter of hours before a missing person became a murder victim. That door of possibility was left ajar by Ertel himself when he conceded the girl may have been killed elsewhere after being kept alive at another location. That would mean being fed the same food she had consumed on the day of her disappearance.

It wasn't Kim Hubbard who was so interested in what Jennifer Hill had to eat the day of her disappearance.

Curiouser and curiouser, not to mention odd and strange…
Then there was the identification of a device in the girl's mouth that I don't know how to explain without wandering off into a wilderness of wondering. It went without notice for several years until Joe Hubbard noticed among the body photos something in the partially opened mouth of the deceased. He enlarged that portion of the photo that can be seen on the website, *Kim Hubbard: The Real Story*. Two funeral directors who were experienced embalmers identified it as a needle injector, commonly used in embalming to compress the mouth and jaw into a permanently closed position.

Now the girl was ultimately embalmed not long after the autopsy, and all the photos were said to have been taken at the body scene and on the autopsy table. The puzzler is that this was an evidence photo supposedly taken in the field before the girl was transported to the hospital morgue.

Does that mean somebody started to embalm the body before returning it to the field? Was the photo taken before the embalming and after the autopsy? If it was there during autopsy, why was it ignored when you consider all the other minutiae in the pathologist's postmortem report? Furthermore, consider the stated point of that photo, Commonwealth Exhibit No. 8, as described in Dr. Miller's testimony, with his hand pulling a cornstalk leaf aside for a better view of her face? Miller had moved the leaf for the purposes of showing the opposite side of the head from a previous photo as well as "demonstrating an earring in the right ear." Otherwise, the mysterious object in her mouth may have gone unnoticed.

The earring brings to mind another oddity mentioned earlier—a reference in CAP records during the search for Jennifer that they were looking for a missing earring. How would they know an earring was missing if they hadn't found a body?

Buying Time to Make a Case for Murder…

We've already tried to make sense of why Jennifer Hill left the Hubbard home wearing one pair of pants and then being found in the cornfield in another pair pulled down and gathered above her ankles. The former were dark blue jeans with colorful hearts sewn on the knees and the same material attached to lengthen the legs in a bell-bottom configuration described by one of her friends as "hippie pants." The latter were light blue pants with a macrame belt. When she left for home, the light blue pants were in a bag she was carrying. When she was found in the light blue pants, the bag was nearby and the jeans she was last seen wearing by several witnesses on record were inside. The witness who had the closest view of Jennifer standing a few feet outside her window looking at Halloween decorations on her front door, Betty Jane Nevel, described every article of clothing, even the distinctly patterned pink Glick shoe bag, but not the pants.

Oddly enough and arousing additional curiosity, Jennifer's mother, who admittedly never saw her that day, reiterated in her testimony: "I am saying I believe when she left their house to come home, she had her light blue pants on…" She didn't. Norma Hill was quite insistent, though, and it seemed important to her that Jennifer was wearing those light blue pants. I've gone into the zagged thread in the ripped seat of the dark blue jeans, which was clearly thicker and a lighter color than the stitching in the seams. Not everyone agrees it was from a sewing machine, so we might dismiss this as odd, if not strange or curious.

It was unlikely Kim Hubbard would be sewing anything by machine or by hand after an assault culminating in her death, whether intended or accidental. It is one reason why it made sense to both Joe and Dorisann Hubbard that Jennifer, who was seen so close to home, made it to her destination and walked into a dispute over the ripped pants. Even discounting a hasty attempt to mend the pants, Kim would have had precious little time to commit murder and dispose of the body between Mrs. Nevel seeing Jennifer get into that car and him answering an acknowledged phone call from Jack Hill.

This leads to a curious disagreement in testimony between Norma and Jack Hill, remembering that the husband was in the courtroom throughout his wife's testimony. All witnesses were sequestered, at the request of the prosecutor, after Norma testified. She said her first call to beckon Jennifer to come home occurred at "about 3:45 p.m." That validates the testimonies of Dorisann Hubbard and Mary Mundrick, a nearby neighbor, confirming that Jennifer embarked on her fatal journey at 3:45. Then came a call to the Hubbards from older sister, Jackie, at her mother's behest, asking if Jennifer had left yet. The part about Jackie's mother asking her to make the call was stricken from the record as hearsay. The thirteen-year-old testified that call occurred at "about 4:25 p.m." Ruthie answered the phone. All agreed about the time and content on both ends of the telephone line. That should have been about five minutes before Mrs. Nevel said she saw Jennifer standing in front of her Halloween-decorated door.

Had Jennifer headed straight home she should have made it well before Jackie's call. It would have been during the missing thirty minutes between Joe Mendez seeing her standing at the corner and when Mrs. Nevel saw her getting into the alleged murderer's car. In the meantime, Mrs. Hill said her husband, Jack, arrived home at 4:05 p.m. which should have been close to coinciding with Jennifer's arrival had she stayed her course.

At the Hill house they were getting worried, according to both Norma and Jack, and now it was Jack's turn to call the Hubbards. This time Kim answered, as Jack would later testify. Norma said that call occurred at about 4:45 and she had looked at the clock while he was calling. Ertel objected to her saying "around quarter of" and she reluctantly conceded it could have been between fifteen and ten of five but no later. Curiously enough, the times of these calls were elicited during Fierro's cross-examination and not established by the Commonwealth.

Ertel never asked about times, except to press Norma into adding a few more minutes to the time Jack made his call. That's because Kim was the one who answered the phone.

Jack Hill sat through his wife's testimony on Thursday, February 21, and he didn't take the stand until the afternoon of Monday, February 25. Ertel was now very interested in the time of his critical call, which his witness estimated at "around five o'clock," reaffirming that it was Kim who answered the phone. He had therefore stretched the time for Kim to commit the murder and dispose of the body from a minimum of fifteen minutes to as much as half an hour. The travel time estimate to complete that circuit as clocked by Cpl. Ronald Barto was twelve to fourteen minutes. My trial runs and those of a defense witness, a former county detective, clocked it in the same range at the same after-work time on a Friday.

Fierro tried to shake Jack Hill from his time estimate, but the witness was stubborn.

Fierro: *... you know that fifteen minutes becomes important in this matter, don't you?*

Hill: *Yes.*

Fierro: *But you are telling the jury it was five o'clock even though you never looked at the clock? Isn't that correct?*

Hill: *I said it was around five o'clock.*

Fierro: *How about five minutes to five?*

Hill: *It could have been, but it was around five o'clock when I called up there.*

Fierro: *Ten to five?*

Hill: *I am not sure.*

It should be noted that the Pennsylvania Supreme Court heard arguments for a new trial in November 1975, though the decision was not issued until January 28, 1977. In their findings, the judges chose the 4:30 to 5:00 p.m. time span in their deliberations:

> Jack Hill testified that appellant answered the phone when he telephoned the Hubbard home at 5:00 p.m. to inquire about Jennifer's whereabouts. This testimony places appellant at his home thirty minutes after Jennifer was observed driving away in the metallic-green automobile.

And so it goes throughout the realm of the odd, strange and curious.

Convenience and timelines even more curious...

Oddities and the coincidences were considerable throughout the trial, but nothing was more convenient and timelier in the production of physical evidence than the impressionable band of clay, two-to-three-feet wide, spread across a dry, grassy, hard-surfaced lane that captured those tire impressions.

To avoid confusion, I'll call it the lane as distinguished from the road, which is Sylvan Dell Road, the paved road bordering the cornfield and the intersecting lane. Had not it been for the band of clay atop the grassy and gravely lane, it is unlikely any prints would have been there. They needed that strip of wet clay to capture prints from tires on both sides of the car. It made their case of the car being there when the body was allegedly placed about 100 feet beyond where the tire prints were said to be impressed in what was described as wet yellow clay material. There is some pretty solid evidence that band of clay may not have been the source of prints in the tire casts, but it was needed to convince jurors it was possible to get physical evidence from the field outside of the immediate body scene. It was part of the cornfield evidence show, and the point was to sound and look impressive, but, at the same time, keep the jurors from grasping what they were seeing.

There was no reason for the car, notably one whose driver must have been in a desperate hurry to get in and out, to stop at that spot 26-29 feet down the lane before proceeding the additional 100 feet where the "official" body scene was located. It should have been a moving tire that left its prints, but the photos of one of the casts in evidence and in a photo on "The Real Story" website show a cast with tire tread marks and more than two inches of its sidewall. Most astonishingly, you can see the letters "ELD" from Kelly Springfield the tire brand. It would be difficult enough to capture this with an immobile tire, let alone a moving tire proceeding up the lane. The tire would then have to back out of the lane after dispatching the body. Because of the narrowness of the lane, a second set of prints should have to have encroached on the other set. Otherwise, the car stopped on the band of clay. Then the killer removed the girl from the car, perhaps after killing her inside the vehicle elsewhere, and carried the body 80 to 100 feet further up the lane to deposit the body. Then again, it would been convenient to place it in the last of the eight sweep rows running parallel to Sylvan Dell Road. The tale of the tires themselves only begins here.

The story of the bulldozer responsible for the clay deposited on the lane couldn't have been more auspicious for the prosecution. Two employees of a Montoursville earthmoving business, Kremser Brothers, testified that they transported a bulldozer via a low-bed truck trailer, known as a lowboy, from another job site in the late morning of October 19, 1973, to do unspecified "work" on the dike wall bordering the Atlantic Richfield (ARCO) Bulk Plant at the far end of the seldom utilized lane.

"The tracks were loaded pretty good with this material," testified H. Luther Dieffenbacher, equipment operator for Kremser Brothers as well as a Montoursville Borough Supervisor, who unloaded the dozer from the lowboy.

Despite all the material compressed in the recesses of the tracks, Dieffenbacher negotiated the dozer up the ARCO compound, completed his work on the dike and then drove the tracked vehicle back down the lane. While waiting for a co-worker to bring the lowboy from the entrance of the compound several hundred yards east of Sylvan Dell Road, he said he "cleaned the mud and stuff off the tracks," apparently with a shovel. He then deposited it in a band across the lane instead of along each side of the dozer at the edges of the lane as would seem to be the logical procedure.

A typical bulldozer weighs at least nine tons, and its tracks exert amazing ground pressure and create deep impressions that remain visibly imprinted in the ground for months. Indeed, several people attested that one set of prints was all that could be seen on the lane from the previous summer and fall.

"I personally searched the entire lane and could only find one set of tracks," said Capt. George I. Rathmell, a US Army Chaplain who observed numerous inconsistencies and contradictions in the case that convinced him it had been "a gross miscarriage of justice." This was confirmed by John Clabaugh and others. "Obviously, the bulldozer could have traveled only one way on the lane in question on the day in question."

According to this testimony, there should have been two sets of prints—one set up and one set back to corroborate the operator's testimony. The only other explanation was that the tread impressions so perfectly meshed each way that it looked like one set of tracks— something very unlikely, if even possible, traveling in opposing directions. The narrow right-of-way lane was just wide enough to accommodate the width of the dozer.

Paul Brouse, who drove the lowboy to haul the bulldozer, said they finished the work and departed from the lane at 12:30 p.m. which would have been about four hours before the killer would have driven up that lane, according to the timeline offered by the Commonwealth for murdering and disposing of the body.

Later attempts to verify this job through Atlantic Richfield revealed no work orders on the dike of their compound during the entire month of

October. The last work of that nature had been done the previous summer after major flooding of the nearby West Branch of the Susquehanna River wrought by Hurricane Agnes in June 1972.

What to make of this, other than adding others to a conspiracy or a growing string of coincidences? Maybe the police got a huge break in their investigation on a seldom used pathway (other than a private place for adolescents necking after dark) on the very day of the alleged crime.

Boot Print Makes Big Impression on Jury...

The boot print found beneath the girl's mud-caked buttocks was the one convincing piece of physical evidence noted by jury members in published comments after their verdict. They wouldn't have known about the discrepancies of the tire prints cast at the time, but they were certainly impressed by one piece of evidence under the body of the murder victim that had to belong to the killer. The problem was that on the same day that Kim's car was taken into custody and impounded, Sgt. Edward Peterson, one of the state police criminal investigators, took possession of the boots at the Hubbard home.

"We asked him if he would voluntarily allow us to make an examination of the boots... and voluntarily make an examination of his vehicle," Peterson testified. Kim brought the boots down from his room. He was not read his rights, Peterson confirmed, because they were "voluntarily surrendered" and "he was not a suspect at the time." By legal definition a suspect is "under suspicion" or "under investigation" for a crime. There was never any known or identified suspect in transcript or case records other than Kim (and, briefly, Joe) after the alleged discovery of the body on October 28th. For a "Miranda warning" to be required by law, the individual voluntarily surrendering potential evidence must be a "prime suspect." When did they reach that point? The state police get to tell us that, but it was clearly an issue with Judge Raup, who observed at the evidentiary hearing a year after the trial that "this is illegal search and seizure."

We know that there was cast making taking place with the car in the borough garage on October 31, the same day the boots were taken into custody. Cpl. Donald Houser, custodian of the evidence who received the boots from Peterson, transported them to the PSP Crime Lab, but added that "I can't give you an exact date at this time" when asked when he took the boots there. Chain-of-custody, which has been so critical in more recent highly publicized murder trials, was clearly an issue throughout the process of gathering the evidence.

Kim and his mother had been puzzled about why the state police were so interested in his boots when he was wearing sneakers that day. They even joked about it before it was clear that Kim was indeed the prime suspect. Dorisann mentioned when questioned by Fierro on the witness stand that Kim was wearing his sneakers that afternoon, which he removed to buff the floor in his socks. He was doing this when he answered the phone call from Jack Hill the afternoon of his daughter's disappearance.

There was a sneaker print on one of the casts that matched one of the sneakers Jennifer was wearing. Had she stood on that farm lane before she was laid to eternal rest in the field? Very curious indeed.

William E. Nixon, an Emergency Room Technician at Williamsport Hospital when her body was transferred there from the field on the evening of October 28, was instructed to go to the morgue and assist in moving the girl's body from an autopsy table to a litter which, in turn, was placed in "the cooler." It was the remarkable condition of the body, which he described as "very hard, quite firm and not decomposed," that grabbed his interest and whetted his suspicions about the sanctity of the evidence.

It was a conversation he had with Dr. Earl Miller, the Lycoming County Coroner and senior member of the medical staff, that occurred weeks after the murder trial that convinced him that something had not been kosher in the testimony about the body in the field. Miller had provided much of the key testimony at the body scene, which went well beyond medical issues and included location of the body and prints and casts made. Nixon and the coroner were in the emergency room one night when Nixon engaged Dr. Miller in a conversation about the case, as described:

"I inquired as to the procedure by which the body of Jennifer Hill was first moved from the site where discovered. Dr. Miller informed me that several Pennsylvania State Troopers lifted the body and when queried why several were used to lift the girl's body, Dr. Miller indicated that (it was) to ensure that the footprint underneath the buttocks would not be disturbed or damaged."

Nixon said he asked how they knew there was a footprint underneath the buttocks, described as "caked with mud" when they moved the body from where she lay that rainy evening. The question seemed to upset Dr. Miller quite a bit, Nixon recalled, and, without uttering another word, the coroner gathered up some papers he had been working on and walked away.

Tire Treads and Footprints and Casts, Oh My...

On the evening of October 31, 1973, Jim Merrick got a call at his home from South Williamsport Police Chief Charles Smith requesting his presence at the borough hall to unlock the tools for which Merrick, a borough employee, had a key. After doing so, he jacked up the car, removed the rear tires and the right front tire from Kim Hubbard's 1967 Oldsmobile, which had been impounded as evidence earlier that day. He then took a tire out of the trunk and installed it on the right front in the presence of Chief Smith and several state policemen, including Cpl. Donald Houser, Property Officer and Custodian of the Evidence, as he later attested.

There was no mention of the left front tire at the time, which was the only tire with deep treads and later determined to be installed by Robert Faust at Poole's Sunoco at 9:00 a.m. on October 29.

Paul Stiner, another borough employee, stated by sworn affidavit in 1975, that he was in the borough garage the day after Merrick removed the tires and observed tire tracks across the garage floor that were "white and faded." He also observed tracks to and/or from one corner of the garage where "it appeared molds had been made."

Several years later, Reporter Brad English, who co-authored an investigative series on the case in the 1980 *Weekender*, said that Captain

Francis Ross, second in command for the South Williamsport Police Department, stated the following in an interview about the case: "… he knew of at least one tire cast being made" at the borough hall and that it had been made "for comparison." He apparently did not comment on why they would need to do that when all tires were allegedly taken to the Pennsylvania State Police Crime Lab in Harrisburg for examination the day after being removed from the car.

Trial testimony by the criminal investigators who made, handled, and examined tire and foot casts tell us that Trooper Joseph Keppick made the casts at the field and turned them over to Cpl. Houser. Cpl. Houser then transported the casts to the Harrisburg Crime Lab about 90 miles away on October 29. However, Leon Krebs, a Pennsylvania State Trooper who examined the casts there, said he received two tire casts on November 1 and two more on November 5.

It was in questioning Krebs, a tool mark specialist in the crime lab who compared casts with tires, that Patrick Fierro came close to revealing the most perplexing mystery about what became known as "the convicting tire." Pointing out that casts of the tires were made at the field on the 28th and 29th of October, according to testimony, Fierro asked Krebs if he could explain how that left front tire, "which was changed (installed on the defendant's car) on October 29th, could make the impression that you got from the state police that was supposed to have been made, let's say between October 19th and October 28th?"

The answer by Krebs would be the only time during the trial that this was brought up, and it wasn't responsive to Fierro's question: "I can't say that it did. I just said it could have."

Ertel objected to the question because, "I don't follow it."

"He answered," said Judge Greevy. "Apparently he knew it."

The question and answer are allowed to stand, and that's when Fierro meekly bows out: "I have no further questions."

Fierro came very close to unleashing some doubts among the jurors about how physical evidence was attained at the body scene, but the subject was never brought up again. It strikes me that Krebs, whose only involvement came after he received this evidence, may have learned something on the witness stand that he didn't know before.

Fierro, contrarily, smelled a rat but allowed it to scurry away.

Now all of this might seem, all these years later, as fodder for a murder mystery that we can't quite construct into a clear picture with our mosaic pieces. But if Kim Hubbard didn't do it, somebody got away with the murder of a twelve-year-old girl. Does that mean a killer continued to be on the prowl in the years or decades after the 1973 murder? The evidence still indicates that it was an "I'm sorry kind of murder," and not the work of a crazed sexual predator as depicted in the Commonwealth vs. Kim Lee Hubbard.

If the killer has any conscience at all, as I suspect he or she does, the only people who paid the price for the crime, the Hubbard family, must be content with getting their part of the story out and being able to move on all these years later. In a way, all of them but Joe Hubbard did. Exoneration through the criminal justice system is still important to Kim Hubbard as an homage to his father. It was because of him that Kim was able to live and thrive in the community to which he returned after serving out his sentence.

CHAPTER 22: TIMELINES

Remember This and Things Will Turn Out OK!

If there is one glaring omission in the Jennifer Hill murder case, it is the obvious lack of suspects and persons of interest, other than Kim or Joe Hubbard, from the day her body was found. It made sense, up to a point, that attention was paid to the Hubbards, with Dorisann and Ruthie erroneously described as the last to see her the day she was declared missing. It was almost too much attention after they learned others had seen Jennifer during her walk toward home with times that corroborated Dorisann Hubbard's clock-verified recall. The curiosity exhibited by the town mayor and chief of police about what she ate and whether she had a bowel movement before heading home seems, in retrospect, somewhat incongruous for a missing person case.

I do not want to do to the Hills what was done to the Hubbards by the DA and state police in their myopic murder investigation, but there never seemed to be suspects other than those who lived in the home from which Jennifer departed to her death. The police procedure over the span during which Jennifer was a missing person was based on her never arriving home after being summoned by her mother. That means the impetus should have been on finding where the girl may have gone, which included the possibility of her being a runaway and, beyond that, a victim of abuse, abduction or, ultimately, homicide.

At first, it made no sense to continue nosing around the place at which she allegedly failed to arrive. There comes a point when foul play must be considered, but, again, the police said they were looking for someone who may have intercepted her. A news item noted they were looking for known sex offenders not long before her body was officially discovered. The first thing you might expect to be done once it becomes a homicide would be to take a closer look at her intended destination and clear family members closest to her as suspects. That's just a matter of procedure, especially when the victim is seen so close to home about forty-five minutes before "all hell broke loose" as Milton rhapsodized in *Paradise Lost*.

After the body was officially found and police had retooled their investigation to find a killer (for the record anyway), ten days had elapsed and physical evidence at any potential crime scene should have been cleansed or removed from wherever the crime scene may have been.

We do know that Kim Hubbard never bothered to clean the interior of his car for weeks as of October 31st when it was impounded. If that was a crime scene or Jennifer had been a passenger, he would have had plenty of time to clean out any evidence. It was an opportunity he never took, but he apparently didn't need to. There was nothing in that car linking it to Jennifer Hill, which included dirt, discarded trash, and even partial fingernails from previous passengers. It takes some time for multiple partial fingernails to accumulate in a vehicle. Then again, Kim was something of a taxi service for schoolmates and other friends. *(Note: Ken Mains mistakenly linked one of fragmented nails to Jennifer Hill in proclaiming Kim Hubbard's guilt.)*

There has never been any admission, evidence, or testimony that any other potential crime scene was considered, other than any related to the Hubbards, in what is a procedural phase-one step for most murder probes. It's not a fun thing for a criminal investigator to do, asking tough questions and searching the premises of family members who, at this juncture, are perceived publicly as victims. If Mrs. Nevel did see Jennifer get into a car in front of her house on Howard Street at 4:30 p.m., it would seem logical that she couldn't have made it home. That is presuming the ride was to get away from home for some clandestine reason, which seems unlikely for a twelve-year-old girl who had heretofore shown no interest in boys other than as playmates at kickball and similar activity as was the case earlier that Friday afternoon. The days-long delay before alerting police came after Nevel knew Jennifer was missing, the object of extensive searching, and not until after the body was found on Sunday, October 28th. Her decision to report seeing Jennifer, she said, was before she knew Jennifer had been murdered. Mrs. Nevel cited a familiar reason for her hesitancy. She didn't want to get involved and especially having to testify in a trial, as she explained when cross-examined by Fierro. Then again, why would she be thinking about having to testify at a trial if she just had information about the possible sighting of a missing person?

The reliance on hypnosis and the white helmet on the back window ledge with very little detail about the car or who may have been the driver doesn't automatically eliminate other potential suspects. The half hour Jennifer was not seen between Mendez and Nevel—a span that would require her to do an about-face from that corner where she was seen standing and walk several blocks in another direction—seems important. If she were intent on not being seen, why was she so prominent to Mrs. Nevel, standing in front of her door and apparently looking over Halloween decorations? There is too much to question for her to be portrayed as the eyewitness who not only saw Jennifer's rendezvous with her killer but, at the same time, removing all other suspects.

Murderers are typically male adults who are family members of the victims, specifically spouses, consorts, and siblings. For too many years, too many murdered children under the age of thirteen have been killed by a family member, according to the US Department of Justice. In fact, most homicides of young children are committed by family members "through beatings or suffocation."

This sad statistic may not have been as commonly known in 1973 as it was in 1993 or 2013. It may be a common oversight by municipal police departments even today, but the Pennsylvania State Police should know better. Is there any reason, other than sympathy, that police seemingly chose to ignore members of the Hill family, their home or even their car? Nothing stands out, other than animosity toward Kim Hubbard or the allure of prosecuting a premeditated murderer/rapist over a case of domestic violence that went too far. I do know the Hills never stepped forward in protest when news media coverage suggested investigators should have paid more attention to Jennifer arriving home after an unlucky thirteen-block that day.

Kim Hubbard's motive for killing Jennifer Hill was proclaimed before, during, and after the trial as a sex-fueled attack that took place in a prearranged liaison between the two of them. The evidence fell far short of sexual assault or intent thereof, but it was legitimized by the forensic pathologist who conducted the autopsy who stated there was no evidence of sexual molestation. Dr. Robert L. Catherman did the prosecution a favor in the following testimony:

> There was no indication of that (sexual molestation). My findings, however, do not exclude some kind, whatever that might be, of sexual molestation. I just didn't find any injury.

Whatever that might be? It might be a way to keep that motive in play. This is the same man of science who said that, despite temperatures and weather conditions to the contrary, the girl's body could have been naturally refrigerated because there may have been "cooling breezes" in that field. This was a fresh body remarkably undisturbed by animal and insects over nine days of exposure to temperatures and minimal winds incapable of refrigerating a human body.

Kim's motive to commit the crime was shaky, but opportunity wasn't much better. The opportunity for Kim Hubbard to commit the crime failed to present itself in the timeline of what he did on October 19, 1973:

> 1:30 p.m.—Paid an insurance premium
>
> 3:35 – 3:40—paid a traffic fine at District Magistrate's office
>
> 3:20-3:30—witness sees him at Hum-Dinger
>
> 3:40-3:45—talks to James Barr who was just getting off work at Barr Hardware
>
> Shortly before 4—Kim leaves after talking with Bill Barr (James's brother)
>
> 4:15—Stopped for a conversation with Ard Stetts on Bayard Street (from their vehicles) near the Hum-Dinger (an estimate).

The above timeline was entered into evidence by Allen Ertel based on the testimony of Commonwealth witnesses like District Judge Ronald Blackburn, who in his testimony estimated the time Kim paid his fine as between 3:30 and 3:50 p.m. It seems Ertel fudged that item in his timeline submitted as evidence. At the same time, any variance in Kim's remembrances of what he did on October 19th was perceived as devious.

"The State said he made some inconsistent statements," Fierro declared in his closing to the jury. "About what? About where he was at a certain time? Whether he paid this bill first or that bill second?"

That Friday, a day off from school for students, started for Kim, by the way, when he arose at 1:00 p.m. after attending school the previous day followed by working the night shift at Stroehmann's.

Sgt. Peterson testified that Kim relayed the following schedule to him when he interviewed the alleged suspect at the Hubbards' home on October 31. He was asked to remember spontaneously what he did twelve days before, and this was the estimated timeline Peterson said Kim provided him:

> Got up at 1 p.m… Went to the store to buy cigarettes and returned home… His mother wanted him to wax and buff the floor so he went to Rent-All Service to rent a buffer… Stopped at Hum-Dinger, got a drink and talked to friends… Came home, but floor was still wet so he went out to work on his car… Came back in. Floor still wet. Went to Fifth Avenue Car Wash and washed his car… Took an estimated total of twenty-five minutes until he got back… Stopped again at Hum-Dinger, talked to Ard Stetts about getting together later… Received the call at 4:45–4:50 from Jack Hill who wanted to know if Jennifer had left. He asked his mother and she said Jennifer left about an hour before… Later his mom asked him to drive around and see if he could find her. It was after 5:00 p.m. and she was concerned it would be getting dark soon… He drove to various places, including Humpty Dumpty, a popular local sub shop, the Hum-Dinger and a playground. Nothing.

He returned home. (He admitted he wasn't looking that hard but just driving around because he believed she had just run off and would show up at her home eventually.)

The bottom line is that Kim's guestimates of what he did twelve days before and the official timeline Ertel had entered into evidence based on witness testimony were not incriminating. They did jump on him for washing his car, supposedly to remove evidence of the car being in that field. They were at most, as Fierro suggested, "inconsistent statements." Kim remembered the places he had been that afternoon, but not necessarily the times. He remembered activities in the Peterson interview that Ertel didn't include in his timeline entered as evidence as well as two—paying the traffic fine and insurance premium—that Kim forgot about but Ertel included.

Nothing pivotal in all of this to show opportunity. That's why it was important for Ertel to destroy the credibility of Kim and his girlfriend, Colleen. He was able to deploy that strategy in another timeline meant to be a personal correspondence between them.

It was an intercepted letter to Colleen, that was written at the urging of Fierro, delivered by Kim's mother and then given to a friend of Colleen's for safekeeping. Not to escape police attention but that of her parents.

"Hi Colleen. These are the things you should know and if I am wrong about anything write and tell about it because we got to know it. 1. You called me at 4:30… Why because you looked at the clock and you was closing early that day. 2. You called me at 7:00. Why because you looked at the clock and you were not ready to come down yet. 3. You come to my house at 7:20 (or) 7:25. Why, because you look at the clock when you got to my house. 4. You stayed at my house and were with me until about 12:45. That's when you went home and I follow you home and when you got home and when home you called me about 1:05 to see if I got home OK. Remember, remember, remember that while you were at my house, we went parking two times 1. By

the railroad tracks 2. Up on the mountain. After we went parking the first time, we stop at the Hum-Dinger and I talked to Ard S. and then we got two Cokes and we went home. 8. Remember that we saw a movie before you got home that night.

Remember this and things will turn out OK. Colleen, you know, I mean I hope you know that I didn't kill anyone. I hope you believe me because I will kill myself before I go to jail for something I didn't even do. Love you always, Kim.

P.S. Here is one of your cassette tapes, so talk to me. I love you. Thank you for everything.

The letter was kept by Susan Shellman, a friend of Colleen's, and brought to the attention of police by her mother, Doris Shellman, who discovered it in a drawer. A handwriting expert testified that it was Kim's handwriting, which was never disputed. It was the result of Fierro urging his client, at the time an inmate in the county jail during the span of two-and-a-half months between arrest and trial, that his case hinged on Colleen and Kim being on the same page about what they did that critical day.

There was nothing there to brand him a liar. It became known as the "Remember Letter" and was characterized as coaching her to lie. It was all about everything they did together that day, including phone conversations. Times were critical, Kim was told. Everything in the Remember Letter took place AFTER Jennifer was allegedly seen by Nevel. The only item of consequence in that timeline was a phone call he said she made to him at 4:30, which would have put him home at the time the alleged crime was unfolding.

Colleen, to her credit, could not state the exact time of that call, and testified that it was "late afternoon" and that she made it from her father's retail store, Clearfield TV. She added that Kim called her later, at about 6:00 p.m. after she was done working at the store. She said she arrived at Kim's house that evening at about "quarter after seven." So, there were discrepancies between the two timelines, but none of those times, except the first call she made to Kim, had any potential links to the crime. And so it went through the evening together.

Kim later recalled sitting in the jail trying to remember what he and Colleen did that evening and at what times. It was weeks after that first interview with Peterson, Ertel and Hynick, and the memories of that day were even dimmer by then. He felt hapless and powerless as he struggled to come up with the times that Fierro said were so critical. He was pretty sure of the 4:30 call and used that time on which to base everything else. In the second call in the evening, he remembered her calling him and she, in her testimony, remembered him calling her. Their time estimates for that call were an hour apart. The times for the rest of the evening and into the early-morning hours fell more into place.

He came to realize his take-charge tone in that letter may have been a mistake, but he felt it was a way to regain control of his own destiny—something he had been unable to do since Jennifer went missing.

It all fell apart when Colleen's father, who played the most dramatic role in the trial by standing up and calling his daughter a liar when she was on the stand, buried her credibility for good during his stint on the witness stand. Kenneth Whitenight testified that he had returned to the store "sometime before four o'clock" and was there until "twenty minutes of five." He said he was certain his daughter never placed a call during the time he was there. Under cross-examination he said he may have talked to a customer but believed it wasn't between 4:00 p.m. and 4:40 when he might have been distracted from whatever Colleen was doing.

> Note from trial transcripts: Ertel, as always prone to exaggeration, in explaining to the judge what Whitenight was going to testify to before he took the stand, said he would rebut Kim's estimate of Colleen's call at 4:30 or 4:35. He then said the girl's father would say "he stayed there until 5:20" and that his daughter called nobody up to that time. In actuality, Mr. Whitenight would testify he was there until "20 of five" or 4:40. That seems a bit close to Kim's estimated time and lends credence to Colleen's contention that she made the call when her father was not there to be an effective rebuttal. Even Fierro never picked up on that forty-minute discrepancy in his cross-examination. The judge didn't. Did the jury?

For Colleen, it had to an ordeal getting through the trial. She was grilled by both Ertel and Fierro—the former to discredit her and the latter who saw her as a witness who could somehow turn the jury in their favor. Instead, she was pressed by Ertel to admit she and Kim had been sexually intimate. And subsequently her father stood up and called her a liar during her testimony—the impact of which may have done more to turn the jury against Kim than any of the Commonwealth's so-called evidence. That was 1970s mainstream American morality. An act that should have resulted in a mistrial turned out instead to be a gift for the prosecution—a gift that Fierro rejected, explaining in a later response to an appeal that he felt Kim's chances of being declared not guilty would be even slimmer in another trial. Little did he know all that would surface in the months after that trial, other than the hypnotized witness he failed to reveal. Had Fierro not left that letter about the Nevel hypnotism in the case file, it, too, may have remained unknown.

It had been a living nightmare from the start of the investigation for Colleen. It would have been easier for her to take flight from the drama instead of fight.

"Well, my parents didn't know I was seeing Kim up until then, and I knew they had to find out," she recalled in testimony. "And I was really upset at the time because the police were sitting there and my parents were sitting there...."

She was scared and still fearful of her parents learning the extent of her relationship with Kim. She admitted being disingenuous then and guessing at when she had called Kim that day. She wasn't really sure of that time, as it turned out, and could only testify under oath that it was "late afternoon."

She and Kim parted on good terms not long after his 1974 conviction, and Kim remains appreciative that she put her reputation and relationship with her family on the line to testify on his behalf.

Ertel ransacked the credibility of the two witnesses—Dorisann Hubbard and Colleen Whitenight—who had to be believed if Kim Hubbard was to be acquitted. In the end it wasn't about motive or opportunity. Ironically, Kim was even discredited for being truthful about lying. He conceded under oath that he chose not to mention a previous employer on a job application because he had walked off that job. When pressed by the prosecutor to explain, he was surprisingly candid. "I lied. I needed a job."

Ertel struck gold by dismissing just about everyone who testified on Kim's behalf as liars. And he made sure, in his closing summation to jury, to take that strategy as far as he could take it:

The defendant said, "I lied to get a job." He said that sort of proud. Would he lie if he murdered? Certainly.

Would Ertel or any of his witnesses lie for a murder conviction? Let's just say the evidence indicates that some went far beyond inconsistent statements to plug the leaks that could have sunk their case.

CHAPTER 23: CHARLIE KING

Death Claims "One Who Persisted"

Charlie King died in his sleep in a rented room where he had been living a solitary existence in Naples, New York. It was so solitary he may have been dead for days, sick and indisposed for weeks, before anyone noticed. It was only a few days before Thanksgiving in 2021, on November 22, when his body was discovered. The exact date and time that he may have breathed his last breath were not clear. There had been no autopsy. No police interest. There was no sign of foul play. Just another old guy, a loner who died in his bed that day, perhaps the day before or even the day before that.

There was no confirmation as to the extent of decomposition. Charlie, who would become something of an expert on decomposition after death, was no murder victim and his time of death would be of concern to few. Sadly, anyone who knew him in the past and had seen him in recent years would probably not have recognized him.

"I met up with him not that long ago, and he pulled up in this piece-of-shit car and the strangest haircut I've ever seen. I couldn't take my eyes off the haircut," Kim Hubbard recalled, noting that the car was crammed with all kinds of stuff as if Charlie had been living in his car. "He acted and talked like Charlie, but he definitely didn't look like him."

Kim could see that the car his old friend was driving was not going to last much longer and he offered him $5,000 in cash to buy another car. He could see Charlie was barely scraping by financially. Although he had been into fishing, trapping, and hunting years back, it didn't look to him that Charlie was fit enough for such activities anymore. Charlie wouldn't take the money he tried to hand him, but Kim wasn't about to leave him like that. He grudgingly agreed to accept $2,000, and Kim could see the relief in his emaciated face after he handed him the money.

It was around 1979 when Charlie moved to Naples to a home owned by his father. After his father died, he lived there alone until a recent fire, apparently of electrical origin, destroyed the building and subsequently forced Charlie to rent modest accommodations in a downtown house that took in boarders.

As bad as Charlie looked the last time Kim saw him, he was more concerned about his financial situation than his health. Charlie had apparently been sick, very sick, for some time, but he never reached out to anyone. What they reportedly found in the room, aside from Charlie's decaying body, was evidence that he hadn't had the strength or reasoning in his final hours to escape even a few feet from his bed. A nearby bathroom must have seemed an impossible journey. Feces was reportedly pervasive in and around the bed in what must have been a horrible ending for him as he lost first his will to live and then his life to a stomach infection that must have developed into sepsis and its inevitable outcome, septic shock. His body, in that event, would have attacked its own tissues and thwarted blood flow to internal organs, including the brain, causing blood pressure to plummet. It is likely he was incapable of thinking or reasoning in the hours before he eventually lost consciousness. His cell phone, his sole contact with the outside world throughout what must have been nightmarish final days was nearby, but he was either unable, unwilling, or resigned to his fate and chose to tough it out. Septic shock is certain death without medical attention. Forty percent under medical care don't make it, so going it alone is a fatal decision if the depleted, deluded mind is even capable of decisions at that stage.

Kim was one of Charlie's few contacts to the outside world, and his murder case, even after Kim did his time, had dominated Charlie's life for years. It was an injustice he took personally, not only because of what they did to Kim but because the real killer got away with murder. Worse yet, that killer had stood by and let Jennifer's death destroy the lives of a family he came to regard as closer than his own.

When Kim returned to South Williamsport to resume his life, he wasn't all that interested in reliving what happened with either his father or Charlie. The pursuit of a new trial had long since run its course. Exoneration was still an option, but who would care now that he had served his time? Kim had expectantly waited in prisons all those years hoping to get out and go to trial with an abundance of newly discovered evidence. Now he was out, and he realized that the publicity his case had generated had given him something not available to most convicted felons—acceptance in his community. That would become even more important when he married and, within a year after that, became a father.

Charlie, a quiet presence in Kim's life in October 1973, was not the only friend who stood by him after his arrest—not at first anyway—but he was the one to whom Dorisann Hubbard turned to stay with Kim on the evening of October 31. Charlie was about three years older than Kim. He was also the one who, due to his proximity to the Hubbards during those emotional few weeks, would commit himself to joining Joe Hubbard in proving the innocence of his son. On October 31, Joe had been hospitalized for a "nervous breakdown," a common term back then for what is generically a loss of emotional control, a crisis in dealing with excessive or abnormal stress, and wife, Dorisann, needed to be with him. That stress had been fueled by a convergence of cops on him and his family and then impounding Kim's car among accusations that either the father or the son was the likely murderer. The father had a solid alibi. The son didn't, in the eyes of the police.

Charlie King was with Kim at the Hubbard house for much of that evening, mostly dealing with trick-or-treaters on Halloween night in South Williamsport. Meanwhile, Kim was pacing around the house trying to understand what was going on and repeatedly wondering aloud, "Why are they messing with me?" The real purpose for Charlie being there were threatening phone calls directed at Kim and his mother's concern that someone might try to follow up on one of those threats. She had already dealt with belligerent accusations of murder the previous week prior to Jennifer Hill's status being changed from missing person to murder victim. Three days before that, men had appeared at the house accusing Kim of a murder before the body was found. Threats, accusations, and the realization that people were already being told that Kim had killed Jennifer contributed to Joe's breakdown. It was all catching up with Kim who, only days before, had expected all the attention to go away soon.

"I think it was dawning on Kim as his father was now in the hospital, his mother was upset over Jennifer's death, that he was becoming a suspect and he was frightened of the potential," Charlie recalled in a 1980 interview.

It was seeing Kim at his most vulnerable on that Halloween night which first convinced Charlie that his friend had nothing to do with what happened to Jennifer Hill. Everything discovered since only cemented his belief in Kim's innocence and realization that he had been framed with manufactured and manipulated evidence.

"I don't think Kim ever mentioned Jennifer Hill," Charlie recalled of that night. "He just had this bad feeling these guys were more interested in getting him than finding the real killer."

"I Had to Go and Check on Charlie"

Kim was driving into Naples to touch base with Charlie on Monday, November 22, 2021. He'd been trying to contact him over the weekend and sensed something was wrong, because Charlie always returned his calls. It's not like he had anywhere to go or the money to spend to do much, including putting gas in a car that might not make it far if he could. Charlie was back into the case. He knew more about it than anyone else. Kim included. The only person who knew more was his father, and he'd been dead for going on thirty-two years.

Kim kept thinking about when he last saw Charlie, and with him not answering or returning his calls, he knew he should make the trip if only to ease his mind.

"I told Suzy I had to go and check on Charlie. I took a thousand dollars with me and headed to Naples."

It was more than a two-hour drive straight north from South Williamsport. Kim was just a few minutes from Charlie's home when his cell phone rang. It was Charlie's sister, Kathy, who knew Kim was one of the few people who cared, informing him that her brother had died. Neither of two sisters, the youngest of the siblings being Margaret, had seen much of Charlie in the previous twenty-five years, although Kathy would talk to him via phone on occasion. Kim would hear from his old friend quite often, and it was usually about the case. Charlie had also been in regular contact with Angela Laskodi, a writer intrigued by true crime cases in which people have been unfairly convicted. She had become engrossed in what she regarded as the framing of Kim for Jennifer Hill's murder.

Charlie had never been committed to much in his life, but he seemed to have a firm belief that he was put on this earth to right this wrong. Angela shared Charlie's fascination with how they must have conspired to convict Kim. Proof was in photos and trial testimony in the conflicting evidence gathered at the cornfield where the remarkably preserved body of Jennifer Hill was conveniently discovered a matter of minutes before a week of searching for her was to be called off.

As for Charlie, apparently, the funeral director who took possession of his body was able to locate one of his sisters from whatever records Charlie had in his possession. Charlie had moved to Naples from South Williamsport several years after Kim was deposited for future withdrawal in the Pennsylvania Corrections system. He was seventy-one years of age, and he was not prepared for the prospect of his own death.

The call went out on December 4 by his youngest sister, Margaret "Maggie" Powell, for GoFundMe contributions. Maggie informed her sister, Kathy Delisle, in Oklahoma of Charlie's death, and Kathy, in turn, contacted Kim. Maggie and Kathy combined their fund appeals, with Kathy raising $3,000 for funeral expenses and Maggie for lawyer fees and property taxes, which indicates Charlie may still have had debts from the family property he had to vacate.

"His death was more than a shock to us," Kathy, the youngest of the three siblings reported. "He lived his life more as a recluse in which little was known about how he lived."

"He never shared that he was sick, and his passing is a shock," Maggie reported. "Although I wasn't aware of his burial wishes, we believe he would want to be cremated and buried beside our father."

Charlie grew up on the mountainside near the southern border of South Williamsport Borough, home of the high school Mountaineers, and had gone to school with Kim. As a child, his sister, Margaret, younger by six years, remembers watching the nearby Little League World Series with her big brother in the late sixties and early seventies. Watching the television coverage of series games in the summer of 2021, she recalled after his death that "they showed the surrounding hills and it reminded me when I would lie on Charlie's back as we slid on a long wooden toboggan down the snowy hill." She was six and he twelve at the time.

Kim was in mourning and in disbelief that Charlie chose to die without a fight. He wasn't that much younger than Charlie, but he worked out regularly and had the physique of someone half his age. "The only thing that gives away my age is my face," he said in an effort at comic relief while sharing the sad news. "Put a bag over my head and you'd never guess I'm sixty-eight." He was also angry that Charlie would not let him know. Not let anyone know. "That son of a bitch didn't have to die. He could have at least lived so we could get the story out. Dad didn't make it. Now Charlie! The next in line is me, and I'm not gonna go down easy."

Death had been pervasive in Kim's life, starting with a younger brother and, after that, Jennifer Hill. His father's death had not been unexpected, and, in a sense, it was a blessing because of the suffering he was going through. His mother lived a full life, including the joys of being with her children and grandchildren over the span of more than two decades. The death of Charlie hit Kim hard, not just because of what he had done for him, but because of the bond formed between them.

When Kim belatedly committed himself to exoneration, starting the website about his case and sharing information with the Pennsylvania Innocence Project out of Duquesne University, he also drew the attention of Angela Laskodi. Angela was fascinated by the case, and it wasn't long before she and Charlie bonded. Charlie had long discussions with Angela who was, at last report, looking into the case with the intention of publishing a book. Angela and Charlie got into the minutia of the evidence used against Kim and particularly the discrepancies at the body scene. Charlie turned many of the documents and photos he had of the case over to Angela.

Angela was particularly infuriated by Kenneth Mains in what she regarded as his biased investigation of the case on behalf of the Office of the Lycoming County District Attorney more than four decades after its conviction of Kim Hubbard. Mains, who bills himself as a cold case detective and "true crime legend," seemed to be offended by Kim's contention that state police tampered with evidence and apparently felt compelled to stymie Kim's quest for exoneration. He made sure to tell a spokesperson for the Pennsylvania Innocence Project that he had found touch DNA evidence on the clothing of Jennifer Hill that showed it had been handled by Kim. Shortly after that, Kim was informed by a professor and coordinator of the Innocence Project that they were no longer pursuing his exoneration.

The clout of Mains stems from his founding of the nonprofit American Investigative Society of Cold Cases which gives him standing among forensic scientists like Henry Lee, defense attorneys, forensic pathologists like Cyril Wecht and true crime television stars like Lt. Joe Kenda. It was quite a climb in prestige for a former municipal cop and county detective, although Mains no longer has a high profile on the organization's website where he is only mentioned as a 2019 attendee of the organization's annual conference.

Charlie's Knowledge Was Invaluable

Charlie King was possessed—make that obsessed—with the case up to his death. It may have been his only continuous interest in the outside world since his role in a 1980 investigative series on the case published over the span of two months in the now defunct *Weekender* newspaper.

He was not one to seek attention, but his knowledge was invaluable. He was an intelligent and talented man, but it wasn't important to him that others knew that. He was proud of his Native American bloodline and painted impressive portraits of Native Americans when young. He was gifted but content not to be categorized in any way. He was a trapper, a hunter with both bows and rifles and an avid fisherman along Naples Creek over the years. These were all things whose solitude brought him solace, and his exposure to American justice that led to the trial and conviction of Kim Hubbard did little to reinforce his trust in a system that, as he saw it, could be abused so readily by the very people who were there for our protection.

He had handled those tires in the evidence room at the state police barracks after the trial and before the evidentiary hearing when everything changed. There was no way that there could be a cast of any tire with deep treads being cast in that field on the evening Jennifer's body was found—even if it was not regarded as "a convicting tire." Convicting tires are those with markings or flaws that directly compare to casts or prints at a crime scene. All four tires on the car when Jennifer was found were bald or balding—until the next day, that is, when a new, deep treaded tire replaced a flat on the right front. Tires that are supposed to be sent to tool mark experts for analysis at the state police crime lab, shouldn't be cast "for comparison" in the borough garage when they should be in as pristine condition as possible when examined by the real forensic experts. Different tires were transported to the lab in Harrisburg days apart, as revealed in trial testimony, allowing more time for comparison casting back in South Williamsport. Talk about broken chain-of-custody and probable contamination.

The shuffling of tires, casts, and photos of tires and casts continued through both the trial and evidentiary hearing to present newly discovered evidence. It even extended to where this evidence was kept through a string of appeals through the higher courts. It was hard enough for Joe and Charlie to sort out the transmigration of the tires and casts alone. Forget about the few footprints captured in the casts—one of which was a sneaker Jennifer was wearing that would indicate Jennifer herself was standing outside the car on the farm lane.

"It took us sixteen days to unravel this mess," Charlie stated in the *Weekender*'s weekly series on the case in the spring of 1980. "As I said earlier, the tires, the casts, and the photos were never together at the same time."

Some of these tires, notably Kelly-Springfields, were mass produced, making serial numbers irrelevant in terms of distinguishing one tire from another. Local distributors and garages were likely to have received dozens of tires with the same serial number. And so it went throughout March and April with an ongoing interview of Charles King in each issue as the heart of the evidence.

Charlie, labeled in the newspaper as "One Who Persisted," became the font of information in that series, which debuted on March 7, 1980. His analytical mind and keen memory sustained the investigative series for reporters Dwight Schmuck and Brad English who would conclude at the end of the series that "we have compiled what we believe to be enough evidence to warrant a new trial AND a full governor's investigation into the entire matter."

That governor at the time was Dick Thornburgh, who would be challenged in his re-election bid in 1982 by the Pennsylvania Democrats' chosen candidate in the spring Primary, Allen E. Ertel. Gov. Thornburgh never did respond to that request to investigate. Ertel, completing his second of three terms in the US Congress at the time, did respond in the April 25, 1980 *Weekender* to a request by Schmuck to answer several questions he had presented to one of Ertel's aides. He chose not to answer specific questions about the Commonwealth's case and evidence by noting that "I have not reviewed the transcript of that case recently." He added that he was not sure any of his trial notes "still exist."

Congressman Ertel did state that "my belief at the time I tried the case was that Kim Lee Hubbard brutally killed Jennifer Hill. It is still my opinion..." He then turned the tables on who was morally responsible at this point by suggesting that if the *Weekender* reporters had information contrary to his belief in Hubbard's guilt, "I suggest that you have a moral and ethical duty to immediately contact the District Attorney's Office of Lycoming County."

Publisher Dick Fenstermacher countered that the "moral and ethical duty" belonged to the prosecutors and that "if there is nothing to hide, let's have the questions answered once and for all." The publisher, in outlining the case, noted that some readers felt that the newspaper needed to go beyond proving Kim Hubbard's innocence by "finding the real killer of Jennifer Hill." Fenstermacher reminded them in what would be the last edition in the series covering the case that a newspaper did not have the responsibility of finding anyone innocent or guilty. Only a court of law can do that, and the press could only urge that justice prevail.

About 36 years later, an investigator employed by the county detective's office at the bidding of the Lycoming County DA did look into the case and then included his findings in a 2016 book, revealing some shoddy investigative techniques, obvious prejudice against Kim Hubbard, favoritism toward police and prosecutors, and convenient DNA technology that could not stand up to the fundamentals of preserving evidence and chain-of-custody. This was detailed in Chapters 17 and 18.

Even three years after my 1977 investigative series in the *Grit* newspaper, many of the key witnesses for the prosecution chose not to respond to the *Weekender*. Ertel offered his opinion of Kim Hubbard's guilt but chose not to answer specific questions about the case, but the list of the unresponsive included the Pennsylvania State Police; South Williamsport Police Chief Charles Smith, Mayor R. David Frey and Maintenance Manager James Merrick, who witnessed tire casting activity in the municipal garage; Carl Pfirman, who accused Kim of murdering Jennifer Hill, while she was still a missing person, perhaps a runaway, several days before her body was found; Jack and Norma Hill; Betty Jane Nevel, the Commonwealth's so-called eyewitness, and Robert Faust, owner of the service station that replaced Kim's tire, used as evidence his car was at the so-called body dump scene after the body was found.

> *Note: Mayor Frey worked with his brother in a family retail business (Frey's Tire Shop) and was a former Justice of the Peace, Lycoming County Democratic Chair, Committeeman*

and Jury Commissioner. The Navy veteran of World War II would have been fifty-eight years old when Jennifer Hill was murdered and lived to the venerable age of 102. Whatever his role in the investigation into the disappearance of Jennifer Hill prior to her body being officially discovered, there is no reason to believe his involvement was anything other than well intended. Chief Smith, however, continued to be involved in the murder probe through Kim's arrest and was the witness Ertel relied on at the trial to set up the key locations to support the perceived activity of their suspect on the day the Commonwealth believed the crime was committed.

It should be stated that both Merrick and Faust signed affidavits acknowledging their roles. My interview of Merrick ended with him confiscating a tape recorder I was holding in clear view and threatening to call police. (The recorder was returned with the interview erased.) I did get to interview several state policemen years after the *Grit* article. They included Steven Hynick and Joseph Keppick, as noted elsewhere, and a retired state trooper, requesting anonymity, who confirmed Kim Hubbard had passed a lie detector test he conducted. Hynick did accuse Ertel of being "politically motivated" in his handling of that case and others, including criminal prosecution of Hynick himself that resulted in his forced retirement from the state police. Keppick, one of several state police who sued former Public Defender Jack Felix for accusing them of manipulating evidence in the Hubbard case, preferred not to comment to any questions, other than he was not aware of evidence tampering.

Charlie King was able to put in plain words the improbability of Kim committing the crime, disposing of the body and being home on time to answer the phone call from Jennifer's father, Jack Hill, in twenty (based on Norma Hill's time of the call) or thirty minutes (based on Jack's). Here's how Charlie, in his inimitable way of breaking down the facts into reality instead of conjecture, laid out the Commonwealth's conception of how their designated killer committed the murder if you really follow the timelines introduced into evidence:

Now, Kim gets his Cosmo (meat and cheese sandwich) from the Humdinger. At this point, Jennifer has been missing for thirty minutes while Kim is still at the Humdinger.

Now, all of a sudden, Jennifer turns up in front of Mrs. Nevel's home on Howard Street which is not anywhere near her home, nor on their path of travel to her home.

Kim leaves the Humdinger, goes home and changes from his sneakers to his combat boots, goes back outside and gets into his car, drives down in front of Mrs. Nevel's house, and picks up Jennifer at 4:30pm. What Kim was doing on Howard Street makes about as much sense as what Jennifer would be doing on Howard Street.

Now, he drives Jennifer Hill all the way down to this cornfield in Sylvan Dell.

There must have been some conversation taking place. I mean, you're not strangling while you're driving. It takes sixty to ninety seconds for unconsciousness, up to four and a half to five minutes for biological death from strangulation, according to what doctors have told me.

Then, Kim takes off Jennifer's dark blue pants and puts on her light blue pants and puts the dark blue ones in the Glick shoe bag she was carrying. Then he changes jerseys, from short sleeve to long sleeve. Then he also, supposedly, sewed the dark blue pants on a sewing machine. He then removes Jennifer from his car, puts her in the cornfield, gets back in the car, drives home in time to answer the phone call from the father of the girl he just strangled.

And nobody saw him on either of these two trips, down to the Sylvan Dell and back, on a Friday when there was no school at 4:30 when people are on their way home from work. This includes Mrs. Nevel who never did identify Kim Hubbard or his car, according to the transcripts.

Charlie's insight was so compelling, along with his detective work with Joe Hubbard, that *The Weekender* was published for the sole purpose of airing discrepancies in that case with "One Who Persisted" featured in interviews over weekly issues throughout March and April 1980.

Despite the seriousness of the crime and his efforts to prove Kim's innocence, Charlie could see the humor even in the worst of times, as reflected in other published comments:

> *Thinking back, to October 31, 1973, Kim wanted to borrow some money. Well, he wanted to borrow three dollars. He wanted cab fare to go visit Colleen Whitenight. I only had a dollar and a half, and I gave it to him. He never paid me back and I hate a guy that leaves town owing me money.*

This was the day they impounded Kim's car. Kim didn't "leave town" by his own choice. Because just sixteen days after they impounded his car on October 31, 1973, he was arrested and jailed—first in the Lycoming County Jail and then at Pennsylvania state prisons at Rockview Correctional in Bellefonte and Chase Correctional a few miles outside of Wilkes-Barre. It would be a decade before he returned home, so interest alone on that dollar-and-a-half would have made repayment today more than nine dollars. Repayment for more than a decade of imprisonment would have been much higher than that, but, then again, it could have been worse. Kim may have assuaged the guilt of some who may have or had knowledge of hanky-panky by looking at a man who was able to do his time and make something of his life.

Charlie also got a kick out of a mayor and chief of police asking Ruthie and Dorisann about Jennifer's bowel movements within seventy-two hours after Jennifer was reported missing by suggesting searchers should have been alerted to "be on the lookout for a bowel movement." A little girl died at someone's hand and that is no joke, but there is no situation too serious for humor.

As was the case with Joe Hubbard, death had denied him from witnessing such an outcome.

Charlie King joins a growing retinue of people closely tied to the trial and conviction of Kim Hubbard and its aftermath who have passed on. His only presence in the digital world—the evidence of his existence, if you will, without even a funeral or "in memoriam" on some mortuary's website—will be his connection with the Hubbard case. His sisters' GoFundMe efforts to cover the costs of his parting are, in a sense, his final and tragic recognition.

The list of survivors is getting thin. Kim is among the younger of those on that list, and he is now well past traditional retirement age. Most of the people in their thirties and forties when Kim was tried for Jennifer Hill's murder, if still alive, would range from their late seventies at the youngest and well into their nineties today.

To those on both sides of this case—
and sometimes smack in the middle of it—
who I've confirmed are no longer with us as
the fiftieth anniversary approaches of the crime
that had a dramatic impact on many of their lives:

Joe and Dorisann Hubbard, Charlie King,
District Attorney Allen E. Ertel, Lt. Steven J. Hynick,
Trooper Joseph D. Keppick, Joseph A. Mendez, Norma J. Hill,
Betty Jane Nevel, Dennis "Denny" Day, Cpl. Ronald Barto,
Sgt. Edward B. Peterson, John Clabaugh, CAP Maj. Louis E. Hunsinger,
CAP Capt. Duane F. Gleckner, Dr. Earl R. Miller, Patrick Fierro,
Kenneth Whitenight, R. David Frey, Peggy Rechel, Cpl. Donald J. Houser,
H. Luther Dieffenbacher, Paul L. Kremser, Mary A. Mundrick, Clair Kiper,
Trooper Alfred R. Gomb, Judges Charles H. Greevy and Thomas C. Raup,
Magisterial District Judge Richard T. Eisenbeis
and several other Commonwealth and Defense witnesses and jurors.

EPILOGUE...

It would be a dismal reflection on society to say that when the guardians of its security are called to testify in court under oath, their testimony must be viewed with suspicion. This would be tantamount to saying that police officers are inherently untrustworthy. The cure for unreliable police officers is not to be found in such a shotgun approach. – **Chief Justice Warren Burger (June 23, 1969–Sept. 16, 1986)**

In trying to understand juries in criminal trials, as well as the judges who preside over them and any resultant appeals, we rely on some historical insight into how our courts regard the testimony of those we rely on to honestly and fairly gather evidence and testify accordingly. That privilege is routinely granted to police in courts of law around the country, whether it is a local police department, state police or a federal agency. Prosecutors work in tandem with these gatherers of evidence, often presented to the trial court as expert witnesses, to convict defendants accused of criminal misdemeanors and felonies.

The introductory observation from Judge Warren Burger, the Chief Justice of the Supreme Court when Kim Hubbard put his fate in the hands and heads of a judge and jury, may shed some light on the assumed credibility of police testimony at the time. The late Justice Burger held them in high esteem as "guardians of its (society's) security," and that calling alone seemingly guarantees their credibility unless shown otherwise. This was the prevailing judicial qualification on weighing the value of police and other criminal investigators testifying on behalf of the state then as it continues to be now.

Police may represent an institution, but they are not institutions onto themselves. That means, as with the rest of us, they are human and fallible and are subject to prejudices and vainglorious visions of their duties to the community they represent as finders of fact. They are therefore subject to dissection of that court-endowed credibility to ascertain the veracity of their testimony.

Judge Greevy never addressed this in his charge to the jury before sending them to deliberate Kim's fate. He did talk at length about expert witnesses who, unlike other witnesses, are allowed to offer opinions based on expertise and experience qualifying them as experts on the particular subject of their testimony, whether tire casts or the estimated time of death of a murder victim.

Expert testimony is not, in and of itself, the truth, and that makes it professional, not personal, for the defense to put that credibility to the test insofar as the court will allow. In high-profile trials, it often seems, expert witnesses take the stand for the prosecution and defense offering opposing opinions. Does that mean one of them is lying, possibly just mistaken, or do they simply cancel each other out?

Sometimes credibility and competency become intertwined in the presentation of evidence, and it is error, not intention, that leads to a falsehood or misconception. The courts have multiple opportunities to confirm guilt or resurrect innocence, starting with the trial and subsequent appeals. The news media empowered with free expression can sometimes do what the courts cannot through the structured accuser-versus-accused system and the attorneys who speak for them.

When evidence becomes complicated and "experts" seem to know what they're talking about, it is perhaps human nature to respect the expertise of the experts and accept their opinions as truth and evidence in and of itself. Before discharging jurors to deliberate, judges customarily caution them that the testimony of police officers should not be given more weight than that of other witnesses, other than presenters of facts sworn to tell the truth. Justice Burger's view of police as guardians who must be held in higher esteem because they are our protectors does not seem to agree with this brief advisory to jurors that seems to level police to the same playing field as others who testify against or on behalf of the defendant.

This issue has certainly been a concern for many a defense attorney and his or her clients. Jonathan M. Warren expounded on it in a 2018 treatise in the *DePaul Journal of Social Injustice* entitled: "Hidden in Plain View: Juries and the Implicit Credibility Given to Police Testimony." Warren, author and professor at the North Carolina School of Law, argues that our courts need to find a fairer way to instruct a jury on police testimony without prejudicing the jury against their sworn testimony above those of other witnesses. Without delving into his recommendations, we can certainly say that police credibility in criminal trials continues to be an issue of jurisprudence as we learn of an increasing number of people unfairly convicted of crimes due to tainted and violated evidence.

"Testilying," or testifying untruthfully, has become what the *New York Times* has called "a stubborn problem" in the criminal justice system as prosecutors, police and even judges participate in what is essentially systemic lying. You can call it bearing false witness or perjury, but it is usually rationalized as achieving justice and protecting the public by ensuring that the guilty don't go free. It may include lying under oath, evidence tampering or failing to reveal exculpatory evidence, and it is often a case of doing the wrong thing to perpetuate a vision of doing the right thing. Testilying may be seen as a way of circumventing the exclusionary rule, blowing a sure-fire conviction with illegally obtained evidence a.k.a. "fruit of the poisonous tree." The end justifies the means, in such cases, because the cops, the DA or both may believe they are protecting the citizenry from a dangerous felon being returned to society "on a technicality." The law itself is replete with technicalities, and they work for and against both sides.

Police or prosecutorial corruption by lying or falsifying evidence for personal gain—politically, financially or reputationally—is not condoned by the police or the public, most of whom would dismiss such cops as "dirty." There is another version of this that is more likely to include people in law enforcement who believe they are doing the right thing. It is known as "noble cause corruption," doing the wrong thing for the right reasons, or so they believe.

In the words of the Public Agency Training Council (PATC), which works with law enforcement and corrections, noble cause corruption makes the corrupt seem honorable:

> *In other words, law enforcement is engaged in a mission to make our streets and communities safe, and if that requires suspending the Constitution or violating laws ourselves in order to accomplish our mission, then for the greater good of society, so be it. The officers who adopt this philosophy lose their moral compass.*

Cops and private detectives were reputable, even heroic figures in the 1970s. It was the decade of police and crime dramas, with the following among the top-rated shows of that decade: *Kojak, Baretta, Police Woman, Starsky & Hutch, The Rookies, The Streets of San Francisco, Hawaii Five-0, The Mod Squad, S.W.A.T., Adam-12, The FBI, CHiPs,* and *Dragnet,* which made a brief comeback from its peak seasons starting on radio in the 1950s and continuing on television, most popularly from 1967 to 1970. There were almost as many popular shows in the seventies about crime-solving private detectives like Cannon, Mannix, Ironside, Jim Rockford (Rockford Files), Matlock and Barnaby Jones. The crime-solvers were always the good guys who sometimes did the wrong things to get the bad guy.

Despite all the negative news about police procedures and conduct in recent years, police officers continue to get high marks for honesty/ethics in Gallup polling. They rated fifth among all professions behind nurses, medical doctors, pharmacists, and grade-school teachers in a December 2020 Gallup Poll. That put them ahead of judges, the clergy, journalists, and lawyers.

It's safe to say that in South Williamsport, Pennsylvania, in 1973, mostly white and middle class, the prevailing belief was that the criminal justice system worked fairly, efficiently and without prejudice or malice. The toll of wrongful convictions that have been revealed in recent decades often point to systemic prejudices against racial minorities and the economically disadvantaged as the root cause of unfair and ill-advised prosecutions.

Kim Hubbard and his family, in my opinion, were among those victimized because a conviction became more important than bringing the guilty party to justice. An incident of domestic violence or an unintended death that was covered up, may have been transformed into something more insidious and premeditated. Premeditation always adds to the weight of a crime when you are a murder defendant. It should be the same for those who are entrusted as our courtroom guardians.

WES SKILLINGS